GOD'S OWN GENTLEWOMAN

GOD'S OWN GENTLEWOMAN

THE LIFE OF MARGARET PASTON

DIANE WATT

ICON

Published in the UK in 2024 by
Icon Books Ltd, Omnibus Business Centre,
39–41 North Road, London N7 9DP
email: info@iconbooks.com
www.iconbooks.com

ISBN: 978-183773-164-0
eBook: 978-183773-166-4

Typeset by SJmagic DESIGN SERVICES, India

Printed and bound in the UK

ACKNOWLEDGEMENTS

I am hugely grateful to my agent, Clare Grist Taylor, for encouraging me to write this book, and to my editors and the team at Icon Books, especially Kiera Jamison, who identified the potential of this project at the beginning, and Connor Stait and Ellen Conlon, who saw it through its later stages and who were such attentive and thoughtful readers.

I was introduced to the Paston letters some 35 years ago, while studying at the University of Bristol. I have such happy memories of my time there, where I was taught by John Burrow, Ian Bishop, Myra Stokes and the inimitable Basil Cottle, and studied alongside my fellow 'Cottlers', including Susannah Chewning, Helen Clarke, Jonathan Glasspool and Martin Nesbit. My interest in Margaret Paston's letters was rekindled a few years ago, when I supervised Jane Clayton's PhD thesis on the letters and wills of some of the other women in the collection. The title of this book was inspired by Colin Richmond's description of Margaret Paston as 'God's Englishwoman'.

Over the past few years, I have spent many weeks in Norfolk visiting sites mentioned in this book and was made to feel very at home in this beautiful and tranquil county, especially at the lovely Heath Cottage in Hickling. The villagers of Mautby were particularly welcoming, and special mention should be made of Maureen Clarke and her son-in-law Simon Bond and daughter Tammy, June Pratt, Emma-Jane and Mark Siddell, Shirley Travis, and Sam Howard's daughters and son, Janet Harper, Trish Durden and Richard Howard. I am also grateful to Sue McGrath and the staff at Blo' Norton Hall, where I enjoyed a magical visit while writing the epilogue to this book.

Thanks are due to the Paston Footprints project, especially Karen Smyth of the University of East Anglia, Rob Knee of the Paston Heritage Society and James Mindham of JMgraphix, and to the Norfolk Historic Buildings Group and Ian Hinton. Several archaeologists and historians offered me encouragement and were patient enough to discuss aspects of my research with me, and special mention must be made of Patricia Cullum, Kate Giles, Jane Grenville and Rachel Moss. Two distinguished literary scholars, Elaine Treharne and Marion Turner, were also generous in their support. All mistakes are of course my own. I am also grateful to the British Library, the Bodleian Library, Oxford, Great Yarmouth Local History and Archaeological Society, Norfolk and Norwich Archaeological Society, the Norfolk Record Office and the University of Surrey Library. Jessica Murphy at the Countway Library of Medicine, Harvard Medical School, answered my queries about MS Ballard 19. The artist Katie Spragg kindly supplied me with photographs of some of her work. The Halls, Norwich, granted us access to photograph the Paston donor doors at St Andrew's Hall. The Church of St Peter and St Paul, Mautby, allowed me to include the photograph of the ruined barn or 'chapel' at Hall Farm House, Mautby.

The research for this book was supported by a fellowship from the Leverhulme Trust (RF-2023-045/1), by visiting scholarships at the Oxford Centre for Life Writing and Wolfson

College, University of Oxford and by a sabbatical from the School of Literature and Languages at the University of Surrey.

Boydell and Brewer granted me permission to quote from my translations in *The Paston Women: Selected Letters*.

The artist Gail Reid worked with Icon's designer, Anna Morrison, to produce the beautiful calligraphy on the cover – thank you so much Gail. My wife, Heike Bauer, accompanied me on our trips to Norfolk with our dogs, and took most of the photographs that illustrate this book. I could not have written it without her support.

This book is dedicated to my sister, Lynne, and to the memory of our mother, Pat, and grandmother, Annie, and to all our mothers who went before.

CONTENTS

AUTHOR'S NOTE

My first encounter with the original manuscripts of Margaret Paston's letters, rather than modern print versions, was some twenty years ago, when I was working on an edition of letters by the women of the Paston family and their connections. Margaret's letters are to be found in four out of five bound volumes in the British Library.[1] My immediate impression was that the volumes resembled old family photograph albums. The history of the Paston collection before it came to the British Library explains why this is the case.

In 1735, a local clergyman and historian, Francis Blomefield, discovered the letters and documents, which are now in the first four of the British Library volumes, in the muniments, or records, room of Oxnead Hall in Norfolk.[2] Oxnead was the former home of the debt-ridden William Paston, 2nd Earl of Yarmouth, who had died three years previously. It was in a ruinous state when Blomefield visited. Subsequently, Blomefield purchased the letters from the executors of the estate, and, over the next couple of hundred years, they passed through the hands of various owners before the British Museum bought them at auction in 1933. The letters in the fifth volume have a different trajectory, having seemingly been handed down through descendants of the Paston family until the British Museum procured them at the end of the nineteenth century.

Although the British Museum rebound all these volumes after their acquisition, the first four retain the eighteenth-century paper mounts, which is why they resemble albums. Within the volumes, the viewer can see both sides of the documents, which are numbered, annotated and marked with the British Museum stamp. The appearance of the individual letters and documents varies considerably. Some are rough drafts, others carefully copied final versions. They are written in a range of hands, some professional, others decidedly less learned. The paper on which they are written is of different sizes and shapes.

To give just one example, let me describe the letter composed by Margaret to her husband, John, on 14 December, around 1441.[3] Margaret dictated its contents to an unidentified member of her household, and the letter's appearance suggests that the scribe then read it through, making occasional amendments. This letter itself is almost square, measuring, roughly, nineteen centimetres by eighteen centimetres. The handwriting is neat, but some words have been erased or scored through, and a few words and phrases have been added between the lines. It looks as if the scribe started to run out of space towards the end of the letter, because the writing in the lower lines is more crowded, and there is only enough room for a brief valediction and the initials 'M.P' in the bottom right-hand corner. The name of the addressee, 'To my right reverend and worshipful husband John Paston', is written on the back of the sheet, so we know it was dispatched. Traces of red wax on the inverse indicate that the letter was locked by folding and sealing. No address was required because the letter would have been carried by a messenger, most likely a servant or another member of the family.

Reading the original letters is more challenging than reading an edited or modernised version; not only is the handwriting difficult to decipher, but there is far less interpretative apparatus. Reading the original letters, however, brings with it its own rewards. Seeing on the page the corrections and changes, no matter how seemingly insignificant, gives these missives an immediacy that is lost in print or online. Reconstructing the act of folding and sealing is a reminder of how vulnerable they were to being lost, damaged or misappropriated. The very fact of their preservation reveals that the letters were valued by both sender and recipient. Letters and letter writing certainly mattered a great deal to Margaret. Alongside other documents such as inventories and wills, letters contained crucial information about the family and its estates. They were also a vital means of communication between Margaret and her husband, her children, especially her sons, and her neighbours and friends. Margaret must often have spent several hours a day reading or having her correspondence read out to her and dictating her replies.

These letters were generally not meant for a wider audience, and they are situation- as well as person-specific. Whether deliberately or not, their meaning is sometimes obscure to the modern reader, and it can be hard to make sense of the events being described or to work out who were the people involved. This book aims to provide enough historical, cultural and literary background to make Margaret's letters accessible and her life comprehendible. The challenges are only exacerbated by medieval naming practices. Within four generations of the fifteenth-century Paston family, there are four William Pastons, and within two generations there are three John Pastons, two Edmonds and two Margerys (one of whom married into the family). I've tried to find as simple a way through this as possible. I call Margaret's father-in-law Justice William, to distinguish him from his son, grandson and great grandson of the same name. Her husband is simply John. Her two eldest sons who share a Christian name are, according to convention, referred to as John II and John III. For the others, especially Margaret's daughter and daughter-in-law, both called Margery, the contexts in which they appear will, I hope, suffice.

The letters were first edited by a Norfolk antiquary, John Fenn, and published between 1787 and 1823 in five volumes under the title *Original Letters, Written during the Reigns of Henry VI., Edward IV. and Richard III. by Various Persons of Rank or Consequence.* The first scholarly edition was by the archivist James Gairdner, who published the four-volume *Paston Letters, 1422–1509* in 1872–5, and another edition in six volumes in 1904. The definitive academic text is the two-volume *Paston Letters and Papers of the Fifteenth Century*, first published in 1971–6, edited by Norman Davis, J.R.R. Tolkien's successor as Merton Professor of English Language and Literature at the University of Oxford. An additional third volume was edited by Richard Beadle and Colin Richmond and published in 2005. In 2015, the British Library made the digitised letters accessible online via its website. Davis's dating and ordering of the letters are considered more accurate than those of his predecessors, so this is the version to which the British Library defers, and it is the one I usually draw on in this book, alongside my own edition and translation of *The Paston Women: Selected Letters*, which was published in 2004. To make the letters and other medieval material more accessible I have modernised the language throughout.

INTRODUCTION

The idea for this book came to me around the time of the death of my mother. Although she had been housebound for the last few years of her life, my mother's final decline took only a matter of months. Admitted into hospital with pneumonia in February 2019, she defied the physicians' initial prognosis that she had only a few days left, and some weeks later moved into the nursing home that would be her last place of residence. After an initial improvement over the spring and summer, which saw her once again enjoying reading detective novels, her daily crossword puzzles and watching Wimbledon, as the nights grew longer and darker her own light began to fade. Unable to fight off yet another chest infection, she passed away with her two daughters and eldest niece by her side, less than a month before her 84th birthday.

During those last few days, sitting holding my mother's hand and talking to her about her family and our lives together, I was unaware of the Covid-19 pandemic still to come, and of a more personal crisis when I was diagnosed with breast cancer some ten months later. Rather, I thought back to the generations of women before me who must have found themselves in a similar position. Living on the west coast of Scotland, some 180 miles away, my mother was unable to be with my grandmother when

1

she passed away, but I do know that my grandmother nursed her mother, my great-grandmother, in her final days, as was the norm in previous centuries. The ensuing rituals of death and mourning also seemed timeless, from the funeral and wake to the reading of the will, and other, more personal acts of memorialisation.

My mother's death also gave me a new perspective on her life as a young woman both *before* and *with* my father, who had died a couple of decades earlier. Going through their letters, papers, photographs and books, and listening to the memories of other older members of my extended family, I suddenly found myself able to understand better, or at least to imagine, their young adulthoods and the early years of their marriage. Often, we can only conceive of our mothers and fathers as we have known them – as parents to us or grandparents to the next generation – but now I started to see the young woman and man who managed to make a life together over the years.

In my grief, the idea of writing a book retelling the life of Margaret Paston began to take shape. Perhaps, unconsciously at the time, I perceived some similarities between Margaret and my mother, both intelligent, forceful, canny, competitive women, who had strong views about how others should live their lives and who weren't afraid to fall out with people with whom they disagreed, even members of their own immediate families. Disputes over inheritance and property loomed large in both their lives, if on different scales. Perhaps this book stands in place of my mother's biography.

Who was Margaret, and why write a book about her? Margaret Mautby was born in the village of Reedham, about twelve miles from Great Yarmouth, in the first quarter of the fifteenth century. She was well-off – her parents, Margery Berney of Reedham and John Mautby of Mautby, were from established and prosperous landowning families – and she married into the upwardly mobile Paston family. She and her husband, John, had seven surviving children: John (II), John (III), Margery, Edmund, Anne, Walter and William. Others may have died at birth or in infancy. What is so remarkable about the Pastons is that, somehow, so many records relating to four generations of the family (from John's parents down to his grandchildren) have survived. Indeed, the Paston letters and papers make up the largest collection of medieval correspondence relating to a single family in England.[1] These documents provide vivid insights into the lives of the gentry classes in late medieval England and include eye-witness accounts of legal disputes, political conflicts and in-fighting in fifteenth-century Norfolk during the turbulent decades of the Wars of the Roses. They describe at first hand forbidden love affairs and clandestine marriages, cruelty and kindness, friendships and animosity, childbirth and child mortality, family arguments and neighbourhood conflicts, battles and violent assaults, sieges and kidnappings, and fear of plague and sudden death. Even more remarkably, given the low levels of literacy of women at this time in history, there are more letters from Margaret than from anyone else in the family.

Although Margaret doesn't seem to have been able to write (she dictated her letters to scribes), she was a prolific correspondent. In total 106 items, including her draft will, are attributed to her in the collection, spanning a period of four decades in the mid- to later-fifteenth century. Until the death of her husband, he is the main recipient. Thereafter, she principally writes to her two eldest sons. The letters are not evenly distributed across time. There are far more from the last two decades of her life, with a marked concentration in the 1460s, a particularly tumultuous time, both nationally and closer to home, with John Paston's disputed claim on the will of the wealthy Sir John Fastolf, the outbreak of civil war, John's death, and, at the end of the decade, the decision of

Margaret and John's daughter Margery to marry the family bailiff, John Calle, against Margaret's will.

It is then no surprise that, like my parents, in my mind, Margaret Paston is fixed in middle age. I think of Margaret as a truculent newly widowed woman in her forties or fifties, who apparently has little time for pleasure, and less still for displays of affection, but who is always focused on the business at hand and the next job that needs to be done. Yet, rereading her letters, I am reminded that there is much more to Margaret than this. The early letters reveal a young woman who loved and worried about her husband, who enjoyed the support of female family members and friends, including her mother-in-law and close companion Agnes, and who was excited by her pregnancies. The later letters tell a different story, as we encounter an ageing widow who increasingly turns for comfort to her chaplain and to her religious devotions, one who fears the spread of plague and struggles with her own ill health, and one who is frustrated by or anxious about her sons and daughters, their behaviour, and their futures. What Margaret's letters offer us is the opportunity to experience something of the course of her adult life from her own perspective; to follow her from marriage and young motherhood through to her widowhood and old age.

I am not the first author to have been inspired by Margaret Paston's letters. In 1929, in *A Room of One's Own*, Virginia Woolf wrote movingly about the absences in history and fiction of what she called the 'infinitely obscure lives' of women in the past:

> For all the dinners are cooked; the plates and cups washed; the children sent to school and gone out into the world. Nothing remains of it all. All has vanished. No biography or history has a word to say about it. And the novels, without meaning to, inevitably lie.[2]

But even as she wrote these words, Woolf already knew of Margaret Paston's correspondence and the rare insights it offers into the everyday life of a medieval gentlewoman. Woolf's copies of James Gairdner's four-volume edition of the Paston letters[3] were sold by Sotheby's in 2011: they are signed 'Virginia Stephen' and dated to 1905.[4] In fact, as early as 1904, she informed a friend about her plans to write a 'large' work on the Paston collection.[5] The following year, she urged her cousin Emma Vaughan 'to visit Paston on the Norfolk coast'[6] and in the summer of 1906, Woolf took Margaret Paston as her inspiration when she composed the short story 'The Journal of Mistress Joan Martyn'[7] while staying in Blo' Norton Hall, a sixteenth-century manor house in Norfolk. Woolf discussed Margaret's letters directly two decades later in her essay 'The Pastons and Chaucer', published in *The Common Reader* in 1925.[8]

Woolf's short story is narrated in part by an unmarried and bookish young woman living in Norfolk in the time of the Pastons, but there is a clear focus on the Martyn matriarch, modelled on Margaret Paston herself. Joan's mother is a woman of considerable authority in the household, who can write but not read, and whose closest confidant is the family priest. In the words of Joan Martyn, 'It is a great thing to be the daughter of such a mother, & to hope that one day such power will be mine. She rules us all.'[9] In Woolf's essay, 'The Pastons and Chaucer', Margaret (Woolf's 'Mrs Paston') also controls the household. She is a brave woman, but she does 'not talk about herself', and she feels angry and frustrated at her eldest son, who rather than attend to his business 'would sit reading Chaucer, wasting his time, dreaming ...'. Woolf, it seems, was fascinated by Margaret, even if she didn't entirely sympathise with her.[10] Woolf was of course drawn to strong women, but perhaps she also found in Margaret her opposite, a woman who didn't seem to have time for literature or the world of the imagination.

Throughout much of my life, I have shared Woolf's fascination. I first encountered the Paston letters when I was a postgraduate reading Medieval Studies at the University of Bristol. As an undergraduate I had developed an interest in medieval women's writing and studied mystical and visionary works such as *The Revelations of Divine Love* by Julian of Norwich and *The Book of Margery Kempe*. The letters by Margaret and other women that I found within the Paston collection offered me something else: the perspective of secular women and insight into lives in which religious experience, although still important, did not entirely dominate. Significantly, my first published essay was on the Paston letters, and it included in its title a quotation from 'The Pastons and Chaucer': Woolf's description of Margaret's letters as 'no writing for writing's sake'. Some ten or eleven years later, I returned to the family and their correspondence, and produced a modernised edition of some of the letters of the Paston women. Since then, I have found myself revisiting them on many occasions.

Despite my enduring fascination with Margaret and the other Pastons, it was only a few years ago that I first followed Woolf's footsteps and travelled to Norfolk to visit the village that bears their surname, and other sites where they had lived or where they were buried. One blustery day in the late summer of 2017, my wife, Heike, and I found ourselves retracing the former road (now marked by a lychgate in the corner of the churchyard), which, to the consternation of their neighbours, was blocked by a wall that Margaret's mother-in-law, Agnes had built because it came too close to one of their homes. Paston Hall has been almost completely rebuilt over the centuries, most recently in the 1800s, so there was little to see there, at least from the outside. Likewise, the notable Great

Tithe Barn dates to the later sixteenth century: a stone over the lintel of the south door reads: 'The Bild[in]g of this Bearn is bi Sir W Pasto[n] Knighte.' The barn is home to a breeding roost of rare barbastelle bats.

On the same visit, we took a walk around the flint church of St Margaret. The Paston village church is not a grand affair. Like the Great Barn it is thatched, with a timber nave roof and carved rood screen, and it is adorned with medieval wall paintings, which include a large late-fifteenth-century image of a bearded St Christopher carrying the Christ child. Remains of a representation of 'The Three Living and the Three Dead' are also visible, a popular late medieval *memento mori* narrative about three royal or noble hunters who encounter three decaying corpses, the hunters' dead ancestors, which admonish the living men for their sins and for failing to commemorate them in masses and prayers. John Audelay, a cleric from Haughmond Abbey, Shropshire, who died only a few years after Margaret was born, wrote a poetic version of the story in English.[11] One of the pew's ends is carved in the shape of a griffin, a mythological creature, half lion half eagle, that the Paston family chose as their heraldic symbol. In its east end, alongside some later Paston monuments, the chancel contains a chest tomb that is thought to be that of Margaret's husband John.[12] When we arrived, the church was empty, but someone had recently placed a candle and a stone on the lid, presumably in his memory.

We then travelled a couple of miles (an easy walk and easier ride for the Pastons) to the remains of the once-imposing Bromholm Priory, which in the Middle Ages was famed for its relic of the Holy Cross. This is where John was originally buried with great pomp and expense, following his death in London in 1466. Margaret presumably oversaw many of the arrangements for the funeral feast. As Nikolaus Pevsner notes, it 'involved 13 barrels of beer, 27 of ale, 15 gallons of wine, 1300 eggs, 20 gallons of milk, 8 gallons of cream, 41 pigs, 49 calves, etc'.[13] In her later years, Margaret was angered by her eldest son's delays in the completion of his late father's sepulchre. Evidently, he didn't heed the warning of the three skeletons on the Paston church wall to remember his predecessors. It is just as well Margaret did not have to witness the Protestant reformers' destruction of the priory which took place in the century after her own death. At least someone seems to have thought to rescue John's remains.

It was only then, when I started to explore these Norfolk villages and their medieval remains, that I began to recognise the importance that other, more material remnants of the family's history might have in making sense of the textual evidence that was already so familiar to me. This journey led me to wonder what more I might find, if I were to visit other villages, towns and churches mentioned in Margaret's letters and associated with her life – places like Mautby, Walsingham, Norwich – and what they might reveal to me about the world in which she lived. Somewhat uncannily, when I opened my copy of Pevsner's guide to North-East Norfolk, it fell open at Reedham, Margaret's birthplace.

This book is not simply a biography. Rather, by focusing on carefully selected letters written by Margaret across her lifetime, from the years immediately following her marriage to those leading up to her death, I take the events described in each of these letters as the starting point for a broader exploration of late medieval social and cultural history and late medieval life, exploring subjects especially pertinent to women, such as love and marriage, childbirth and childcare, running a household, recipes and cooking, trade and shopping, sport and games, and medicine and religion. I pay attention to, if not quite, as Woolf has it, the cooking of the dinners, the washing of the plates and cups, and the sending of children to school, then at least some of the details of Margaret's everyday existence within and beyond the household. But I also try to do much more than this, discussing Margaret's experiences alongside the history of the Paston family and the lives of some her family, friends and even enemies. I include accounts and anecdotes of my travels around contemporary Norfolk, in search of remaining traces of the castles, manors and chapels described in Margaret's letters, and I include my reflections on what light these visits throw on her correspondence. But most importantly, I try to recreate the world of late medieval England as viewed from the perspective of a courageous, intelligent and forceful woman who lived through, and survived, battles, plagues and family conflicts.

1. 'THE GENTLEWOMAN FROM REEDHAM'

*20 April, probably 1440 (Agnes Paston to
her husband, Justice William)*

The church of St John the Baptist, Reedham, with its distinctive chequer-patterned exterior, stands in relative isolation some way outside of the modern village above the River Yare. It is an ancient Christian site, dating back to the seventh century, but although there is evidence of reused Roman building materials, most of the existing structure dates to the thirteenth or early fourteenth century. Reedham was where Margaret Paston's mother's family lived, but the medieval hall has not survived, although the church tower was built in Margaret's lifetime, paid for by a legacy in the will of her uncle Thomas Berney.[1] In a copy of her will, written a couple of years before her death, when she was in her early sixties, Margaret left a bequest for repairs to the Reedham church, specifying that this was 'where I was born'.[2]

When Heike and I visited Reedham one quiet Sunday in midsummer, the churchyard was open, but the building itself remained closed. Below the rainbow 'Welcome' sign on the door hung another notice, informing us that access was possible only on Wednesdays and Saturdays. Because much of the medieval interior was destroyed by a fire in 1981, the loss was not so very great. We were able to walk along the paths cut through the unmown grass, dense with ox-eye daisies, buttercups, Queen Anne's lace and cow parsley, and around the outside of the church, where a gathering of bees clamoured for access through a gap in the stonework, high on the south-facing wall.

Sitting on a bench looking across in the direction of the Yare, I enjoyed listening to the chatter of the rooks, almost drowning out the birdsong and the crowing of a cockerel on a distant farm. I was reminded of the soundscape of my late mother's home in North Yorkshire where the birds conversed loudly from the rookery high in the trees of the manor house opposite. But I didn't have a strong sense of Margaret's presence. And indeed, without her letters as guidance, it can seem as if her life didn't start with her birth but began only two decades later, when arrangements were being made for her marriage in the spring of 1440, or thereabouts.

At that time, the wealthy Norfolk 'husswyf' Agnes Paston wrote to her husband a brief, and somewhat cryptic, letter recording the first meeting between two young people, Margaret Mautby and their eldest son, John.[3] The term 'huswyff' – in modern English 'housewife' – described a woman, usually a wife, responsible for a family and its servants.[4] In the case of Agnes and her husband, William, her dominion extended to several manors and estates across Norfolk and extending into Cambridgeshire, Hertfordshire and Suffolk. The meeting was important to both Agnes and William, because both families were hoping the two would marry. John was not only being given the opportunity to assess his future bride; Agnes was, in effect, interviewing the woman who would become her successor. This is also *our* first encounter with Margaret, and although it is Agnes who provides this first-hand account, we can choose, if we like, to see Margaret through John's eyes: a strong, perceptive, confident and resourceful young woman who, as she stepped through the doorway and moved her hood back from her eyes, quietly began to assert her authority over the household which she would, in due course, come to control.

Agnes liked Margaret. That much is clear from the letter that Agnes wrote to her husband. But, in her letter, Agnes doesn't mention Margaret Mautby, as she was then, by name. Instead, she refers to her as 'the gentlewoman, whom you know of, from Reedham'. The marriage arrangements for Agnes and William's son, although apparently progressing as smoothly as might be hoped for, were at a sensitive stage, so discretion (or secrecy) was paramount. A good bride was a precious commodity and letters could be intercepted or lost and then fall into the wrong hands. It wasn't worth taking unnecessary risks. Agnes reports to William that Margaret addressed her prospective husband 'kindly and courteously, and said he was truly your son'. Despite the brevity of this description, Margaret's charisma is already evident. With her first greeting, a mere handful of words, she demonstrated grace and sensitivity, good manners and diplomacy.

William was a formidable figure, a successful lawyer and a Justice of the Common Pleas who owned extensive estates in Norfolk. John had followed his father into the law. He was educated at Trinity Hall and Peterhouse at the University of Cambridge, and, at the time this letter was written, had recently been admitted to the Inner Temple, one of the Inns of Court in London. John and his parents would all be delighted to hear that he took after his father. But, nevertheless, in this account, John remains in the shadows. Agnes has nothing to say about him, or about his reaction to being introduced to the woman with whom he would expect to spend the rest of his life, the woman who would, it was hoped, give birth to and bring up children, who would run the household and manage the servants, and with whom he would share oversight of the family manors and estates. Perhaps Agnes doesn't say anything because she doesn't need to. William could confidently assume that his son would quite rightly be impressed by any woman his parents might choose for him. Perhaps John had suggested the match himself, having heard of Margaret and her suitability through mutual connections. Perhaps it didn't really matter what he thought.

Agnes is confident that the negotiations will be swiftly resolved. The parson of Stockton, who was going to conduct the ceremony, was also involved in the discussions, even down to the details concerning who would pay for the bride's clothing. The parson had reassured Agnes that if William would buy Margaret a new gown, Margaret's mother would give her a fine fur. But the colour of the gown mattered to Margaret: it must be either a fine blue or a bright sanguine, that is, a vibrant blood red. William was in London, while Agnes was at home in the village of Paston (whence the family took their surname), so he regularly assumed responsibility for any purchases that couldn't be made locally but had to be brought back from the metropolis. Still, he sometimes made mistakes, so it was imperative to give him unambiguous instructions. Agnes also asks him to buy her some gold thread for hair decoration. It isn't clear if this is for herself or for Margaret. Almost as an afterthought she adds a reassurance that William's fishponds are doing well.

It might seem surprising that, in the lead-up to this special event, Agnes should wish to update William on the state of the ponds, but fish were a valuable resource, and the Paston ponds an indicator of the family's status and wealth.

Fishponds were an essential aspect of the managed and agricultural landscape in late medieval England. They would be carefully constructed with a system of dams, sluices, leats and causeways. Some survive to the present day, for example at the moated manor house of Hindringham Hall, around 25 miles northwest of Paston. The ponds would be grouped together and stocked with different species of fish such as bream, carp, perch, roach and eel. Eels were popular throughout Europe, and they were a dietary staple in Norfolk where they thrive in the fens and waterways. Ely, in the neighbouring county of Cambridgeshire, derives its name from the 'Isle of Eels'. *Le Ménagier de Paris* or *The Good Wife's Guide*, a famous late-fourteenth-century French guide to running a household, includes a variety of recipes for eel sops, eel in white garlic sauce, eel pasty and 'reversed eel', which is a little more complex and involves ginger, cloves, cinnamon, nutmeg and grains of paradise.[5] These last are seeds from the plant *aframomum melegueta,* a member of the ginger family, related to cardamom. They were commonly used in medieval cooking and medicinal recipes.

Rural Norfolk was one of the most thriving areas of late medieval England. It was characterised by swathes of fertile arable land, where crops of barley, oats and rye were grown. The coastal towns grew wealthy from overseas trade, especially wool from the county's pastures. Bishop's Lynn, modern-day King's Lynn, was the first British town to join the Hanseatic League, a defensive trade federation centred in Northern Europe. Situated inland, Norwich was a staple port, a centre of import and export, which enjoyed specific rights and privileges. It was also one of the largest and most prosperous cities in England, second only to London. Walking along King Street as it runs parallel to the River Wensum, with its restored medieval trading hall, the Dragon Hall, it is possible to get a sense of this busy centre of commerce. Further along King Street is a distinctive pink building known as the Music House or Wensum Lodge, the earliest parts of which date back to the twelfth century. It was owned in the early thirteenth century by Isaac of Norwich, a financier and prominent member of the Jewish community, and over two centuries later bought by one of John and Margaret's sons. The Paston family, with its extensive manors and estates, was certainly well placed, quite literally, to accumulate further wealth, and thus to rise quickly up the social hierarchy.

Norfolk, at the end of the Middle Ages, was also a centre of culture and a hotbed of religious enthusiasm. The anchoress Julian of Norwich is well known today for her two written accounts of the 'showings', or divine visions which she received in 1373, when she was 30 years old. Julian lived in strict isolation, confined to a cell or anchorhold attached to a church situated in the heart of the old city. To find the church, which was rebuilt after the Second World War, with its reconstructed anchorhold, you can turn off King Street down a narrow alley which now takes her name, just a stone's throw from the Dragon Hall. Julian may not have been a recluse at the time of her first mystical experiences, but she was formally enclosed in her later years. Around 1413 she was visited in her cell by another famous local visionary, Margery Kempe, whose *Book* records her spiritual life and adventures, including her pilgrimages in England and to Rome and Jerusalem. While we don't know for certain whether Julian was a nun, Margery Kempe certainly wasn't. As a reasonably well-off laywoman (her father was a former mayor of Norwich and member of parliament for Norfolk) whose religious fervour took precedence over her sense of responsibility to her husband and family, Margery Kempe enjoyed considerable freedom from the ties of domesticity.

The late fourteenth century saw the emergence of the non-conformist Lollard movement, which is sometimes seen as a form of proto-Protestantism. 'Lollard' was a term of abuse, which is thought to come from the Middle Dutch word lollaerd ('mumbler' or 'mutterer').[6] It was applied to those who followed (albeit to varying extents) the reformist teachings of John Wyclif and who held a range of beliefs antithetical to the dogma of the Roman church, including denying the divine authority of priests and the sacrament of the Eucharist and denigrating practices such as confession, pilgrimage and the worship of the saints. William Sawtrey, a priest at St Margaret's Church in King's Lynn (now the Cathedral), was the first heretic to be executed on English soil when he was burned at the stake in 1401. Between 1428 and 1431, William Alnwick, Bishop of Norwich, led a sustained campaign against the Lollards that resulted, notably, in the trials of Hawise Mone, who came from the village of Loddon, not far from Reedham, and Margaret Baxter from Martham, located further north in the direction of Paston itself. Both were redoubtable women, ardent in their beliefs, who had little fear of the ecclesiastical authorities. Despite having been subjected to a series of brutal public floggings, Baxter was rearrested only six months after her first trial. Both women seem to have managed to escape execution. Many others did not. The site of the Lollard executions in Norwich is commemorated today in the name of the Lollard Pit Pub, across the river from the Cathedral on the far side of Bishop Bridge.

The family into which Margaret Mautby was to marry did not share the heterodox beliefs of some of its Norfolk neighbours. On the surface, it was a far cry socially from those of the Norwich Lollards, who were on the whole lower-class craftsmen and artisans. But, in fact, the Paston riches had only been recently won. According to one document from the time purporting to describe the family 'Kin and Ancestry', Justice William's father, Clement, was 'a good plain husbandman', who had only 100–120 acres of land to plough in the village of Paston and a 'little poor watermill running by a little river'; in other words, Clement's farmland was around a tenth of the size of a small medieval manor.[7] It claims that he 'drove his cart' to the market at the coastal town of Winterton to sell his grain 'as a good husbandman ought to do'. The same document describes Justice William's mother, Beatrice, as 'a bond woman', a peasant woman and indentured servant, in other words as someone from one of the very bottom rungs of medieval society. It was Beatrice's brother, Geoffrey Somerton, who provided his nephew with the opportunity to rise in the world. Geoffrey had found a way to escape servitude and to qualify as an attorney, and he helped Clement pay for William's education and legal training in London.

The 'Kin and Ancestry' record was produced in the years immediately following Justice William's death, and clearly by, or on behalf of, someone who resented the Pastons' rise to a position of considerable power and influence. Its assertions concerning the family's roots are completely at odds with the genealogy drawn up in the later seventeenth century by one of William and Agnes's even more socially elevated descendants, Sir Robert Paston, Viscount Yarmouth.[8] This family tree traces William's pedigree back almost to the invasion of 1066, and a man called Wulstan, cousin to a Norman earl. Despite its evident anti-Paston bias, the earlier account is the more authentic. Justice William did not have exalted ancestors, but he had benefited from the patronage of his successful uncle and made good on the investment in his education. He also purchased land, especially around the village of Paston, establishing it as a manor, and accumulated extensive estates across the county.

Agnes's background, in contrast, was far more distinguished. Agnes was something of a trophy bride for William, if such a thing can be said to have existed in fifteenth-century England. When they married in 1420, Agnes was only around fifteen years old, and William was some 27 years her senior. Agnes was the daughter and co-heir of wealthy Sir Edmund Berry of Horwellbury, Hertfordshire, so in order to secure this socially and financially advantageous match, William agreed to gift his bride the manor of Oxnead. William's investment was a good one; following her father's death in the 1430s Agnes inherited the manors of Horwellbury, Marlingford and Stanstead. The marriage between Agnes and William seems to have been a successful one, but it is striking that in this, the only surviving letter from Agnes to her husband, her tone is respectful, but almost brusque. She addresses him simply as 'Dear husband' and abbreviates the formulaic opening, 'I recommend myself to you, etc.'. By way of comparison, one of Margaret's first letters to her new husband, John, begins, 'Right reverent and worshipful husband, I recommend myself to you with all my simple heart'.[9] It would be a mistake to read too much into these greetings, governed as they are by the strict epistolary conventions of the time. Nevertheless, Agnes, by now some twenty years married, clearly felt able to circumvent some of the formalities and get directly to the business at hand. After all, her letter was signed off with, 'Written at Paston in haste'. Perhaps that is one reason that the marriage worked so well: husband and wife recognised the importance of cutting to the chase and prioritising the family interests above everything else. They expected their children to do the same.

Because we first meet Margaret in the letters when she was around nineteen years old, we know relatively little about her childhood and young adulthood. Her father's family was from Mautby, where Margaret lived towards the end of her life, where she died, and where she was also buried. There is no space in her letters for reminiscing about her early years, and other evidence about them is sparse, but it is possible to imagine something of her life. Her infancy was spent in an exceptionally beautiful part of the world. Reedham is in what is now the Norfolk Broads and is rich in bird and animal life. The Broads themselves, which today are such an important feature of the area, were formed where peat had been dug for fuel in the Middle Ages, leaving behind pits which gradually filled with water, and there isn't any documentary record of their existence before the fourteenth century. Our current understanding of the Broads as human-made rather than natural occurrences can be credited primarily to the botanist Joyce Lambert, who studied them in detail in the mid-twentieth century.[10] Located east of the Broads, and just a few miles from Great Yarmouth, Mautby sits at the edge of the marsh, also lovely, but bleaker, at least on the rainy day we first walked there with our dogs, spotting hen and marsh harriers in flight, and listening to the call of the golden plover and the cry of the curlew. Margaret's father, John Mautby, owned estates across East Anglia, so Margaret certainly would not have experienced any physical hardship or deprivation. Quite the opposite. Her family enjoyed high status as well as riches. Her mother, Margaret or Margery Berney, had a genuine claim to illustrious family links as she was related to the wealthy soldier and literary patron Sir John Fastolf, whose family also were from Reedham, a man whose death was to have a huge impact on Margaret, her husband and her sons.

Nevertheless, despite being born into such privilege, Margaret's options would have been severely curtailed simply by dint of her sex. While not all young women of her social class chose to marry, the alternatives were largely limited to entering a convent or into service in the household of another, higher-status, family. Some women, single or married, entered trade and were able to run their own business (as her older contemporary, Margery Kempe, did for a time, trying her hand at both milling and brewing, although with little success), and the less well-off might learn a skill such as needlework that would help them find employment, but these options wouldn't have been available to someone of Margaret's standing. In fact, according to canon law, her parents could have arranged for her to have married when she was as young as twelve, because by then she would have been considered to have reached adolescence, although her consent (and that of her husband) would still have been required. It would have made sense to wait for a few more years, not least because that would mean her parents could hold off from providing her with the expensive dowry that would prove crucial in the transaction. When Margaret was only around ten or eleven, her father passed away, leaving her his sole heir. There was therefore even less incentive for her mother, who subsequently remarried, to rush into finding her daughter a husband.

Unlike her university-educated future husband, Margaret wouldn't have received a formal education. Her mother would have taught her prayers such as the Pater Noster and Ave Maria, instructed her in the rudimental tenets of the Christian faith, provided essential training in morality and conduct, and introduced her to the skills needed to run a large household and estate. We can get a sense of some of the guidance the young Margaret might have received from her mother from medieval conduct literature, a genre that included works like *Le Ménagier de Paris*, intended to introduce its readers to appropriate social norms. Another example, written in English in the century before Margaret was born and also aimed specifically at women, is the poem *How the Good Wife Taught her Daughter*.

In this work, the character of the Good Wife provides advice on married life and housewifery. While we should be wary of taking the text too much at face value, it does provide us with insights into the sort of counsel Margaret's mother might have provided. Margaret's own first words to her husband are certainly in keeping with the Good Wife's recommendation that 'If any man proffer thee to wed, / A courteous answer to him be said'. [11]

A young girl's education did not entirely depend on her own mother. Margaret may have been placed temporarily with another family to improve her comportment and manners and to prepare her for married life. Her parents might even have sent her to be schooled informally at one of the Norfolk convents, where she could have learnt enough Latin to enable her to read a psalter, a book of biblical psalms, and a book of hours, a collection of prayers and texts intended for private devotion. Yet, although as an adult Margaret did own at least a couple of devotional books, it is possible that she had never learnt to write because, not untypically for the time, none of her many letters are written in her own hand. If that were the case, then she didn't find it an insurmountable barrier to communication. A vociferous letter writer throughout her adult life, she turned to her sons, the family chaplain, and her servants to act as her scribes.

As her late father's heir, Margaret brought nine manors in East Anglia into her marriage to John. William and Agnes had succeeded in netting an exceptional match for their eldest son. Margery Mautby in turn had found a son-in-law from a family that was clearly going places. But how much of a voice did either Margaret or John really have in selecting a spouse? Romantic love was, in a sense, invented in the High and late Middle Ages, in its literature and visual culture. Writers like Marie de France, Geoffrey Chaucer and Thomas Malory celebrated and critiqued its ideals in their poetry and prose. And while such works may originally have been aimed at an aristocratic, courtly audience, both women and men, by the fifteenth century courtly romances were also being enjoyed by less elevated readers. Indeed, Margaret and John's eldest son was a keen bibliophile, who over the years managed to build up an impressive personal library. It is worth pausing for a moment to glimpse at its contents, for the insights it gives into the meaning of love at the time.

The Paston library was reasonably eclectic. It contained works about statecraft and good governance, heraldry and chivalry, and devotion and religion, but it also includes material that is more familiar today, such as at least three of Geoffrey Chaucer's works – *Troilus and Criseyde*, *The Legend of Good Women*, and *The Parlement of Foules* – as well as some of John Lydgate's, a translation of Alain Chartier's *La Belle Dame sans Merci*, Arthurian literature and other romances. Of these books, two stand out: *Troilus and Criseyde* and *The Parlement of Foules*. Chaucer's epic poem, *Troilus and Criseyde*, is often considered to be one of the most poignant love stories in the English literary tradition. It follows the fortune of the couple from the first thralls of passion through to their enforced parting, Criseyde's subsequent inconstancy and Troilus's suffering and pain. *The Parlement of Foules* is, in contrast, a fable about a gathering of birds presided over by Nature. It is also a debate poem in which opposing sides argue their case, in the hope of winning the dispute. In the poem, three tercel, or male, eagles claim the hand of a formel, or adult female, eagle. At the end, none of the tercel eagles is successful in his suit as the formel eagle requests a year's respite before she makes her decision, although the other birds in the parliament do pair off.

What these works reveal is that romance was culturally important in the later Middle Ages, and that while it was sometimes associated with forbidden or secret love (Troilus and Criseyde hide their relationship from those around them) and rejected suitors (Criseyde ultimately abandons Troilus), it was also consistent with open courtship and marriage. So, while Chaucer's account of Criseyde's intoxicated response to seeing Troilus return triumphant from battle, 'Who gave me drink?',[12] is a far cry from Margaret's far more sober and politic reaction to meeting her future husband, *Parlement of Foules* emphasises the importance of the woman's choice in marriage (at least within the appropriate social hierarchies), and her right to refuse the suitors that are presented to her.

The relationship between Margaret and John was then quite different from the grand passions of the literature of medieval romance but typical of the conventions of their time. Marriages arranged by the families of both parties became even more prevalent in England in the fifteenth century, as greater social, as well as religious, control was exerted over the practice. Among the highest social classes, it was not uncommon to arrange marriages for very young children for dynastic and political reasons, although as noted the minimum acceptable age for marriage was generally seen to be that of puberty: twelve for girls and fourteen for boys. In families of the social status of the Pastons, the bride would usually be in her late teens and her husband a few years older. Margaret's future parents-in-law, Agnes and William, with their 27-year age gap, were something of an exception. Before a couple could be formally betrothed or engaged to be married, the financial settlement between the two families had to be agreed, and Agnes's letter alludes to this discussion. The bride's family would provide a dowry: money, property and moveable goods which would be transferred to the groom, but which were intended to support her financially throughout her marriage and possible future widowhood. This is not to be confused with the dower, which the groom gave to his new wife when they married, and over which she would have control. Marriage was not only a social contract. Although it did not have to be formalised in church and could be contracted privately, it was also seen as a sacrament, a Christian rite. Individuals were not supposed to be forced into marriage. Consequently, the couple would usually be given the opportunity to get to know one another and courtship would be encouraged. It is for this reason that the first meeting between Margaret and John was considered by Agnes to be so very pivotal.

2. 'YOU HAVE LEFT ME SUCH A REMINDER'

....

*14 December, probably 1441 (Margaret Paston
to her husband, John)*

....

Margaret and John's wedding went ahead, as planned, sometime in 1440. It may have taken place at the Church of St Michael and All Angels at Stockton, a location chosen because Stockton was owned by the family of Margaret's stepfather, Ralph Garneys, who lived with Margaret's mother in neighbouring Geldeston. The village of Stockton is some six or seven miles south of Margaret's birthplace in Reedham, if you take the ferry, which dates to the seventeenth century. The morning Heike and I arrived at the crossing, there was a queue of vehicles on the opposite bank and on our side two men were dubiously scrutinising the mechanism of the chain ferry. The ferryman's prognosis was not good: he estimated it would take at least an hour to repair. But it was still early, the sun was blazing, we had our three dogs in the back of our Land Rover, and the pub was not yet open, so we decided to take the alternative, longer, road route.

When we made it to Stockton, we found a charming, if isolated, church of late Saxon origins located along a narrow tree-lined lane leading to a farm. There is little evidence now of the important manorial centre of Margaret's time. Pleasingly, there was a fingerpost announcing 'Church Open Today' propped against the entrance. The brick porch with its curved Dutch gable is postmedieval but the pretty round tower is fourteenth century. According to an information notice, the church has been recently renovated and re-thatched. Inside, the light streams through the leaded pains. The carved, fifteenth-century stalls are carefully polished. The remaining medieval stained glass includes a depiction of the Virgin Mary holding the infant Jesus. If this is where Margaret and John were married, no physical traces of Margaret or the Pastons remain, but within the nave I almost felt I could sense her youthful spirit, like a movement glimpsed out of the corner of an eye.

Margaret and John's wedding would have been a public affair, with much of the ceremony, including the exchange of rings, taking place outside rather than within the building. Chaucer alludes to this practice when, in 'The General Prologue' to *The Canterbury Tales*, he states that the Wife of Bath has had five husbands 'at [the] church door'.[1] Unlike Chaucer's Wife, Margaret was only to have one husband, a man whom she quickly came to love dearly. In an undated letter from very early in their marriage, addressed to John at Peterhouse in Cambridge, Margaret complains that he had been unable to return before Whitsun, adding, 'I suppose you will be home before long.'[2] She was already finding it hard to be apart from him.

By the end of the following year Margaret was pregnant with their first child. Another of Margaret's early letters to her husband, dated to 14 December in around 1441, makes playful and affectionate allusions to her condition.[3] This was written from Oxnead, bought by William Paston in 1419, just prior to his marriage, where the family often now resided. The medieval village of Oxnead, which was situated some 30 miles north of Stockton, has vanished. All that remains is the church and the hall, and both have been added to, or rebuilt, over the centuries. Despite a sign directing visitors to the hall, which is now a wedding venue, it was surprisingly hard to find, and we overshot it on our first attempt. Having finally parked up, we walked down the drive and after a few minutes came upon the Church of St Michael in a magical spot amid a small wood. Inside, the most notable features are postmedieval: the late-sixteenth-century alabaster tomb of Sir Clement Paston and his wife, Alice, and the seventeenth-century stone bust of Lady Katherine Paston. Oxnead Hall, located slightly further along the drive, would be unrecognisable to Agnes and William. The servants' quarters and garden terraces are all that remain of the Tudor hall that Sir Clement had built, and to which nineteenth- and twentieth-century additions have been made. No externally visible traces of the medieval manor house remain. Nevertheless, Oxnead Hall still makes an impressive statement about wealth and privilege, when viewed from the public footpath running along the other side of the Bure.

At the time when Margaret was in Oxnead writing this letter, or having it written for her, John was some 120 miles away in London, where he stayed in lodgings at the Inner Temple for much of his time. With his frequent and extended absences, the friendship between Margaret and Agnes was to prove to be an important one. Margaret would spend a great deal of time in Agnes's company, especially in the years following William's death in 1444, only three years after this letter. Agnes was still bearing children of her own when Margaret joined the family. While Agnes's relationship with her son John became increasingly strained, she and Margaret remained close, offering each other support during family crises and conflicts with neighbours and opponents of the Paston family. At the time when Margaret was writing ('in very great haste' as she, or her scribe, notes), she and Agnes would have been busy with their Christmas preparations. The festivities would begin just ten days later, on Christmas Eve.

The first half of Margaret's letter does not make any *direct* reference to her pregnancy, but centres on another dress purchase. It seems that Agnes had asked her husband, William, to obtain some 'musterdevillers' – a woollen cloth from Normandy – from which she planned to have a new gown made for her daughter-in-law. William had returned without it, claiming he had passed the request on to his son. Margaret complains that her father-in-law had also failed to buy her a new girdle as instructed, and that once again he tried to shift the blame onto John. She dismisses William's claims, insisting that she doesn't believe them and that 'he only said it as an excuse'. Margaret stresses the urgency of the purchases: she now has only two winter dresses left, that one is so cumbersome she is tired of wearing it, and that she 'has grown so shapely' that only one of her girdles still fastens around her. Here, then, are the first hints of Margaret's condition.

Margaret's request for a new girdle is laden with symbolic significance. Girdles were belts that fastened loosely around the waist to which purses and keychains might be attached. For wealthy women these were expensive commodities, often adorned with jewels. At the end of her life, in her will, Margaret was to bequeath three girdles to other women: her best blue girdle adorned with purple and gilt was left to her daughter Anne; a purple girdle adorned with silver and gilt was left to one of her daughters-in-law; and a black girdle adorned with silver, gilt and enamel was bequeathed to a servant.[4] Girdles weren't simply valuable items and indicators of status. They also had a figurative meaning: they could represent virginity and chastity. The Holy Girdle (or Girdle of Thomas) was a much-worshipped relic of the Blessed Virgin

Mary, which, according to legend, had been dropped as she ascended to Heaven and caught by St Thomas the Apostle. The Holy Girdle is associated with miracles relating to pregnancy and childbirth. It is particularly venerated in the city of Prato in Tuscany, where the 'Sacra Cintola' was brought by a merchant in the mid-twelfth century, and where it is still exhibited several times a year. One of the peculiarities of the medieval cult of relics was that many religious houses claimed to possess the same holy object and insisted on its authenticity in each instance. In the Middle Ages, other examples of the Holy Girdle were to be found in Westminster Abbey and, even nearer to home, in the Priory of St Leonard in Norwich.

In the context of Margaret's letter, the Middle English word that I have translated as 'shapely' is noteworthy: 'fetys'.[5] Chaucer uses it on a number of occasions in his translation of the French allegorical dream vision, *Le Roman de la Rose*.[6] The word can describe men as well as women, but it is more frequently applied to beautiful damsels or maidens, in other words to virginal young women who were more likely to maintain a slender figure. Medieval women's lives were understood to have three stages or states: maidenhood, wifedom and widowhood. As a maiden, a girl or young woman was in the control of her father or guardian. When she became a wife, her husband assumed authority over and responsibility for her, at least in theory. But while in financial terms a wife was certainly dependent on her husband, women and men would often work together in a close partnership, and this seems to have been the case for Margaret and John. In referring to herself, ironically, as 'fetys' or 'shapely', and no longer fitting any of her girdles, Margaret is teasing her husband about her new state, no longer a maiden, but now a mother-to-be as well as a wife.

Margaret was around five months pregnant at this time. In the Middle Ages, there was no reliable way of detecting pregnancy in the first weeks and months. The cessation of a woman's periods would be an important indicator, of course, but she would be aware that this might be due to a variety of causes, including ill health or poor diet. The speculative tests that did exist, such as examining the colour of a woman's urine, seeing if a needle rusted when placed in it, or mixing it with wine, would have had limited, if any, success. For example, while there doesn't seem to have been any scientific basis for the rust test, alcohol can react with proteins in a pregnant woman's urine so this may have been somewhat effective. However, the earliest sure indication was the quickening, the sensation of the unborn child moving in the womb that occurs at around four or five months. This means that at the time when Margaret was writing, her certainty concerning the pregnancy was still very recent and the couple had yet to make any sort of public announcement. But Margaret's expectant state was already showing. As she puts it: 'I can no longer live by deception; I am found out by everyone who sees me.' This is a secret that cannot be kept.

Margaret tells her husband that his mother, Agnes, had in fact already revealed the secret of the pregnancy to a recent visitor, John Damme. A close and loyal friend of the family, John Damme had in turn responded by assuring them that this was the best news he had heard all year. In so doing, John Damme was not merely congratulating the family on the imminent arrival of a new baby. Rather he was acknowledging an even more momentous event: the possible advent of the future head of the Paston family. According to the laws of primogeniture, the first-born son, on the death of his father, inherits his estate. Margaret and John would feel the full weight of familial and social pressure to produce a Paston heir, and so no doubt Margaret's first pregnancy came as an especial relief. At this stage, neither John nor Margaret could possibly know whether the baby would be a boy or a girl, although contemporary medicine and lore might provide some guidance. Consumption of certain foods, for example, was thought to encourage conception of a male foetus, and there were tests that were believed to reveal the sex of the baby. A useful source of information about this is a manuscript copied and compiled by Robert Thornton, a fifteenth-century Yorkshire landowner, which is, as it were, a library in miniature: it contains romances, religious texts and medicinal recipes and remedies, including advice on fertility and procreation. Among the last is the recommendation that to determine the sex of the child the mother should drop some breast milk in water: the milk should sink if she is carrying a boy and float if she is carrying a girl.[7] Margaret may well have tried something like this out, though it is likely that she and John were simply happy to be having any child so early into their marriage. Only when the baby was born the following spring did they find out for certain that it was a boy.

The family would not have a great deal of time to prepare for the birth. The delivery itself was a private affair, and a first-time mother like Margaret would turn to the experience and expertise of other women to advise and assist her. Given her wealth and status, in order to preserve her own health and that of her unborn child, she would be able to retire to her chamber a month before the birth for the 'lying in', an extended period of confinement which would last for several weeks after the birth, until the churching or purification ceremony. Thus, the responsibilities of running the household had to be delegated to others. Margaret was also in the privileged position of being able to employ a midwife to assist with her confinement, and she writes to John about the arrangements that have been put in place. This was by no means the norm in the period. While midwives had become more common by the 1400s than in previous centuries, there were far fewer in rural areas, and their assistance was largely the preserve of the well off. Poorer women would have to rely on their family and friends to help them out.

Unfortunately, the midwife or *obstetrix* whom Margaret had approached, a woman named Elizabeth Peverel, had been incapacitated with sciatica, but she assured Margaret that this would not prevent her attending. She informed Margaret, via Kate, a family servant, that 'she should come here when God should grant the time, even if she must be wheeled in a barrow'. Unlike modern midwives, Elizabeth Peverel is unlikely to have received formal training. Rather she would have developed her practice out of her own experience and learnt it from other women in the community. Midwifery was also still unregulated – the earliest licences recorded in Europe date to the following decade, when they began to be issued in Regensburg, in modern-day Germany.[8] There were obstetrical and gynaecological texts in circulation that provided guidance on caring for women in labour, and the topic was also addressed in many more general medical handbooks and encyclopaedias. The most well known of these is *The Trotula*, an influential anthology of works on women's medicine that was attributed to Trota of Salerno, a twelfth-century woman medical practitioner. It was translated into English in the mid-thirteenth century.[9] Yet, it is perfectly likely that, like Margaret herself, Elizabeth would have had limited literacy, if she were able to read or write at all, and therefore may not have had a use for any of these works. Nevertheless, she was still a medical professional, with highly prized and specialist skills, and her contemporaries would have acknowledged this.

If Elizabeth did in due course arrive in a wheelbarrow, she would no doubt have come armed with the tools of her trade, including her scissors, some additional clean linen, and a birthing stool. Nor would Elizabeth have been the only woman present during Margaret's labour. The birthing chamber has been characterised by scholars as a particularly feminine space, from which men were largely excluded. Agnes, with whom Margaret was staying when she wrote this letter, may not have been present because she was also pregnant at this time, expecting John's youngest brother, Clement, who in due course was born shortly before Margaret's baby. Margaret's mother, Margery, would no doubt be in attendance – Margaret would subsequently give birth to her second son at her mother's home in Geldeston. Other female relatives, friends, neighbours and servants would also be gathered around.

A similar situation is described over 200 years earlier by the courtly poet Marie de France. In her lay 'Le Fresne' or 'The Ash Tree', Marie depicts a lady giving birth to twins in a room surrounded only by women and attended by a trusted maiden.[10] Another source, more contemporary with Margaret's letter, is *The Book of Margery Kempe* (it was completed just three years previously), which provides vivid insights into the practical preparations that had to be undertaken. It describes Kempe's visions in which she imagines herself providing 'a half-gallon of sweet, spiced wine' for the confinements of St Elizabeth, the mother of St John the Baptist, and the Virgin Mary, and gathering cloths for swaddling bands, as well as bedding and food.[11] It was important to have as many caregivers around to offer help and support as was realistically possible, but a male physician would be unlikely to be invited unless serious complications were expected or there were grave concerns about the health of the mother. Similarly, a priest would be summoned only if a need for the last rites was anticipated. John himself would, it is to be hoped, return from London to be near his wife at this crucial time, but he would be expected to remain outside the birthing chamber.

Margaret signs off her letter of December 1441 by reminding her husband that she has sent him a ring 'with the image
of St Margaret' and requesting that he wear it 'as a reminder'
until he is reunited with her. She adds playfully: 'You have left
me such a reminder that makes me think about you both night
and day when I would like to sleep.' Margaret, presumably, sent
John the ring when she notified him that she had conceived, or
perhaps the ring was *the* notification, because St Margaret of
Antioch was the patron saint of pregnant women. When John
wore the ring, others who saw it would also realise that his wife
was expecting a baby: it would serve as a public statement. By
her repetition of 'reminder', Margaret figures this an exchange
of gifts: a pregnancy (John's gift to her, which keeps her awake
at night and therefore ensures she is unable to forget him)
is traded for a ring (a promise of love and fidelity). Around
thirteen or fourteen years later, and after having already given
birth to four surviving children, Margaret continued to see the
humour in pregnancy when she signed a letter, 'by your groan-
ing wife, M.P.'.[12] Margaret's gift to John was not simply a love
token, or notification of her expectant state, it was also apot-
ropaic or talismanic, a lucky charm intended to safeguard its
wearer. Indeed, in this case, it must surely have been intended
to offer protection to the giver and her unborn child as much
as the receiver, because as well as being the patron saint of
pregnant women, St Margaret of Antioch was also the patron
saint of childbirth.

The connection between the legendary saint and pregnancy
and childbirth, to the modern mind at least, seems somewhat
tenuous and even bizarre. St Margaret's cult was widespread in
late medieval England: there are many churches dedicated to
her, and her story circulated in many hagiographies, or saints'
lives, written in Latin and in English. One of the most popular
of these collections was Jacobus de Voragine's *Legenda aurea*

or *The Golden Legend*, which was originally compiled in the thirteenth century.[13] According to the version recorded there, St Margaret was devoured by the devil in the form of a dragon, but when she crossed herself its belly 'burst open and the virgin emerged unscathed'.[14] Aspects of this unlikely narrative were regarded as far-fetched even at the time, and the clerical author of *The Golden Legend* includes the qualification that 'the beast swallowing the maiden and bursting asunder is considered apocryphal and not to be taken seriously'. Nevertheless, Margaret's escape from the belly of the dragon was seen as an appropriate metaphor for a successful birth, where the baby is delivered from its mother's womb alive and well.

Margaret was not an excessively religious woman, but she took her devotions seriously. One noteworthy characteristic of her letters is that she dates them according to the liturgical calendar. This letter, for example, was written 'on the Thursday before St Thomas's day' (the feast of St Thomas the Apostle, the same apostle who received the Virgin Mary's girdle; his feast is now celebrated on 3 July). Even if she doubted the literal truth of St Margaret's encounter with the dragon, she clearly held her in high regard. In this respect she was typical of pregnant women of her day. This was an era of exceptionally high infant mortality, and many women died in childbirth. What is more, the pains of childbirth, like menstruation, were seen as an indication of the sinfulness of the female body, and those who died in childbirth or soon thereafter might not be buried in consecrated ground. It is then no surprise that women turned to prayers, incantations and charms to help preserve themselves and their unborn babies, and that the birthing chamber became a devotional space.

Margaret may even have taken a manuscript with the text of the Passion of St Margaret, or even relics of the saint, into her birthing chamber. Some manuscripts included the instructions that they should be used to bless pregnant women. The British Library has an example of an amulet roll, made from parchment, that dates to around this time, which is inscribed with a prayer asking the Holy Cross to protect the wearer, specifically in childbirth.[15] The amulet also alludes to the passions of some of the saints (although not, in this case, St Margaret herself). It seems to have been used as a birthing girdle or belt, in which case it would have been placed around the woman's distended stomach when she went into labour, while her companions uttered prayers and invocations. Another, well-worn and evidently much used, birthing girdle, now preserved in the Wellcome Collection, promises explicitly that its use will preserve the lives of both the child and mother, at least until the former has been baptised and the latter blessed in a churching ceremony which would take place following the lying-in.[16] Such girdles, if they proved efficacious, were highly valued, and would be lent to female friends. There is also mention in a fifteenth-century will of a mother bequeathing one to her daughter, alongside other devotional objects.[17] Even if Margaret did not make use of a birthing girdle or of relics, she and her companions would certainly have called upon God to ensure a safe delivery.

John may well have returned the ring of St Margaret into her possession for good luck, so that even though he could not enter the chamber himself, he would be there in spirit. The ring certainly seems to have been efficacious. Margaret and John's eldest son, John, was born sometime before the middle of April 1442. The future lineage of the Paston family was guaranteed, or at any rate, more secure. But, in an age of incredibly high infant mortality rates, Margaret and John decided to hedge their bets. When Margaret gave birth to a second son two years later, they also called him John.

3. 'NOT EASY IN OUR HEARTS'

....

28 September 1443 (Margaret to her husband)

....

Almost two years later, in September 1443, Margaret found herself in a similar situation. Once again staying at Oxnead, with Agnes, she wrote to John at the Inner Temple in London, and made a somewhat cryptic reference to her second pregnancy: 'I shall send my mother a token that she gave to me, because I believe the time to send it to her has come, if I keep the promise that I made – I believe I told you what it was.'[1] As Margaret was to give birth on this occasion in Geldeston, she may be signalling to her mother that it is time to begin the preparation for her lying-in. Perhaps the token exchanged between Margaret and her mother was a ring, like that which Margaret had previously given John, or perhaps it was something else, such as a brooch or purse. Presumably Margaret had felt her child moving in her womb and her expectant state was beginning to show because she reminds her husband that once again she needs a new girdle. The purchase of new clothing is certainly not an important concern in this letter, as Margaret herself acknowledges, because at the time John was recovering from a bout of serious illness.

The affection and love that Margaret felt for her husband did not diminish after the birth of their first child. Quite the contrary, this letter is testimony to the depth of Margaret's feelings for John. Margaret opens the letter by asking about the state of John's health, and by giving thanks to God that it is improving, and goes on to tell him: 'I have never had such a sorrowful time as I had from the time I knew of your illness until I knew of your improvement, and my heart is still not much at ease, nor shall be until I know that you are completely well.' Twice in the letter, she asks John to write back and reassure her about his welfare, if he is strong enough to do so, and she emphasises how much she is missing him. She insists, poignantly: 'I would rather you were at home, if your comfort and illness could be as well looked after here as it is where you are now, than have a new gown, even if were of scarlet'; scarlet in this context is not necessarily colour-specific and may simply refer to a rich luxurious cloth. She urges him to seek permission from his father to return home just as soon as he has recovered enough to bear the journey on horseback: 'Because I believe that you would be looked after as tenderly here as you are in London.' She closes the letter by sending John both Agnes's blessing and her own, and by urging him to 'eat and drink well, for that would be the greatest help to you now in respect of your health', and by reassuring him that their infant son continues to thrive.

That Margaret wishes to see her husband return home, where he can be cared for properly, rather than remain in London, might not seem an unusual sentiment, but the reasons behind it are more complex than appears on the surface. In a letter written to her husband over twenty years later, Margaret warns him, 'for God's sake, beware what medicines you take from any physicians of London', and adds that she has lost all trust in them after the past negative experiences of family members, including John's own father.[2] Margaret's suspicion of professional medical practitioners may also reflect a personal sense of discomfort about the displacement of women from some areas of healthcare. In the twelfth century, the renowned German visionary and polymath Abbess Hildegard of Bingen had been responsible for composing the medical treatises *Causae et Curae*, or *Causes and Cures*, and *Physica*; the latter of these two encyclopaedic texts includes a detailed herbarium (a book about medicinal plants) as part of its account of the healing properties of the natural world. The ensuing centuries saw university-educated physicians, who were exclusively men, increasingly dominating the practice of medicine. Women continued to be involved in the more practical aspects of medicine, as midwifes and nurses for example, but, with limited access to books and learning, they found themselves almost entirely excluded from the medical scholarship of the time.[3] There were, inevitably, some exceptions. In the mid-fourteenth century, Philippa of Hainault, wife of Edward III, employed a woman called Cecilia of Oxford as her surgeon.[4] But only a couple of decades before Margaret's letter, in 1421, a group of surgeons in London petitioned parliament to introduce greater medical regulation, and recommended that any woman practising medicine should be punished by imprisonment and a heavy fine.[5] Nevertheless, within the households, women continued to have responsibility for looking after the sick.

In the Middle Ages, bodily and spiritual health were closely interconnected, with cure of the soul being seen as an essential aspect of the care of mental and physical illnesses. Medical practices operated alongside devotional and penitential ones, such as invocations, prayers, charitable donations and pilgrimages, as Margaret's letter of September 1443 vividly illustrates. Unable to tend to her husband's ailments in person, Margaret reassures him that she and Agnes are nevertheless labouring spiritually to bring about his healing. Agnes, she reveals, 'has promised another image of wax, of your weight, to our Lady of Walsingham', indicating that a previous image had already been given, and she also records that she had donated four nobles to the Norwich friars. These were generous gifts. The noble was a gold coin, worth six shillings and eight pence, and four of them would be enough to buy a horse. While we can only guess at John's weight, we do know that beeswax was a valued commodity. Beeswax candles were cleaner, odourless and much more expensive than the pungent tallow candles made of animal fat, so the former were largely used only for church ceremonies or in the households of the wealthy. We can be certain then that the beeswax votive, possibly a representation of John himself, would have been extremely costly, perhaps equivalent to a gift of at least a couple of thousand pounds today, or roughly the value of four horses at the time.

Votive offerings would be placed as close to the shrine as possible, while older offerings would be hung from the roof. Agnes's votive was clearly custom made, but off-the-peg offerings would be sold by vendors from stalls near the entrance to the shrine. A unique example of a late medieval votive offering was discovered during the Second World War in Exeter Cathedral. Shaped like a woman, it was located in a canopy above the tomb of the fifteenth-century bishop Edmund Lacy (it is now preserved in Exeter Cathedral Library and Archives). In this case the wax is hollowed out and the figure is only just over twenty centimetres high, so it is far lighter and smaller than Agnes's offering. It was found alongside several more typical examples of the genre such as wax models of limbs of humans and animals, each representing injured or diseased body parts. Such offerings were made by pilgrims who sought healing either for themselves, members of their family or their livestock, and by pilgrims whose prayers had been answered.

Margaret herself doesn't mention any specific charitable contributions that she had made or planned to make, but she does resolve to travel on pilgrimage to Walsingham, some 22 miles from Oxnead, and to St Leonard's Priory in Norwich some ten to eleven miles away.

The origins of the Shrine of Our Lady at Walsingham are recounted in the 'Pynson Ballad', so called because it was first published in a short pamphlet by the printer Richard Pynson in the late fifteenth century. [6] According to tradition, the shrine was founded in 1061 after a devout laywoman, 'Rychold' or Richeldis de Faverches, received three visions of the Virgin Mary in which she was shown the *Santa Casa* or house of the Annunciation in Nazareth, where the Angel Gabriel had in turn appeared to Mary and announced that she would become the mother of God. In Richeldis's vision, the Virgin Mary asked Richeldis to have a copy of the *Santa Casa* constructed in Norfolk as a site of pilgrimage, promising that 'All that seek me there shall find succour'. Richeldis complied, and, after miraculously overcoming some difficulties in its construction, built a wooden replica, the Holy House, which was subsequently encased in stone to ensure its durability. In reality, the foundation of the shrine may well date to the following century and the establishment of the Priory of Our Lady.

By the fifteenth century, Walsingham had become one of the most renowned pilgrimage destinations in England and across Western Christendom. The Pynson Ballad enumerates in some detail the miraculous cures available to 'all who are sick, bodily or spiritually' and who seek the intervention of Our Lady at Walsingham: the dead are revived, the lame, blind, deaf and wounded are healed, as are lunatics and lepers, and those possessed by fiends have the evil spirits driven out of them. The spiritual needs of the multitude of pilgrims who visited it were met by the priory's Augustinian canons. The Walsingham devotions of Agnes evidently proved effective, and John recovered from his illness. Much later in life, when Margaret was in her early sixties and her own health was starting to decline, her third son, Edmond, suggested that he accompany her on another planned visit there.[7]

In the early 1930s Walsingham was revived as a pilgrimage site, having been destroyed in the Reformation. Only remnants of the priory survive, and the original medieval 'Holy House' and Marian statue have been lost. Arriving at the Anglican shrine one late morning in early summer, I was surprised to find it almost deserted. The shrine church was empty, except for one woman sitting in prayer or meditation or perhaps just thinking. Inside the church is a reconstruction of the Holy House at Nazareth and, within it, of the statue of Our Lady of Walsingham. Fragments of the original stonework are embedded within the house's exterior and interior walls, and a window looks out at the church's main altar. Having the shrine to myself, I found it exceptionally peaceful, lit by the rows of lamps and candles lining the walls, and of course I stopped to light one for my mother, and one for myself.

On our visit to Walsingham, we had planned to go on to the Roman Catholic shrine at the fourteenth-century Slipper Chapel, so called because it was the final station for medieval pilgrims, who would remove their shoes to walk the last mile barefoot. Some modern pilgrims still do. But the sun was directly overhead, and we had our dogs with us, so we retired instead to the shade of Walsingham Abbey grounds, the site of the medieval priory, to eat our picnic lunch. Almost immediately inside the abbey grounds, visitors are greeted by a striking view of a towering arch, a folly constructed out of the east window of the medieval priory. There are other ornamental features built or adapted from its original structures and stones in the elaborate nineteenth-century gardens, but the imposing late medieval gatehouse remains, as do the refectory ruins, two wells and a room referred to as 'the crypt' (albeit with an added door and windows). The crypt contained some information boards which referenced Agnes Paston's donation and stated that, by the beginning of the fourteenth century, the demand for votive candles was so great that Walsingham had to import them from Russia.

The second shrine that Margaret proposes to visit in her letter is the Priory of St Leonard in Norwich. St Leonard of Noblac is famously the patron saint of prisoners, but also, fittingly given Margaret's expectant state, another patron saint of women in labour. The son of a fifth-century Frankish nobleman in the court of King Clovis I, St Leonard converted to Christianity and devoted himself to healing the sick and petitioning on behalf of the imprisoned. Rejecting an ecclesiastical appointment, he chose to become a hermit in a forest in Limousin. According to his legend, Leonard was summoned by the then king (Clovis's grandson) to assist his pregnant wife, who had gone into premature labour, and whose own health was rapidly deteriorating. Following Leonard's prayers, she recovered miraculously and gave birth to a healthy son. The priory dedicated to the saint in Norwich was a dependant cell of the cathedral priory. It was located outside the city, across the fourteenth-century Bishop Bridge at the end of the Bishopgate, next to a road now known as Gas Hill (referring to the former gas works that later occupied the site). In contrast to the Priory of Our Lady at Walsingham, little physical evidence remains, though it is memorialised in the present-day St Leonard's Road, which runs along its eastern border, and number 85, located on the site of main buildings, is called 'The Priory'. On our own pilgrimage there, we struggled to locate the address, which is not visible from the road, only to realise, eventually, that we had by chance parked directly in front of its drive.

Although, in comparison to Walsingham, St Leonard's was a minor local pilgrimage site, by the fifteenth century, the priory church nevertheless drew a regular stream of visitors, who were attracted by its images and relics.[8] These included, as one would expect, a famous bejewelled statue of St Leonard himself, as well as one of the saint's bones, and his cap. Alongside the girdle of the Blessed Virgin, which was located in a pyx beneath the altar, there was also an icon of Mary, adorned with an Agnus Dei, or Lamb of God, around its neck, a sapphire ring, a pectoral or ornamental breast plate, jet beads and a brooch. The Virgin Mary's girdle may have been lent out by the priory to aristocratic or noble women for their birthing chambers (as was the famous Westminster girdle), but a woman of Margaret's status, wealthy but not of the highest social ranks, would have had to be content to leave offerings at the shrine. Like the Walsingham Virgin and that of St Leonard, this statue would have been adorned with votive items relating to illness and childbirth. Margaret very probably intended her visits to Walsingham and to St Leonard's to serve a dual function, to facilitate both her husband's ongoing recovery and the safe delivery of her second child.

Margaret's letter of September 1443 is not solely focused on her husband's health and her own pregnancy. Other, more mundane matters are also addressed and, in the midst of Margaret's concerns about John's recovery, she mentions that her father-in-law, Justice William, had recently travelled on business to Beccles in Suffolk, staying overnight in the home of her mother and stepfather at nearby Geldeston. Margaret had hoped that William would return with one of her gowns, presumably one that would fit her during her pregnancy, but once again she was disappointed: William had come home without it. Her mother said she would have to collect it herself when she next visited, and her stepfather and uncle offered to come to Oxnead and take her home with them. Margaret was not keen on the idea of travelling to Geldeston at this point because it would delay her receipt of any updates on John's progress. She confides to him, 'So God help me I will excuse myself from going there if I can.' Ralph Garneys and his brother-in-law were not acting entirely selflessly in proposing their trip: Margaret explains that while in Oxnead they planned 'to amuse themselves with their hawks'.

Hawking was a popular sport in late medieval England, and it is one in which the men in the Paston family participated. An expensive pastime, as the birds had to be trained and maintained, in its most elite forms it was mainly the privilege of the royalty and nobility, although at the other end of the social spectrum fowlers also used birds of prey in their hunting. Information about the sport can be found in the so-called *Book of St Albans,* or *Book of Hawking, Hunting, and Blasing of Arms* (in other words, heraldry), which was printed in the later fifteenth century. Intriguingly, parts of this text are attributed to a woman, Juliana Berners, usually identified, probably inaccurately, as the prioress of Sopwell Nunnery, close to St Albans.[9] While Berners may not have written all or any of the treatises that comprise the *Book,* she probably assembled it. The essay on hunting, which is written in verse and is for the most part a translation of an earlier Anglo-Norman work, takes the form of instructions by a 'dame' (which could mean either a mother or simply a teacher) addressed to her 'child' or 'son'. Within the text, correct hunting practices are seen as inherent to correct gentlemanly conduct.

The section on hawking in the *Book of St Albans* includes a classification of the birds of prey according to the size and magnificence of the bird and the social rank of its handlers. The gyrfalcon, the largest falcon in the world, is the bird of kings; the peregrine falcon is that of princes; the rock falcon or merlin that of dukes; and the tercel or tiercel that of earls (the term tiercel is applied to male peregrines because they are a third smaller than the females). This hierarchy continues down to knaves, servants and children, who would all handle kestrels. Knights, squires and yeomen, men of the Paston rank, would usually own saker and lanner falcons, and goshawks or hobbies.

Hawking was a sport that, unusually for the time, was also open to women as well as men, although if the written record is anything to go by, it does seem to have been largely enjoyed only by ladies of the highest ranks. The appropriate bird for a lady, at least according to *The Book of St Albans*, is the female merlin, although the late-fourteenth-century conduct book *Le Ménagier de Paris*, translated as the *Good Wife's Guide*, suggests it is the sparrowhawk.[10] The reality may well have been that, as for men, the size of the raptor depended on the status of the woman who was handling it.[11] Even if Margaret did not frequent the royal and aristocratic courts where hawking was such a popular activity, she would have been involved, albeit indirectly, in the sport. *Le Ménagier de Paris*, ostensibly written by an elderly husband for his young wife, includes guidance to the woman on how to look after and train birds of prey, with the explanation, 'so that in the hunting season you can divert yourself with this pursuit if you so choose'.[12] Margaret may well have known how to handle and fly the falcons and hawks that belonged to the men of the family, and she would have on occasion had to oversee their care. While Margaret never mentions going hawking herself, it is liberating to imagine her as a young woman, putting aside her worries about her husband for a little while and setting off on horseback across the fields around Paston or Oxnead in pursuit of small game and vermin, with her spaniels by her side and a goshawk perched on the thumb of her deer-skin gauntlet, the jesses looped loosely around her fingers.

4. 'CROSSBOWS AND WINDLASSES'

In the early years of her marriage, Margaret's letters were mainly concerned with pregnancy and motherhood, punctuated by anxieties about her husband's health, but, although she continued to bear children, by the end of the decade her situation had changed dramatically, and other worries took precedence. In a justifiably famous but undated letter that must have been written in the autumn or early winter of 1448, when Margaret was still in her twenties, she wrote to her husband requesting that he urgently obtain for her 'crossbows and windlasses ... poleaxes ... [and] jacks' and suggesting he might borrow them from their friend Sir John Fastolf.[1] Margaret was writing from the village of Gresham. Its castle, a fortified manor house, had been seized by enemies of the family, but in the absence of John, who was still in London managing the legal and diplomatic challenges to this assault, Margaret had taken up residence on site, asserting ownership of the estate and leading, in person, the defence of its properties.

Margaret may have been pregnant with her first daughter, Margery, at this time, but if that were the case she makes no mention of it, nor does she comment on the location of her young sons during these hostilities. Rather, she complains to John about the practical martial difficulties she encountered: 'Your houses are so low that no one can shoot out with longbows, even if we might have ever so much need.' Margaret was very much in the thick of the action, and fully informed about the practicalities of warfare. She describes in some detail the defensive structures that their opponents have put in place to defend the castle: 'They have made bars to bar across the doors, and they have made loopholes in every quarter of the house to shoot out of, both with bows and with handguns. And those holes that have been made for handguns are scarcely kneehigh from the floor, and five such holes have been made. No man could shoot out of them with hand-bows.' Margaret also reveals the source of her information – a Paston spy had been drinking with the enemy and had reported back to her, providing a full account of what he had heard.

The mid-1440s marked a turning point for the Paston family, with the death of Margaret's father-in-law, Justice William. His widow, Agnes, remained at Oxnead, and soon after a man called John Hauteyn took advantage of her more vulnerable state and made a claim on the property, asserting that it was his rightful inheritance. This resulted in a dispute that was to drag on for some years. These were by no means the first conflicts over property in which the Pastons had become embroiled. The previous decade the manor of East Beckham had been claimed by force by the son of a former owner even before William's purchase of it was finalised. The matter was apparently resolved shortly before his death. But with William's passing, the family lost their claim once and for all. Now the ownership of John and Margaret's own residence was also being challenged, and the threats against them were escalating.

Justice William had bought the manor of Gresham in 1427 from Sir William Moleyns and the courtier Thomas Chaucer, the son of the poet Geoffrey, who served as Speaker of the House of Commons in the early fifteenth century. Justice William subsequently gifted it to John and Margaret on their marriage. It was Margaret's jointure, which meant that it would be owned by her if she outlived her husband. Gresham became their main home. However, in 1445, Sir William Moleyns' heir, his daughter, Eleanor, married Robert, 3rd Baron Hungerford (referred to in the Paston correspondence as Lord Moleyns). Working with a lawyer called John Heydon, a neighbour of the Pastons, Hungerford asserted his wife's claim on Gresham and in February 1448, when neither John nor Margaret were in residence, he took possession by force.

The dispute over Gresham continued in the months that followed and culminated in a violent attack on Margaret in January 1449 by, allegedly, a thousand of Moleyns' men. It is vividly recorded in a petition to Henry VI that John presented to parliament later that year.[2] Having blown up the walls, and broken down the gates and doors, Moleyns' army, described by John as a 'riotous people', then 'came into the said mansion, the wife of your said beseecher [i.e. Margaret] at that time being therein, and 12 people with her, which people they drove out of the said mansion and undermined the wall of the chamber wherein the wife of your said beseecher was, and bore her out of the gates'. The houses were then destroyed, their contents ransacked and robbed, and the tenants terrorised. John reports that Moleyns' men had said that if they had found him on the premises, they would have killed him.

No letters survive from Margaret describing these events directly, and perhaps her silence is revealing about the extent of the horror that she faced. Even though she must have feared for her life, she was not going to stand down or leave her post voluntarily. The following month, Margaret writes to her husband from Sustead, around a mile away from Gresham, from the home of their ally, John Damme, where she had fled following the assault.[3] Margaret wants to update him about the ongoing problems at Gresham, yet she says nothing of her own recent experience. Margaret was clearly not the only brave woman in the household. Tellingly, Margaret describes sending her trusted servant Kate to deliver a message to the men threatening the Gresham tenants loyal to the Paston cause, 'because I could get no man to take it'. Margaret takes the opportunity of this letter to remind John that even in London he is not safe. She advises him to ensure that he does not go out on his own because 'Lord Moleyns has a company of ruffians with him who do not care what they do, and they are the sort to be feared most'.

In Sustead, Margaret soon realised that she too was still at risk, and in the second half of February, having heard rumours that Lord Moleyns' men planned to kidnap her and imprison her inside Gresham Castle, she made her escape to Norwich on the pretence that she was going to have new clothes made for herself and her children. Margaret finally admits to feelings of fear when she confesses that, 'after I heard these tidings, my heart was not at ease until I got here', and asserts: 'I would be very sorry to live as close to Gresham as I did, until this business with Lord Moleyns and you is fully resolved.'[4] When John and Margaret did finally succeed in reclaiming Gresham, the ransacked castle was so dilapidated it was uninhabitable. It was never rebuilt.

Margaret's account of the battle for Gresham in her letter of 1448, and that provided by John in his petition (which must have been based on what Margaret and others told him), provide valuable insights into late medieval warfare. Castles and castellated manor houses like that at Gresham were designed to withstand raids and offer refuge from enemy forces but were vulnerable to being besieged. In a letter written to his brother John III over two decades later, Margaret's eldest son asks for the measurements of the site and includes a crudely drawn plan.[5] This reveals that the walls formed a square, and with towers of varying dimensions projecting from each corner, one substantially larger than the others. According to the sketch, there was a drawbridge which would offer access across the encircling moat; John states in his letter that this was on the north side. The manor house was situated within the castle walls; it is in this house that Margaret and her family would normally have resided.[6]

The ruins of Gresham, overgrown by trees and vegetation, stand today on private farmland, but the arial view offered by Google Earth clearly reveals the location of the moated fortification. Shortly before our trip to Norfolk, the Paston Footprints project, a National Heritage Lottery Fund collaboration which has developed a series of Paston heritage trails, posted their new circular walk around the area, so my wife and I, accompanied of course by the dogs, were able to christen it.[7] Our drive into Gresham from Sustead took us along the evocatively named Hellgate Lane. Having left the Land Rover near All Saints Church in the village, we walked past the village sign, with Gresham Castle as its central image and the Paston coat of arms in the top-left corner. As we turned down off the main road, we spotted a cul-de-sac called Paston Close. Leaving the village and its morning school run behind us, we found ourselves in welcome solitude, save for the military jets flying overhead, reminding us of the martial past of this otherwise remote spot. On the remainder of our outing we only encountered one other dog walker, and a BT Openreach engineer undertaking repairs in the area. The best view of the Gresham Castle site is from the corner before the junction, where there is a clearing in the trees and hedgerows, although we had to make our way behind the Openreach van to see it.

Driving or walking past it on the road, you would not realise it was anything more than a small wood. Nevertheless, looking across the crops in the field, it is possible to discern the shape of the castle and its moat.

The weapons and protective gear that, in her letter of 1448, Margaret asks her husband to send are typical of the time. The crossbow had an extended range, which would prove invaluable in a siege situation, and it was also reasonably accurate. It had the additional advantage of being relatively easy to use, so it would have mattered less that Margaret did not have the support of a trained militia at Gresham. The windlass was a mechanism for bending back heavy crossbows or arbalests, which had greater force and could hurl larger projectiles. The poleaxe, in contrast, was designed for close combat. It took the form of a long wooden shaft topped with a relatively small metal head that comprised an axe on one side, a spike or hammer on the other, and a spike projecting from the top. It was particularly effective for fighting opponents wearing armour. Jacks were defensive coats. Margaret may well have been referring specifically to the jack of plate, which was made of overlapping iron plates sewn between layers of fabric and designed to protect the upper body from assault. The jack offered a light-weight alternative to full plate armour. Plate sleeves, constructed in a similar way, could be attached to protect the arms.

Margaret also reports on the weapons used by Moleyns' men: bows and 'handguns'. Archery was an important ancient skill used in hunting as well as warfare. Handguns were more recent introductions, and were so called because of their portability, which distinguished them from cannons. Whereas the modern term handgun refers to the pistol, its medieval predecessor was more like a rifle, with a metal barrel and a handle. It was unwieldy to fire as it did not have a trigger, but was ignited by applying a lit cord. It was also less exact than the crossbow. Margaret's description of the low apertures made for the handguns suggests that they were being fired from a kneeling or crouching position rather than from standing.

John's petition indicates that when Moleyns' men-of-arms came to evict Margaret from Gresham, they were far better equipped than the Paston band. These men wore cuirasses, or metal body armour that included both a chest plate and back piece, as well as jacks and brigandines (similar to jacks but with the metal plates rivetted rather than sewn into the fabric). They also wore sallets, bowl-shaped metal helmets that flare out at the back of the neck, often worn with a visor or a bevor, which was designed to protect the neck and lower half of the face. They were armed with glaives or spears, bows and arrows, handguns and long, rectangular shields known as pavises which could be used with bows, crossbows and handguns. These men also carried cauldrons filled with burning rods, long hooks, mattocks and long tree trunks to use as battering rams. They were intent upon knocking down the walls, breaking through the gates and doors, and demolishing and burning down the houses. With only twelve people there to support her, Margaret must have been terrified by the arrival of this hostile and dangerous army determined to take Gresham by force. She may well have taken up weapons against the invaders. Certainly, medieval manuscript illustrations depict images of women bearing arms, such as a representation of a woman aiming a crossbow at knights in an elephant tower that is found in the margins of an important fourteenth-century legal manuscript, the Smithfield Decretals.[8]

One of the key figures behind the dispute over Gresham was the Norfolk lawyer John Heydon, who owned neighbouring Baconsthorpe Castle, less than four miles to the west. Today its substantial ruins give some sense of how Gresham would also have looked before its almost complete obliteration.

Like Gresham, the remains of this fifteenth-century fortified and moated manor house are now located in open countryside and access is via a rough pot-holed track. Baconsthorpe enjoyed a longer history than Gresham. Heydon's son converted part of it into a textile factory, and the site includes the remains of a turreted Elizabethan outer gatehouse. An ornamental lake and formal gardens were added in the sixteenth or seventeenth century, but by the 1750s the family could no longer afford the castle's upkeep, so much of it was pulled down and the materials from which it had been built were sold off. Only the outer gatehouse remained inhabited, until in the early twentieth century it became structurally unsound. By the time we had made our way from Gresham to the castle, evening was already drawn in, and the flint skeleton of the inner gatehouse, the towers and wall all appeared somewhat sinister, even a little threatening. I wasn't entirely surprised to learn that the castle was said to be haunted by a spectral sentry, even though I didn't see him myself. Heydon would no doubt have insisted a guard remain on duty, even after everyone was long dead.

Heydon was a long-time rival of the Paston family, involved in the claims against William concerning the ownership of East Beckham: his father-in-law was William's opponent in that case. Heydon's background was similar to William's; he was a man of humble birth whose success as a lawyer brought him money and influence. He served as a Justice of the Peace and Knight of the Shire but, after operating against the interests of the city in a dispute with the cathedral priory, he was dismissed from his position as Recorder of Norwich. His blatant ambition and self-interest made him a hated figure across much of East Anglia. He was nevertheless a shrewd political player with several high-ranking clients, and from the mid-1530s he served as agent for the powerful William de la Pole, 1st Duke of Suffolk, married to Geoffrey Chaucer's granddaughter Alice.

In a letter written in 1444, some years prior to the outbreak of troubles at Gresham, Margaret took the opportunity
to relay some local scandal about Heydon.[9] Heydon, claiming
that his wife Eleanor's children were not his own, cast his wife
out, and threatened to cut off her nose and murder her new-
born child. Medieval religion and culture were somewhat at
odds over the question of adultery. It was frowned upon by
the church because sexual activity was only sanctioned within
marriage, and adultery was seen fundamentally to undermine
that sacrament. Despite this, in the literature of the time, adultery, especially when committed by women, was often seen as
a subject of comedy, as in Chaucer's fabliaux (or short bawdy
tales) such as 'The Miller's Tale' or 'The Merchant's Tale'.
Alternatively, it was idealised, as is illustrated by the chivalric romances featuring the relationships between Lancelot and
King Arthur's wife, Guinevere, or Tristan and King Mark's
wife, Isolde. The twelfth-century French author Andreas
Capellanus, or Andrew the Chaplain, wrote a satirical treatise
entitled *De Amore*, known in English as *The Art of Courtly
Love*, which justified adultery with the claim that only affection but not passion can be experienced in marriage.

In medieval society, women were often subjected to much
stricter punishments for sexual infractions than men. In
fact, facial mutilation as a form of punishment of the sort
threatened by Heydon had a long history. According to a law
introduced into England in the eleventh century by King Cnut:
'If a woman during her husband's lifetime commits adultery
with another man, and it becomes known, let her afterwards
become herself a public disgrace and her lawful husband is
to have all she owns, and she is to lose her nose and ears.'[10]
Although this punishment seems to have been enacted rarely,
if ever, it does feature fictionally in the short narrative poem
'Bisclavret' written by Marie de France.[11] 'Bisclavret' is a tale

about a noble knight with a terrible secret: for three days of every week he transforms into a werewolf. On finally discovering his secret, his wife takes another lover as part of her plan to rid herself of him by trapping him as a werewolf forever. The werewolf gets his revenge, attacking the lover and tearing off his wife's nose. 'Bisclavret' is sympathetic in its portrayal of the werewolf, who is ultimately rewarded: not only does he turn back into a man, but his land is restored to him by the king. Meanwhile, his wife is tortured and, with her lover, banished, and Marie tells us that her facial disfigurement is passed on to her daughters and female descendants.

Even within the world of literature, then, double standards were applied to men and women, and it was the case that in real life a woman adulterer was likely to receive much stronger public disapproval than a man who committed the same act or even worse crimes. The woman's own family would, almost certainly, feel that they had been shamed by her actions, and she might well be disowned, as seems to have happened in this case for Heydon's wife, Eleanor. Heydon meanwhile remained in the favour of his in-laws; he was even named as a beneficiary in the will of Eleanor's father. The husband would feel personally dishonoured by the betrayal, especially if, as in the Heydon case, he believed that his wife had given birth to another man's child, thus disrupting lines of succession and inheritance. He would also feel humiliated. Despite the positive treatment of Bisclavret, medieval cuckolds (the husbands of adulterous wives), such as John the carpenter in Chaucer's 'Miller's Tale', are often presented as figures of ridicule. While his wife, Alison, goes unpunished for her extramarital sex, John ends up with a broken arm, publicly shamed and labelled as mad.

Margaret's account of the Heydon scandal is matter of fact. On first reading her letter it isn't immediately clear where her sympathies lie, although there was certainly no love lost between Margaret and Heydon. Perhaps Margaret was simply relaying some nasty gossip about a Paston foe; perhaps she thought that Heydon deserved his bad fortune, or that his accusations were misplaced. She may even have felt some sympathy for Eleanor and her offspring. Whatever the case, Margaret didn't commit her views to writing. Even before the outbreak of hostilities at Gresham, she didn't want anyone outside her family and trusted circle of servants and associates to know what she really thought about the affair.

Somewhat unexpectedly, despite the crisis unfolding at the time, Margaret's 1448 letter about the Gresham conflict is not limited to martial matters. Margaret also somehow finds the time to append a request for provisions that includes '1lb of almonds and 1lb of sugar', as well as some 'frieze', or woollen cloth, for gowns for the children and 'a yard of black broadcloth for a hood for me'. Lamenting the lack of good fabric that can be obtained locally, she instructs John about where he should go to get the cheapest and widest range of material for the dresses, and about the price that should be paid for the fabric for the hood.

In her earlier letter of 1444, alongside the gossip about Heydon, Margaret also includes instructions about shopping for their infants. She asks John to make some purchases on her behalf, sending him samples of lace for him to match. John, like his father, was evidently not always the best shopper. Margaret reprimands him gently for purchasing caps that are too small for their two young sons. He may have obtained them ready-made rather than from a cap or hat maker's workshop. Evidently, they were not high quality either: Margaret asks him to buy replacements that are 'finer' as well as bigger. Four years later, Margaret is wiser and more attuned to her husband's shortcomings: she gives very precise directions as to weights and measures; she also specifies exactly where he should make his purchases.

What these two letters reveal is the sheer breadth of women's household duties, as well as the extent to which Margaret, and other women of her social class, relied on their husbands and male family members to help with the purchasing of clothing, fabric, more exotic foodstuffs and household goods that couldn't be obtained locally. The 1448 letter also reveals the continuing importance of such seemingly mundane activities even when trapped in what was, effectively, a war zone. Indeed, another way of looking at this would be to recognise that, with its very specific requests for weapons and armour as well as for nuts, sugar and fabrics, the letter of 1448 begins as well as ends with a shopping list. After eight years of marriage, Margaret was used to planning, scheduling, delegating and giving orders and instructions. It is no surprise then that she approached martial conflict in the same way that she approached household management.

5. 'A POT OF TREACLE'

By the summer of 1451, Margaret and her husband had settled in Norwich and were still looking for a permanent residence, but this was not an ideal time to be hunting for a new house. In a letter dated 1 July of that year, Margaret sent John news of illness at home, telling him that 'both I and your daughter have suffered greatly since you left here'.[1] Neighbours and friends were also affected: 'One of the most handsome young men of this parish is very ill with the pestilence; God knows how he will get on.' Margaret goes on to report on a death: 'Sir Harry Inglose passed to God last night, may God absolve his soul, and was carried to St Faith's at 9 o'clock today, and will be buried there.' The term 'pestilence' that Margaret uses could refer to 'an infectious or contagious disease; a fatal epidemic or disease, plague', or more specifically to 'an outbreak of bubonic plague'.[2] Margaret was writing in the middle of the 1449–52 pandemic. Margaret and John's daughter, Margery, was just an infant at this time, so this public health crisis must have been particularly worrying for her parents.

Scientists and historians now believe the medieval bubonic plague pandemic, or Second Plague Pandemic, originated as early as the late twelfth or early thirteenth century. The so-called Black Death spread across Asia, Europe, Islamic North Africa and possibly also Sub-Saharan Africa,[3] reaching England in the mid-fourteenth century. The fourteenth-century Italian writer and poet Giovanni Boccaccio described its horrendous symptoms in his famous work *The Decameron*: 'In men and women alike there appeared, at the beginning of the malady, certain swellings, either on the groin or under the armpits, whereof some waxed of the bigness of a common apple, others like unto an egg, some more and some less, and these the vulgar named plague-boils.'[4] These boils, or buboes, then started to appear all over the body, and were followed by 'black or livid blotches' which like the buboes were 'a very certain token of coming death'.

The Black Death decimated the population of Europe. A monk of St Albans, Thomas Walsingham, recorded in his chronicle that: 'Towns once packed with people were emptied of their inhabitants, and the plague spread so thickly that the living were hardly able to bury the dead. In some religious houses not more than two survived out of twenty. It was calculated by several people that barely a tenth of mankind remained alive.'[5] East Anglia was badly hit by the Black Death, especially in its cities and towns, with Norwich seeing its population reduced by up to three-quarters. Many of the dead were buried communally in pits. The Black Death was followed over the coming decades and centuries by waves of epidemics of bubonic and pneumonic plague, sweating sickness and other diseases. Pneumonic plague is a form of plague that affects the lungs causing coughing and shortness of breath as well as fever and vomiting. It kills extremely quickly. Sweating sickness, sometimes called English sweating sickness, was a contagious disease that was first recorded in 1485 and spread from England to continental Europe where it circulated until the mid-sixteenth century. It involved cold and hot sweats as well as a range of other symptoms and lasted for around 24 hours before the patient either recovered or died.

The impact of the Black Death and ensuing epidemics was enormous, economically as well as socially, causing labour shortages and widespread unrest. Walsingham observed: 'Rents dwindled and land was left untilled for want of tenants (who were nowhere to be found). And so much wretchedness followed these ills that afterwards the world could never return to its former state.' One of Chaucer's *Canterbury Tales*, 'The Pardoner's Tale', is set in a time of plague and explores the corruption and immorality that, according to some contemporaries, caused its outbreak in the first place, and which certainly followed it in many areas. It tells of three riotous men carousing in a tavern, who set off to kill a 'thief men call Death, / that in this country all the people slays' and who 'has a thousand slain in this pestilence'.[6] At the other extreme, the intense and sometimes zealous religious enthusiasm of the late fourteenth and the fifteenth centuries has been seen as a response to pandemic and epidemic devastation. All this suffering and upheaval inevitably offered opportunities to some of the survivors. One chronicler, Henry Knighton, wrote that in the autumn following the arrival of the Black Death, 'it was not possible to hire a reaper for less than 8d [pence] and his food, or a mower for 12d with his food'.[7] In the later fourteenth century, Justice William Paston's father, Clement, seized this chance to accumulate wealth, enabling his son to climb sharply up the ranks.

Nevertheless, even if the Paston family line benefitted from the Black Death, it also suffered as result of the later waves of plague, and the letters include numerous references to the pestilence. In 1452, a year after Margaret's letter, Agnes informed Margaret's husband that in Norwich 'people are still dying, but not so grievously as they did'.[8] Despite these positive signs, the following summer both Agnes and Margaret sent John news of two deaths. One was that of Margaret's uncle, Philip Berney, who, in the words of Agnes, 'passed to God last Monday in the greatest pain that I ever saw in a person'.[9] The second was Sir John Heveningham, who returned home from attending mass and went into his garden where he collapsed. According to Margaret, 'his sickness took him on Tuesday at nine o'clock before noon, and by two after noon he was dead'.[10] But, given how sudden this latter death was, it could have been due to another cause.

In her letter of July 1451, Margaret asks her husband to obtain medicine for herself and the infant Margery. Margaret's domestic healthcare responsibilities were not limited to treating minor ailments or nursing sick members of the family but included prescribing and even dispensing medicines for the most serious of illnesses. As her letters reveal, Margaret kept a supply of treatments to hand, and through them we can get a glimpse of the contents of her medicine cabinet. Some Margaret would have made herself out of plants she would have found in her kitchen or utilitarian garden, where plants for culinary, medicinal and general household purposes were grown. Alongside brassicas, legumes and root vegetables such as cabbage, sprouts, peas, beans, cabbage and carrots, herbs such as dandelion, fennel, peppermint, rosemary, sage and the evocatively named feverfew, knitbone (comfrey) and self-heal would be found. Margaret had a strong sense of the efficacy of plants in treating illnesses and injuries and was willing to offer advice or to distribute remedies to neighbours and friends. When one of her kinsmen fell sick, Margaret recommended offering him an infusion of mint or milfoil (yarrow) to increase his tolerance of food.[11] She also suggested that he be treated with some of her white wine, which was widely prescribed, often in diluted form, as a general tonic and panacea. Wine was also used to sterilise wounds and equipment.

I benefited from some insights into the natural medicine that Margaret favoured when I went to visit her parish church of St Peter Hungate in Norwich. At the time of my visit, the building, which was deconsecrated in the first half of the twentieth century and is now an arts space, was hosting works by the ceramicist Katie Spragg. This exhibition combined the medieval past with medicinal plants and traditions of healing and care. In the accompanying leaflet, Spragg comments on the influence of medieval herbals, or collections of natural remedies, on her art: 'I was interested in the way fact and fiction blurred in these manuscripts, but also that this doesn't matter, different types of knowledge merge in the meeting of plant and human worlds.' Spragg's ceramics incorporated spring wildflowers from the churchyard, including daisy, dandelion, chickweed, poppy, violet and primrose, all of which were at one time thought to have healing properties. Two pieces, 'Doctrine of Signatures: Hair, 2021' and 'Doctrine of Signatures: Hands, 2021', were inspired by the ancient belief that ailments of the organs or limbs can be treated by plants that resemble the affected body part. An artwork entitled 'Medicinal Plants of Hungate' was located so that it was illuminated by the light flowing in from the windows. My attention was drawn to the east window with its late medieval stained glass. The angels at the top were installed as part of Paston-funded repair work. At the bottom of the window, in the centre, is the figure of St Agatha, patron saint of breast cancer patients.

Margaret would have recognised the medicinal qualities of the local plants that featured in Spragg's exhibition, many of which are still to be found growing in the churchyard of St Peter Hungate. Other medical supplies had to be purchased from further afield, such as 'triacle' (treacle) or theriac, a remedy that was used as an antidote for toxins and poison and as a cure for a wide range of complaints. The compound theriac was developed in late Antiquity by the Imperial physician Galen, whose work became hugely influential in Europe in the High Middle Ages.[12] It was complicated to produce and contained an extensive list of ingredients including viper flesh, opium from poppy seeds and the roots, bark, flowers, seeds and fruits of a wide range of other plants, mixed with gums, oils, resins and honey. Some of the ingredients may well have been quite effective in combating toxins and bacteria. Theriac was quite distinct from treacle of 'mummie', a substance extracted in the medieval and early modern periods from embalmed corpses, originally taken from Ancient Egyptian tombs, which was believed to have healing qualities. 'Triacle' of the sort with which Margaret was familiar was taken orally, mixed with water or wine, or applied directly to the skin.

'Triacle' was widely used to treat victims of plague and pestilence. In her 1451 letter, Margaret explains to her husband that she has already sent on to her uncle a pot of treacle that John had purchased on his behalf, and she asks him to send her another from London as soon as possible. Because treacle was valuable commodity, it was manufactured in a number of cities, including Cairo, Constantinople, Genoa and Venice, and exported across Europe. In a subsequent deadly wave of the pandemic, in the spring or early summer of 1479, Margaret's eldest son, John II, sent his mother 'three pots of treacle of Genoa', asking her to pass at least one on to his brother, John III.[13] John II, like Margaret, was sceptical of the medical practitioners in the city: he was concerned that the seal of one of the treacle pots may have been tampered with, even though his London apothecary had promised him that they had not been opened since they were sent from Genoa. In November of the same year, the newly married John III included a postscript in a letter to his eldest brother, asking for a further two pots of treacle of Genoa because he and his wife, Margery, and their young children had already used all they had.[14] He specified that the treacle should cost sixteen pence, roughly the equivalent of two days' wages for a skilled craftsman. John III lamented that 'the people die in agony in Norwich, and especially near my house, but my wife and my women don't come out, and we cannot flee further'.

While no book of medicinal recipes from Margaret's early married life survives in the Paston collection, we do know that, a quarter of a century later, Margaret's son John II commissioned the copying of a 'little book of physic', or a book about medicine.[15] This book is actually a compendium of texts about a range of medical and medical-related matters, including astrology, uroscopy (the examination of urine for diagnostic purposes) and tracts on the treatment of the plague by John of Burgundy. The last make several recommendations concerning lifestyle and diet (including avoiding baths and citrus fruit, keeping the window shut and burning juniper branches), and provide advice on treatment with medicinal herbs and phlebotomy or bloodletting. Medieval medical science emphasised the impact of the planets and stars on physical health. This manuscript includes, as well as illustrations of urine glasses with labels describing the colour of their contents, an image of a zodiac man showing the correspondence between parts of the body and the astrological signs.

It is quite possible that John II sought out some of the books he commissioned or purchased for the use of other members of his household and wider family, and his mother is likely to have had a keen interest in this one. It is worth noting that alongside the Latin John of Burgundy plague tracts there is also an English version, which would make it more easily accessible to someone like Margaret, without a formal education. Nor is Margaret likely to have been the only woman in the family who would have found the contents useful. Margery Brews

Paston, the wife of John III, continued her mother-in-law's engagement with matters of medicine and healthcare. In one letter to Margery, John III asked for her to send him a compress to treat knee pain and full instructions on its use.[16] His questions about how to apply it and for how long indicate that it is Margery and not John who has the medical knowledge.

Women shared their recipes with, and dispensed treatments to, relatives and friends. The earliest recipe in the Paston collection, for a 'fair wholesome drink of ale', was one that Margaret's father-in-law obtained from a Norfolk gentlewoman, Lady Sibylle Boys.[17] The recipe involves chopping sage, wood avens (or St Benedict's herb), rosemary and thyme, and placing it in a bag with a newly laid hen's egg. This is then hung in the barrel of ale along with another bag containing ground cloves, mace and spikenard (an aromatic plant). The combination of the herbs and ale would make a tonic. The addition of a newly laid egg to the barrel 'for preservation' may relate to the bloom which protects such eggs from bacteria. On one occasion, Margaret was confident that, if requested, her friend Lady Elizabeth Calthorpe would provide herbal infusions for a seriously ill cousin,[18] while on another her friend and kinswoman Alice Crane enquired of Margaret 'if the medicine that I sent you with my last letter does you any good'.[19]

Margaret, like most of her peers, was part of a women's circle of lay medicine and healthcare. She was also at the heart of a network of local politics. By the time she wrote to John in the summer of 1551, Gresham had finally been reclaimed by the Pastons, albeit in a ruinous state, but the troubles rumbled on. In the same letter in which she updates her husband on the progress of the pestilence in the city and asks him to send her medicine, Margaret assures John that he had the full support of the wife of a north-Norfolk landowner, Lady Catherine Felbrigg. Lady Catherine, the widow of Sir Simon Felbrigg,

Standard-Bearer to Richard II and a member of the Order of the Garter, was an influential figure, whose estate was just a couple of miles from Gresham. John, on hearing that one of the Felbrigg servants had spoken out against him, asked Margaret to intervene. Lady Felbrigg in turn insisted that even if these rumours were true, this had occurred without her knowledge, and she would take the servant to task. Margaret writes: 'I have spoken to Lady Felbrigg about what you asked me to talk about. And she said openly that she would not, and never intended to either, let Lord Moleyns or any other to have their way in that business for as long as she lives.' Margaret goes on to report that she had attended a dinner hosted by a relative at which Lady Felbrigg and her companions had lamented John's absence and 'said they would all have been the merrier if you had been there'. Margaret had succeeded in dampening down a potential falling-out between her husband and an influential neighbour.

Margaret often served as her husband's intermediary or representative on matters of politics and business. In this respect she was far from unique. It is too easy to dismiss royal and aristocratic women, whose marriages were arranged to form or strengthen political allegiances, as mere pawns. In fact, such women were often also involved in negotiating or obstructing marital alliances, influencing policies and acting as intermediaries at home and with other realms. Figures like Eleanor of Aquitaine, queen consort of England and France in the twelfth century, or, in Margaret's own lifetime, Margaret of Anjou, wife of Henry VI, and Lady Margaret Beaufort, mother of Henry VII, demonstrated considerable authority and power.

A key writer who addressed the importance of women's skills in diplomacy in the later Middle Ages was Christine de Pizan. Christine de Pizan was born in Venice but moved to France as a young child and lived there until her death around 1430. She is often thought of as the first professional woman author and poet in the European tradition, in so far as she supported herself financially by her writing. Christine de Pizan is also sometimes described as one of the first feminist writers because she wrote in defence of women and advocated on their behalf. Two of her most famous works are *Le Livre de la Cité des Dames* or *The Book of the City of Ladies* and *Le Livre des Trois Vertus* or *The Book of Three Virtues* (often known as *The Treasure of the City of Ladies*), which were both written in the early fifteenth century. *The Book of the City of Ladies* is a celebration of the achievements of famous mythical, Biblical, and historical women and of women's virtue in and positive contribution to marriage. In its sequel, *The Book of Three Virtues*, de Pizan offers advice to women of all ranks in society, from princesses to prostitutes, covering practical issues such as the running of the household, appropriate behaviour and how to dress.

Although Christine de Pizan also wrote about love and religion, she had a very varied repertoire, and did not allow herself to be constrained by her sex. She addressed topics such as statecraft, kingship, chivalry, politics and warfare. In a chapter of *The Book of Three Virtues* entitled 'How the good and wise princess will make every effort to restore peace between the prince and barons if there is any discord', de Pizan gives the following advice: 'If any neighbouring or foreign prince wishes for any reason to make war against her husband, or if her husband wishes to make war on someone else, the good lady will consider this thing carefully, bearing in mind the great evils and infinite cruelties, destruction, massacres and detriment to the country that result from war; the outcome is often terrible.'[20] Going further, she advises active intervention: the lady must 'ponder long and hard whether she can do something (always preserving the honour of her husband) to prevent this war … she will wish to work and labour carefully, calling God to her aid, and by good counsel she will do whatever she can to find a way of peace'.

De Pizan effectively argues that consorts and wives should do their best to counter the martial ambitions of their husbands.

From Margaret's letters, it is evident that lower down the social hierarchy, women as wives and mothers also had central roles to play in forming or cementing political relationships within the localities. There are many examples in the letters of occasions where Margaret or other women in the family try to diffuse a difficult situation before it gets out of hand. Early in the Gresham affair, Margaret recorded that she has spoken with the widowed Isabel de la Pole, Lady Morley about a dispute over dues which Lady Morley believed were owed to her. Lady Morley planned to bring legal proceedings against John, and Margaret had done her best to dissuade her, but 'she said she was only a woman, she must do as her advisors say, and her advisors had advised her, and she said she would act accordingly'.[21] Margaret explains, 'There was no way I could get her to undertake to leave off until you come home.' Margaret's mother-in-law, Agnes, proved to be more successful: she 'applied herself in this very faithfully ... And she has obtained an undertaking from my lady not to act against you in this matter if you are willing to come to an agreement with her and do as you ought.'

Margaret learnt from Agnes how to be an ambassador for the family into which she had married. When the Gresham troubles were at their height, Margaret warned her husband that his well-wishers 'have counselled me that I should counsel you to use other means than you have used' and to seek the help of other people than previously to further their cause.[22] While Margaret supported John in his struggle to hold on to Gresham and even led its defence, she was fully cognisant of the power of negotiation and peacekeeping, and, like Christine de Pizan, she saw combat as a last resort. Margaret understood that, just like healthcare, diplomacy was a key responsibility of a wealthy medieval housewife.

6. 'SOMETHING FOR MY NECK'

In the spring of 1453, Margaret of Anjou, Queen consort of Henry VI, came to Norwich. Margaret provides her husband with a short account of the two-day royal visit, focusing on an exchange between the Queen and Margaret's kinswoman and friend, the widow Elizabeth Clere.[1] The Queen had summonsed Elizabeth specifically, 'and when she came into the Queen's presence, the Queen made much of her, and encouraged her to find a husband'. Margaret of Anjou may well have been supporting the cause of a member of her own household when she suggested that Elizabeth remarry: a possible suitor is one of her esquires, Edmund Clere of Stokesby, a relative of Elizabeth's late husband.[2] Margaret comments wryly to John: 'But as for that, he is no nearer than before.' Elizabeth was not convinced by the Queen's proposition. Yet, the Queen was impressed by Elizabeth. Margaret reports that she was 'pleased with her [Elizabeth's] answer, and spoke of her very approvingly, and said on her honour that since she came to Norfolk she had seen no gentlewoman who pleases her more than she does'. Elizabeth's well-honed diplomatic skills meant that she avoided offending the Queen.

Margaret does not express any jealousy about her friend being singled out in this way. She informs John that one of the King's half-brothers has sent for him, and that the messenger, the bailiff of Swaffham, on discovering John absent, assured Margaret that he would be called for again when the King's brother returned to London. But, in among the other business of her letter, Margaret complains that she had to borrow a 'device' or ornament, some sort of piece of jewellery, from Elizabeth Clere for the event, 'because I dare not, out of shame, in my beads go in the midst of so many lovely gentlewomen who were here at that time'. She urges her husband to purchase her a piece as soon as possible: 'I entreat you to spend some money on me before Whitsun, so that I can have something for my neck.' In fact, some months earlier, at the end of January, she had already asked him to buy her a new necklace, perhaps in anticipation of just such an occasion occurring when it might be required.[3] John, it seems, had once again proved negligent in making purchases on Margaret's behalf.

Margaret of Anjou's visit to Norwich occurred at a pivotal moment in the Queen's personal and political life. After prolonged negotiations in the spring of 1445, just a few years after Margaret and John's far less exalted wedding, the fourteen-year-old Margaret of Anjou had married Henry VI of England, some nine years her senior. Henry VI had inherited the English throne at the age of nine months and his minority had lasted fifteen years. At ten years old, he was also crowned King of France, a claim that was disputed by Charles VII, uncle to both Henry and Margaret. The marriage alliance between them was designed to bring an end to the drawn-out war between England and France – the so-called Hundred Years War (1337–1453). Unlike Margaret and John, the royal couple were not obviously well matched. Henry was an educated but reserved and ineffective man, whose faith was important to him and who was averse to war, while Margaret was highly intelligent, strong-willed and determined. Nevertheless, the early years of their marriage were successful, with Margaret offering support to her husband and acting as a generous patron to their subjects. In 1450, Margaret issued a pardon to the rebels in Jack Cade's Rebellion, a popular uprising against the government. Nevertheless, Margaret's popularity was marred by ongoing troubles with France. The peace that the marriage promised was not long lived. Margaret proved to be a disappointment in another crucial respect: for several years she did not provide the King with an heir. All this changed in January 1453, when she finally conceived. She was, therefore, expecting a child when she arrived in Norwich that April. She also travelled to the Shrine of Our Lady of Walsingham to give thanks for her pregnancy, and no doubt to pray for a safe birth. She presented the shrine with a bejewelled pax, a decorated tablet which would be ceremonially kissed by participants during mass.

By the time Margaret of Anjou had given birth to Edward, Prince of Wales, in October of that year, her situation had changed dramatically. At the beginning of August, after receiving the news of a devastating defeat of the English troops in Gascony, Henry had experienced a dramatic breakdown which completely incapacitated him, physically and mentally. It is not particularly helpful to try to diagnose his condition retrospectively, but contemporary accounts reveal how it manifested. Initially, Henry became frenzied, and this was followed by months in which he was almost completely immobile and unresponsive, unable even to feed or wash himself. In medieval terms, he appeared to be suffering from a severe melancholia, extreme despair and sadness accompanied by psychological disturbances and physical symptoms. At Windsor, Henry was cared for by the royal physicians and placed under the constant attention of his servants. He was oblivious to the arrival of his son and heir. According to one report in January of 1454:

> at the Prince's [Edward's] arrival at Windsor, the Duke of Buckingham took him in his arms and presented him to the King in a godly manner, beseeching the King to bless him; and the King gave no answer. Nonetheless the Duke waited quietly with the Prince next to the King, and when he could get no manner of answer, the Queen came in and took the Prince in her arms and presented him in the same way as the Duke had done, wanting him to bless him. But all their efforts were in vain, because they departed from there without any response or acknowledgement, except only that once he looked at the Prince and cast down his eyes again, without saying or doing anything.[4]

Henry was irresponsive to what was going on around him.

In January 1454, Margaret of Anjou, inspired by formidable French antecedents such as her mother, Isabelle of Lorraine, and her grandmother Yolande of Aragon, petitioned parliament to be appointed regent during the King's illness. This was the moment at which she made her first significant bid for power. Her proposal was rejected, and instead parliament named Richard, 3rd Duke of York, as Protector of the Realm, although this arrangement proved to be short lived. The King's continued absence from official events was silently noted in a letter sent to Margaret's husband in June of 1454: 'The Prince will be invested at Westminster on Pentecost Sunday, the Chancellor, the Duke of Buckingham, and many other lords of estate present with the Queen.'[5] It was not until January of the following year that John received the news that 'the King is restored to health, and has been since Christmas day, and on

St John's Day [the Feast Day of St John the Evangelist] commanded his almoner [an officer responsible for distributing alms] to ride to Canterbury with his offering, and commanded the secretary to offer at [the shrine of] St Edward'.[6] A significant moment marking the King's recovery was when he finally acknowledged his son: 'The Queen came to him and brought my lord Prince with her; and then he asked what the Prince's name was, and the Queen told him Edward; and then he held up his hands and thanked God for it.'

Based on her central role in the events that followed the rise to power of the Duke of York and the outbreak of the Wars of the Roses with the 1st Battle of St Albans in 1455, Margaret of Anjou's prevailing reputation is that of a ruthless, cruel and power-hungry woman. In Shakespeare's *Henry VI, Part 3*, the future Richard III describes her as unnaturally vicious and evil: 'She-wolf of France, but worse than wolves of France, / Whose tongue more poisons than the adder's tooth! /How ill-beseeming is it in thy sex / To triumph, like an Amazonian trull, / Upon their woes whom fortune captivates!'[7] This tirade is a misogynist response to Margaret of Anjou's ambition and single-mindedness. A letter written to Sir John Fastolf in February 1456 states: 'The Queen is a great and much petitioned woman, for she spares no effort in pursuing her matters with the aim of successfully achieving power.'[8] Despite facing strong opposition, Margaret's determination inspired some of those around her to support her cause. In her proactive involvement in the events of the Wars of the Roses, the Queen was not simply self-serving. She was motivated by the determination to ensure that her husband, and ultimately her son, should rule the realm, and that their enemies must be overthrown.

The Paston family inevitably got caught up in the civil war that resulted from the dynastic struggle between the Lancastrians who supported Henry VI and the Yorkists who

took the side of Richard of York. The Pastons' most powerful
political ally was John de Vere, 12th Earl of Oxford, a staunch
supporter of Henry VI and the Lancastrian cause, who was
executed for treason in 1462. The biggest threats to the family
and its property were John de la Pole, 2nd Duke of Suffolk,
whose father was murdered in 1450, and John Mowbray, 3rd
Duke of Norfolk, and his son, the 4th Duke. In the years that
followed Margaret of Anjou's visit to Norwich, and after some
initial prevarication, the Pastons shifted their allegiance to
the Yorkists, with Margaret and John's two eldest sons serving in the court of Edward IV and the household of the Duke
of Norfolk, respectively. After the Yorkist defeat at the Battle
of Bosworth, the family once more shifted their support, this
time to the 13th Earl of Oxford. John Paston III fought on
Henry VII's side at the Battle of Stoke, where he received a
knighthood. By that time, Margaret of Anjou was dead: she
passed away two years before Margaret Paston in 1482, some
eleven years after her seventeen-year-old son was killed at the
Battle of Tewksbury, and her husband had died (probably having been murdered) in the Tower of London.

When Margaret Anjou arrived in Norwich in 1453, her reputation was still intact, and the Paston loyalties had yet to be
tested. The city was at the time very much a thriving metropolis, and evidence of this is visible today, its centre dominated by
Norwich Castle. The castle keep, constructed on top of a grass
mound with a surrounding ditch, is in a prominent position,
abutting the Castle Quarter shopping centre. Its highly decorated external walls were refaced in the nineteenth century,
giving it a rather artificial appearance. It has an inner bailey, or
enclosure, and a semi-circular outer bailey. At the time of writing, the floors and rooms in the keep are currently being rein-
stalled. The motte and bailey were originally built as a fortified
residence for William the Conqueror when he came to the city,

but by the mid-fifteenth century the castle had long been used as a prison, and in the late eighteenth century a new jail was built by Sir John Soane. A hundred years later it was converted into a museum, and it remains such to this day, housing the city's art collection.

As the castle was no longer a royal residence, Margaret of Anjou would have been welcomed at the Benedictine priory attached to the city's Cathedral, where in the previous century both Edward III and Richard II had stayed with their queens.[9] Pevsner's evocative description of the Cathedral would have been as true in Margaret of Anjou's time as it is today:

> The spire makes the cathedral, as one approaches Norwich. When one is nearer and happens to have found a good vantage point, the other distinguishing features enter the picture: the exceedingly long nave and the strange geometrical richness of the decoration of the crossing tower. The interior is at its most powerful when one first sits down in the nave.[10]

The Romanesque Cathedral continues to dominate the skyline, despite the differences in the scale of the surrounding city, and its interior, especially when studied closely, draws us back in time.

There have been many changes to the Cathedral since the mid-fifteenth century, some of which were made in Margaret's lifetime. The magnificent painted and guided bosses in the nave and choir, which narrate events from the Old and New Testaments, were carved when the roof was replaced following a fire, ten years after her meeting with the Queen. Most of the original glass was destroyed in the Reformation and has had to be replaced. The Chapel of the Holy Innocents, which replaces the shrine to the murdered child William of

Norwich, the subject of a popular medieval antisemitic cult, was installed as recently as 1979. William was found stabbed to death in 1144 and some years later, Thomas of Monmouth, the monk of the Cathedral Priory who wrote his hagiography, claimed that he had been abducted and crucified; this false accusation of ritualistic killing is the first example of blood libel in medieval Europe.[11]

Still, a considerable amount of the medieval interior and furnishings remain that would have been seen by Margaret and her friend Elizabeth in 1453, including traces of the wall paintings and painted panels, and the wooden stalls with their carved elbow rests and misericords (ledges under the seat which give support when standing). A huge range of subjects are carved onto these, including scenes from the Bible and apocrypha, kings, queens, bishops and angels, heraldry, signs of the zodiac, agricultural tasks, activities, mystical beasts, and animals and birds. There are also donor portraits commemorating the citizens of the city who paid for the building work or furnishings. In the choir, one fourteenth-century misericord, for example, represents Sir William Clere and his wife Denise Wichingham, grandparents of Elizabeth's husband, with a coiled greyhound at their feet. Another depicts her father-in-law standing next to his mother who is praying and wears a rosary at her waist. In both cases, the heads of the figures have subsequently been chiselled off, but in Margaret and Elizabeth's time they would have been complete. The coat of arms of Sir Robert Berney, a relative of Margaret, appears on the elbow rest of the second of these stalls. These carvings, demonstrations of civic pride, would have been very familiar to the two women.

From its Norman foundation, Benedictine monks were placed in charge of the Cathedral church. The Bishop's Palace was built to its north, but the building that remains today is mainly Victorian. The monastery was constructed on the south side. Particularly remarkable is the cloister, which was rebuilt in the fourteenth and early fifteenth centuries. It is the only two-storey cloister in the country, and like the Cathedral church itself, it is decorated with wonderfully ornate and colourful carved-stone ceiling bosses. They are not limited to Biblical scenes, but, like the misericords, include monsters and animals, hunts and battles, domestic scenes, and even the twisted torso of an acrobat. Because the vaulted ceiling of the cloister is so much lower than the roof of the nave, it is much easier to view these bosses and to appreciate their breathtaking artistry and beauty.

Remnants of the medieval city wall and towers also remain visible today, and the beautifully carved Ethelbert and Erpingham Gates in Tombland (the former market area) still provide access to the expansive Cathedral Close; covering some 44 acres, the Close gives a sense of the sheer scale of the monastery in at its height. Margaret's father-in-law, William, was buried in the Lady Chapel, although her husband, John, had ignored his father's wish to found a perpetual chantry there, where prayers would have been said for his soul. The Lady Chapel was destroyed in the late sixteenth century – it was located on the site of the modern St Saviour's Chapel, by the grave of Edith Cavell, the British nurse executed by a German firing squad in 1915.

A three-minute walk from the Cathedral is another institution with a royal history: Norwich Great Hospital, which dates to the thirteenth century, when it was called St Giles's hospital. It has offered care to the sick and infirm from its foundation to the present day. It now provides sheltered housing for the elderly but was originally built to look after elderly priests and the ailing poor. The surviving medieval buildings or parts of them include the Infirmary Hall,

Refectory and former Master's House, former Chaplain's House, Cloisters and St Helen Bishopgate (which still serves as a parish church). In 1383, some 70 years prior to Margaret of Anjou's arrival, Norwich was visited by Richard II and Anne of Bohemia, and the wooden ceiling of the chancel, now the Eagle Ward, was decorated with paintings of 252 eagles, interspersed with gold bosses, in honour of the new queen, whose arms included the two-headed Imperial Eagle used by the Holy Roman Empire. The importance of this establishment would be recognised in the will of Elizabeth Clere, who also chose the Cathedral as her final resting place: she left bequests to the hospital monks, priests, choristers, and residents in return for requiem masses, dirges and prayers.[12] It is also acknowledged in Margaret's will.[13]

At the time of her audience with Margaret of Anjou, Elizabeth Clere had been widowed for seven years, was very rich, and was in control of considerable property. Born around 1416, the daughter and sole heir of Thomas Uvedale of Tacolneston, she was just a few years older than Margaret, and close to both Margaret and her mother-in-law Agnes. Elizabeth's birth family was not so exalted as those of her two friends, but she had made a good marriage. She had wed Robert Clere in 1434, when she was about eighteen years old, and the couple had had four children. The Clere family's estate was in Ormesby, a village near Great Yarmouth and only a couple of miles from Mautby, although Elizabeth, like Margaret and Agnes, mainly resided in Norwich. When Elizabeth was only 30, her husband had died, and she inherited his estates unconditionally for life. Despite the Queen's recommendation that she remarry, Elizabeth preferred instead to hold on to her financial autonomy and social independence until her death, in Tacolneston, some 40 years later.

Elizabeth's and Margaret's lives were intertwined domestically and financially, as well as socially, and Elizabeth was more than capable of holding her ground against the Paston family. In later years, when Margaret's children were of a marriageable age, Elizabeth resisted suggestions that the Pastons should marry into her family. Margaret's second son, John III, considered himself a possible suitor for Elizabeth's daughter,[14] while Margaret herself contemplated a match between her younger daughter, Anne, and one of Elizabeth's sons.[15] The two families were finally united in the next generation, but only after the deaths of both Margaret and Elizabeth, when one of Margaret's granddaughters, also called Elizabeth, married Elizabeth Clere's grandson, William.[16]

The friendship between the Pastons and the Cleres was one that brought benefits to both families. Margaret's husband, John, provided the widowed Elizabeth with valuable advice regarding legal issues such as grazing rights and property disputes and may well have acted formally on her behalf.[17] Elizabeth set great store by John's opinion – Margaret reported that Elizabeth had said 'that there is no man alive that she has put her trust in so much' – and so was distraught when, at a time when John was at his lowest ebb, rumours circulated that she had spoken out against him.[18] Margaret's intervention succeeded in reconciling her husband and friend. In turn, in times of need, Margaret found herself borrowing money from her wealthy kinswoman, as did other members of her family. This was not in itself that remarkable. The Bank of England was only founded in 1694 and in an age before modern banking, borrowing from family and friends was the norm. On at least one occasion, to her considerable embarrassment, Margaret struggled to repay a very significant debt accrued on behalf of her eldest son, which Elizabeth Clere had asked to be settled.[19] Yet, this did not prevent Margaret from subsequently borrowing money from Elizabeth for her son, and conse-quently facing further personal losses.

It is in this context that Elizabeth's loan of jewellery to Margaret for the royal visit should be understood. As Margaret's relative and friend, Elizabeth was using her greater wealth to help her out of a difficult situation by ensuring she was appro-priately accessorised for meeting the Queen. Jewellery was not simply a reflection of the taste of its wearer, or of the current vogues. Rather, it was in indication of the status of the wearer and her, or often his, affluence and social aspirations. Medieval sumptuary laws, which dictated how people were allowed to spend their money and attempted to restrict what they wore depending on their rank, were mainly ignored. The item that Elizabeth lent Margaret would likely have been made of silver or gold. It may have been intricately decorated, and set with precious gems such as sapphires, garnets, rubies and pearls, or enamelled, or both. In Elizabeth Clere's will, two pieces of jewellery are mentioned – a gold rosary and a 'brooch with a chain and a pearl at the end' – but it need not have been either of these.[20] The term Margaret uses to describe it – 'device' – suggests that it was artistically worked, in contrast to her own unfashionable 'beads'. Whether a rosary, pendant, collar or brooch, it would certainly have been designed to complement the low necklines of the dresses of the time.

What sort of necklace would Margaret have wanted to replace her own beads? Like Margaret's ring of St Margaret, etched with an image of the saint, much jewellery was devo-tional as well as decorative, taking the form of adorned crosses and small reliquaries (which contained sacred relics of the saints), but perhaps that wasn't what Margaret, still a relatively young woman in her mid-thirties, had in mind. She may have preferred something that was simply ornamental. According to the medieval lapidaries, or books of stones, precious and

semi-precious stones had different 'virtues' or healing properties, so this might be an additional factor to be considered,
although Margaret doesn't indicate this in her letters. In asking
John to buy her new jewellery in London, Margaret would
have expected him to seek out the shop of a talented goldsmith. Today, the Worshipful Company of Goldsmiths is based
in Goldsmiths' Hall in Foster Lane in the City of London. In the
Middle Ages, Foster Lane, which is near St Paul's Cathedral,
was also the centre of gold and jewellery production, and
when John finally purchased Margaret's necklace, he would
have surely bought it from one of the shops there.

Some beautiful examples of jewellery of the time have survived, such as the items found in the Fishpool Hoard, now
in the British Museum, which was discovered by construction
workers in Ravenshead, Nottinghamshire in the mid-1960s.[21]
This treasure included well over 1,000 gold coins and two gold
chains as well as four rings, three pendants and a brooch in the
shape of a heart, all made of gold and decorated with precious
gems or enamel. The hoard seems to have been buried in 1464,
during the Wars of the Roses. Of the three pendants, one is in
the shape of a cross set with rubies and amethysts, one is a sapphire and enamel roundel, and the third is an exquisite padlock
locket with the words 'de tout' and 'mon cuer' ('all my heart')
engraved on its sides and a chain attached. Closer to home for
Margaret, a fifteenth-century gold reliquary pendant depicting
the Crucifixion was discovered in the nineteenth century, just
a few miles from Gresham in the village of Matlaske; it is now
held in the museum at Norwich Castle. But the example of a
late medieval English necklace that really catches my imagination as I think of Margaret is that of the Middleham Jewel.

The Middleham Jewel, which is part of the permanent collection of the Yorkshire Museum, is a lozenge or diamond-shaped
pendant reliquary, set with a large blue sapphire.[22] It has a

depiction of the Trinity and the Crucifixion on the outer face, and a Nativity scene and the Lamb of God on the inside. There are also engravings of short extracts from the Latin Mass and other words around the front edge, which probably have talismanic significance, and there are fifteen miniature images of saints, many of them women, on the reverse. The jewel was produced by a London goldsmith around the time that Margaret of Anjou went to Norwich, or shortly thereafter. The Middleham Jewel would have been made for a pious royal or aristocratic woman of the time, and it no doubt was also seen to have medicinal qualities: sapphires were believed to help with a range of ailments. The pendant was designed to offer protection during childbirth, as is indicated by the depictions of the Nativity and of St Margaret of Antioch and other saints believed to give assistance to women in labour. Given that it was found near Middleham Castle, the residence of Richard III, it could well have been owned by a member of his immediate family, perhaps his mother, Cecily Neville.

We cannot know for certain what sort of necklace Margaret had in mind, but we can assume that it would reflect her sense of her own social standing, and her family's ambition. Even if it is unfeasible that John would have bought anything anywhere nearly so fine for Margaret, the Middleham Jewel is revealing about the high quality of artistry that would have been available in the capital, for a price.

7. 'REMEMBER MY SISTER'

Among the many remaining medieval sites and churches in
Norfolk, the three of the greatest significance to Margaret
were St Andrew's and Blackfriars' Halls located in the former
Dominican friary, her parish church St Peter Hungate, and her
home on the cobbled slope of historic Elm Hill. All of these
are tightly clustered together in an attractive area north of the
castle. Remarkably, Margaret and her husband have left very
tangible traces of their presence in this tiny locale.

In 1413, a fire substantially destroyed the thirteenth-century
friary church and monastery in Norwich, and its rebuilding took
six decades, partially coinciding with the Pastons' residence in
the city. After the Reformation, the nave of this church became
what is now St Andrew's Hall. The choir turned into Blackfriars'
Hall, taking its name from the habits of the Dominicans and of
their predecessors at the site. Margaret and John Paston contrib-
uted to the restoration of the church, paying for new roof-beams.
Their gift was memorialised in the doors they had installed in
the south porch of St Andrew's Hall, carved with the arms of
Paston impaled with Mautby, which remain in place today.

Just one minute's walk from the Halls is the former church of St Peter Hungate, where, in 1460, the couple also financed expensive restoration work; the year is commemorated on the porch doorway. The decommissioned church building is structurally complete, with its elaborate wooden ceiling still intact, but the interior has been very much stripped away. Despite this, the role of Margaret and John as benefactors is apparently acknowledged in the decoration of the church. A corbel in the south transept is said to represent Margaret. It depicts the head of a woman wearing a headdress, comprising a caul in the form of a gold or wire mesh confining the hair and a short, scalloped veil.[1] Another corbel carved with the head of a bearded man wearing a turban-like chaperon or hood is thought to depict John. It is within this peaceful former church in Norwich, with its beautiful wild yard, the place where the Pastons worshipped regularly in the years that they lived nearby, that I have felt the strongest sense of the presence, not just of Margaret, but also her whole family, including her young children.

St Peter Hungate is located at the top of Elm Hill, an exclusive residential location then and now, which was occupied by successful merchants and lawyers in the later Middle Ages. Pesvner calls it 'the most picturesque street in Norwich', and states, with typical understatement, 'there is not a single house in Elm Hill which could be disturbing'.[2] It is certainly very beautiful with its timber-framed houses, the upper floors overhanging the street below, although nowadays there is something of the film set about the location and it bustles with tourists rather than with the hubbub of late medieval urban life and business. A blue plaque on a sixteenth-century house at numbers 22–24, now a private members' club, states that it is the site of the Paston family home, the original buildings on the street having been destroyed by fire in 1507. Whether this really was exactly where the Paston residence was located is open to question.

We do know that Margaret and John moved home several times in Norwich before they were finally able to settle. The winter before she met Margaret of Anjou, Margaret complained to her husband that their accommodation was too cramped: 'As for your being here when you come home, the houses are too small for your men and your horses, and therefore you need to come home sooner to buy yourself another place.'[3] The following summer, a more suitable town house had been found to let, with space where a stable for John's horses could be built, but Margaret felt the rent was too high and the landowner refused to let them the neighbouring warehouse.[4] Finding a residence in the city that could meet the demands of their growing family proved challenging, but eventually Margaret succeeded.

In a letter sent from Norwich in January of 1454 or thereabouts, Margaret, once again pregnant, writes about the alteration work to their home that she is undertaking.[5] Margaret reports that she has obtained vital materials from Sir Thomas Howes, the chaplain and servant of Sir John Fastolf: four large supporting beams for the floors or ceilings. Margaret complains that although the supporting beams will soon be installed, further progress can't be made until joists and planks are obtained. Her description provides some insight into the arrangement of the building. Three of the beams, which had already been obtained, were for the malthouse, the brewery and the 'withdraught' or withdrawing chamber. It was common for medieval town houses and halls to have their own malthouses and breweries as well as bakehouses. The 'withdraught' was an inner chamber, or suite of rooms, used for conducting business.[6] But the house was not purely functional, it was designed to allow Margaret some personal space. The fourth and biggest of the beams was to be brought from nearby Hellesdon as a gift from Fastolf for her private chamber, a generous gesture signifying the high regard in which he held Margaret.

Margaret goes on to outline some problems with the planned arrangements for John's 'withdraught'. The room John had chosen proved too small. He wanted his chests and counting table together in the room alongside his bed, but Margaret had measured the area and found that even if the bed were to be moved, there still would not be enough space for him to sit and work. Instead, she tells him he will have to continue to use the room he has previously, and she reassures him that she has put plans in place to protect his belongings when they are moved.

While the main business of the letter of January 1454 is Margaret's renovations of the new house, she also mentions, somewhat obliquely, another matter; one that relates to one of the most infamous episodes recorded in the letters of the Paston women, and one that deserves far more attention than Margaret's brief allusions would seem, on the surface, to justify. Margaret urges John to 'remember my sister', meaning her sister-in-law, Agnes's daughter Elizabeth, and 'to play your part faithfully in helping her to get a good marriage before you come home'. At the time of this letter, Elizabeth Paston was already in her mid-twenties and was still single; this despite the family's apparent efforts to secure her a husband. Margaret passes on to John the name of a widower; Agnes has asked if his financial situation might make him an appropriate suitor.

Women in the upper echelons of medieval society could struggle to find a husband for a variety of reasons, such as their family's failure to provide a sufficient dowry or the absence of a suitably moneyed and influential match. Both were no doubt factors in Elizabeth's case. John, as head of the household following the death of his father, was responsible for making the arrangements, but he had shown himself more than parsimonious when it came to his siblings. Elizabeth herself would have to agree to any proposals put to her via her family, but she would have limited choices available to her. If a woman of her social standing wanted to remain single, she could become a nun and join a convent or enter service. If she were to remain at home, she would be perceived as a drain upon the household expenses.

In encouraging John to seek a husband for Elizabeth as a matter of priority, Margaret reminds him that his mother, Agnes, has lost patience with the whole affair, telling him that 'it seems from [her] words that she would never be so glad to be free of her as she is now'. This is quite a claim because, five years previously, Agnes's relationship with her daughter had completely broken down after she failed to secure a match between Elizabeth and Stephen Scrope, the stepson and sometime secretary of Sir John Fastolf. Scrope was a cultured and sensitive man, with an interest in literature and medicine, but without even meeting him, Elizabeth judged him to be less than desirable. He was a widower, 30 years' senior to his prospective bride, and Elizabeth had heard that he was 'unattractive' – in fact, Scrope had been scarred by an illness he had experienced in his youth. But the question of the financial arrangements was also influencing her.

One of the uncertainties surrounding the marriage to Scrope was that, until Fastolf died, he was unable to receive his inheritance from his parents (his mother having passed away a few years earlier) and as a consequence, he struggled with debt. Another issue in question was what would happen to Scrope's inherited estate if he were to remarry. It wasn't clear to the Pastons if it would pass in due course to Scrope's daughter by his first wife, a girl Scrope had felt pressurised into marrying off when she was still an infant, or whether it would come to any children he might have with his second. Agnes wanted to be sure of the legalities before pursuing the matter any further. Despite her reservations about her prospective husband's age and appearance, Elizabeth was apparently also willing to countenance the marriage if her eldest brother could confirm that it would be her children who stood in line to inherit, and that she would be granted sufficient jointure.

It is a letter from Elizabeth Clere to Margaret's husband, John, in which she intervenes on behalf of her younger relative that provides real insight into the negotiations, and it makes painful reading.[7] She reports that in order to pressurise Elizabeth Paston into complying with her wishes, Agnes is keeping her a prisoner in her home and isolating her from all social contact; she is unable to receive any visitors or to talk to the servants. Even Scrope has been unable to meet her in person, causing him some disquiet. John's sister has been forced into surreptitious communication with Elizabeth Clere via a local mendicant, Friar Newton, who is acting as their intermediary. Even worse, Agnes is subjecting her daughter to horrific and sustained physical violence: 'Since Easter she has for the most part been beaten once or twice a week, and sometimes twice in one day, and her head has been broken in two or three places.' Having been thrashed into submission, it is unsurprising that John's sister is in a state of absolute misery and despair; she has never been 'so sorrowful as she is nowadays' and is desperate to escape. Elizabeth Clere urges John actively to seek an alternative match if possible, warning him that 'sorrow often causes women to bestow themselves in marriage on someone they should not'. She also entreats him to burn her letter before anyone else sees it, because if Agnes finds out about it she will never forgive her.

Terms like 'coercive control', 'domestic violence' and 'emotional abuse' are modern ones, and in the past the physical punishment of minors was not simply acceptable but even encouraged, as is captured by the early modern expression 'spare the rod and spoil the child'. Medieval canon law gave those it considered superior, those in a position of authority, whether husbands, parents, teachers, religious leaders or masters and mistresses, the right to correct and to chastise physically the inferiors placed in their care, their wives, children, pupils, novices or servants. There were of course some constraints on this, and theologians and lawyers argued about how much physical violence was acceptable and in what circumstances. Certainly, in theory at least, any corporal punishment meted out should not be life threatening or cause very serious injury. It is evident from Elizabeth Clere's reaction that Agnes's attacks on her daughter exceeded what she saw as reasonable discipline.

We don't have direct access to Elizabeth Paston's own point of view – no letters written by her from this time have survived – but the ill-treatment of children and young people was widespread, and Scrope too had been a victim of psychological trauma. Reflecting as an adult on his childhood experiences, Scrope complained that soon after Fastolf became his stepfather, Fastolf illegally 'sold' him and then subsequently repurchased him: 'So he bought and sold me like a beast.'[8] Scrope was referring to the legal concept of wardship, whereby a guardian takes control over the estate of a minor following the death of one or both parents, and through this gains the right to arrange their marriage. Wardships could prove commercially advantageous because the guardian would benefit from the profits of the ward's estate during the minority. They could also ensure a marriage that furthered their own interests. Wardships were often traded for financial gain, which is exactly what Fastolf had done with Scrope. Often little care was paid to the needs of the vulnerable ward, and Scrope blamed his long-term health problems on Fastolf.[9] Scrope also claimed that even after he had come of age, Fastolf had continued to deprive him of his rightful inheritance.

The corruption of the wardship system and the resultant abuses of those vulnerable young people it ostensibly protected was widely recognised at the time and is reflected in contemporary culture. The exploited ward is a topic addressed in the medieval romance *The Tale of Gamelyn*, in which the hero lives with his wicked older brother who deprives him of his inheritance, wastes his lands and mistreats his tenants.[10] Perhaps Scrope was familiar with the story, and identified with Gamelyn's struggle to regain what he had lost. Certainly, he described himself as being (like Gamelyn) 'outlawed' by his guardian.[11] While Scrope no doubt felt that an alliance with Fastolf's good friends the Pastons would serve his interests well, it is entirely probable that, like Elizabeth, he was hoping to execute an escape from his domestic situation, in his case from a man who acted *in loco parentis* in name only. Perhaps if Agnes had not prevented them from meeting, Elizabeth would have found that she had more in common with Scrope than she realised. As it was, the negotiations floundered.

Elizabeth's story is so important because it reveals just how limited were the options of a young woman from a wealthy family who was not an heiress, and whose mother perceived her as a burden rather than a companion. Four years after Margaret's letter of 1454 and almost ten since the failed match with Scrope, Agnes finally got her daughter off her hands when Elizabeth moved to London, having found a place in the service of an aristocratic family, the Poles. Agnes wrote a memorandum to herself to remind Elizabeth that 'she must accustom herself to work willingly, as other gentlewomen do, and thus help herself somewhat'.[12] Agnes clearly felt that Elizabeth brought her misfortunes upon herself.

With her escape from her mother's cruelty, Elizabeth's luck had finally changed, at least for a while. Later that same year, at the age of 30, she married. Her husband was Robert Poynings, a controversial figure who had joined Jack Cade's Rebellion in 1450, had been imprisoned and accused of treason, and had only recently been pardoned. In a letter from Elizabeth to Agnes, written shortly after her wedding, she asked her mother to pay the dowry that the couple had been promised and the expenses she had incurred during her period of service as well as another debt.[13] Not surprisingly, the tone of the letter is distant, even reproachful. Even with some distance between them, relations between mother and daughter had evidently not improved much. Elizabeth and Robert lived together in Southwark and had a son, but their marriage was short lived. Robert, who was fighting on the Yorkist side, went missing sometime in 1461, and was presumed dead.

Elizabeth was widowed for a decade before she married Sir George Browne, of Betchworth Castle in Surrey, a member of the household of Edward IV. George was around ten years younger than Elizabeth. The couple had a son and a daughter and seem to have been content together. They were certainly very wealthy. Today Betchworth Castle is an atmospheric ruin on the outskirts of Dorking, approached through an avenue of trees originally planted in the eighteenth century; its grounds have been transformed into a golf course. Most of the remains that are now visible are early modern and, except for part of the tower, there is little indication of the crenelated building that replaced the medieval manor house in the time of George's father, Sir Thomas Browne. The castle itself is fenced off for safety reasons, but the location, perched in the Mole Valley, and now overlooking a fishing lake, is striking. It is certainly possible to imagine Elizabeth lavishly entertaining guests, including perhaps royalty, in what must have been an impressive and, at the time, newly modernised residence.

Sadly, once again, the political conflicts of the Wars of the Roses cut short Elizabeth's happiness. George had been knighted following the Battle of Tewkesbury, but changed sides again in 1483, joining Buckingham's Rebellion against Richard III. He was executed in the Tower of London, whereupon his estates were seized. Elizabeth herself was involved in the rebellion but was pardoned and her jointure was returned. She outlived Sir George by five years. In her will, she asked that she be buried alongside him at Blackfriars in London.[14]

There are no records of Elizabeth visiting Margaret and John after her marriages, or of Margaret travelling to see her either in London or Surrey, but we do know that the family remained in contact. In a letter from Elizabeth to Margaret's eldest son, written during her first period of widowhood, after she had been dispossessed of her lands by Robert Poynings' niece and her husband, she asks for his assistance reclaiming her estates.[15] On another occasion, John II reports to his mother that he has spent an enjoyable Christmas with his aunt and Sir George Browne,[16] and Sir George was also a good friend of John III.[17]

We cannot be certain what Margaret made of this dark episode in the Paston women's history, when Agnes was so cruelly abusing her daughter; no letters from Margaret survive in which she discusses it explicitly. But it seems likely that she shared her friend Elizabeth Clere's concerns. Certainly, on a separate occasion, Margaret sympathetically passed on a message to her husband from his sister in which Elizabeth complained of Agnes's hostility.[18] Also, as in her letter of

January 1454, Margaret made a point of repeatedly urging John to find Elizabeth a suitable husband. Margaret no doubt felt some affection for her sister-in-law, given that even after almost twenty years of marriage her love for her husband, Elizabeth's brother, was unwavering. Margaret signs off her letter to John of January 1454: 'I entreat you not to be reluctant to write letters to me between now and when you come home. If I could, I would have one every day.'

8. 'ONLY BACKGAMMON, CHESS AND CARDS'

On 5 November 1459, Sir John Fastolf died. His passing marked a significant change in Margaret and John's fortunes. In recent years, Margaret's husband had been employed by Fastolf as part of his legal team, and Fastolf had become his close friend and ally. Indeed, Fastolf once described John Paston as his 'heartiest kinsman and friend', a substitute for the biological son that he never had.[1] Despite proving such a poor stepfather to Scrope, Fastolf stepped into a paternal role, and in return John devoted himself to pursuing Fastolf's interests as well as his own. Margaret, aware of the effect Justice William's death had had on her husband, encouraged this relationship, which could only benefit the rest of the family. John even posited to Fastolf, no doubt with Margaret's approval, that one of his young daughters should be betrothed to a cousin of Fastolf whose wardship he sought to secure.[2] Fastolf's passing had huge implications for Margaret and her family that extended far beyond the emotional turmoil one would anticipate following the loss of a cousin, neighbour and mentor.

In the days before Fastolf's death, John Paston had been summoned with the news: 'It is high time. He draws fast homeward and is brought very low and sorely weakened and enfeebled.'[3] After his arrival at Fastolf's main Norfolk residence, Caister Castle, John remained by his side to the end, where he claimed to have heard his dying wishes. John announced that Fastolf had named him as his heir in an oral will made on his deathbed, with the vital caveat that John should ensure that Fastolf's plans for Caister should be fulfilled posthumously.[4] John claimed that he and Fastolf's chaplain, Thomas Howes, were to take responsibility for administering the estate, thus side-lining the other executors. This will, so John claimed, replaced that which Fastolf had drafted earlier in the same year, in which Fastolf explicitly warned against those who would falsely claim 'to be next inheritor to me after my decease'.[5]

Unluckily for John and Margaret, despite the presence of Fastolf's priests at his bedside, ready to perform the last rites, and his servants and physician waiting nearby, there were no other witnesses who could confirm John's version of events. Even so, Margaret didn't question it. She was firmly of the belief that Fastolf would want his estate to stay within his extended biological family. But this was not the first time that John had asserted a questionable claim on an inheritance. According to his mother, Agnes, when Justice William died fifteen years earlier, John had ignored his deathbed instructions which would have been more generous to her and would have provided for his younger brothers. This led to long-term conflict within the family, with Agnes never fully forgiving John, although she remained close to Margaret. Following Fastolf's death, in contrast, the wrangling over the will was very public. Although John and his family took immediate possession of Caister and the other properties, Fastolf's other executors were determined to challenge his claims, and the Pastons became embroiled in extensive physical disputes and legal battles as they tried to secure this inheritance. Two years later, the Duke of Norfolk claimed Caister, in the years that ensued claims were made on other estates, and, in 1464, the proceedings initiated by one of the co-executors, William Yelverton, came to court. But as the year 1459 drew to its close, much of this was still to come.

In the month after Fastolf's death, Margaret's main concern was the correct etiquette for celebrating Christmas in a bereaved household. John was unable to return home to Norwich for the festivities because he was in Caister, claiming ownership of the castle and its contents. His brother William travelled to London to secure the properties there. Margaret was very conscious of the family's sudden rise in status following their inheritance, and of the social obligations this entailed. On Christmas Eve 1459, Margaret writes to her husband that she has been seeking advice from her more elevated friends about the most appropriate forms of entertainment.[6] She had sent John II, who was now seventeen years old, to visit the widowed Isobel, Lady Morley, 'to find out what games were played at her house on the Christmas following the death of her husband', while the fifteen-year-old John III was deployed to another influential Norfolk household, that of Katherine, Lady Stapleton, second wife of Sir Miles Stapleton. Margaret was particularly pleased with the way in which her eldest son had fulfilled his task, but both young men returned with similar responses.

Having assured her husband that the Paston Christmas festivities will be conducted with appropriate decorum, Margaret then goes on to raise some concerns about the staffing situation in their Norfolk residence. The main problem was that the man in charge of the buttery was refusing to do his accounting daily, as requested, but insisted that he could only tally up the costs on a weekly basis. The buttery not only stored the food supplies for the household but also wine and ale; 'bread' and 'beer' as the recalcitrant servant put it to Margaret. The servant in charge of managing the buttery was the 'butler', a role which at the time did not have the high status among servants that it was to gain in ensuing centuries. A well-run buttery was essential, and in the lead up to Christmas, Margaret would have been particularly anxious that it was fully stocked and that the finances were in order. Perhaps she also suspected the servant of stealing from the family, which would explain why she wanted to keep a close eye on his calculations. At any rate, Margaret urges John to find a servant from Caister Castle to take on the role instead, likely assuming that Fastolf had had more reliable and trustworthy staff in his employ. No doubt Margaret felt that the family could afford better servants now that they had come into such incredible wealth. Almost as an afterthought, Margaret adds that a second servant, Simond, should also be replaced because of his stupidity; according to her own proverbial expression, 'you are never nearer a wise man with him'. With its attention turning to mundane domestic matters, Margaret's Christmas Eve letter certainly suggests that she had no inkling of the troubles that would soon descend upon her family.

To make sense of the calamitous events that were to follow, it is important to understand the man whose death precipitated them. Sir John Fastolf is a historical figure whose fictionalised reputation precedes him. He is immortalised in literature in the character of Sir John Falstaff in *Henry IV, Parts 1* and 2. Shakespeare's Falstaff is the debauched companion of the future Henry V, an ageing and corpulent reveller and minor criminal, 'fat-witted with drinking of old sack',[7] who haunts the brothels and taverns of London and proves himself dishonourable on the battlefield. Despite his dissolute life, in Shakespeare's *Henry V*, Falstaff dies as well as could be hoped.

His passing is witnessed by the innkeeper Mistress Quickly, who reports that he 'made a finer end, and went away an[d] it had been any christom [Christian] child'.[8] Fastolf, a wealthy and cultured former soldier, could hardly be more different to his literary counterpart, although there are some points of convergence between their lives, and both men at their ends focused their thoughts on God and the afterlife, experiencing what was known as a good death.

Fastolf's background was not dissimilar to that of the Pastons. Born at Caister in 1380 into a Norfolk gentry family, he rose to prominence because of his distinguished military career in France, where he fought alongside Henry V at Agincourt, and was subsequently knighted. In 1426, he was made a Knight of the Most Honourable Order of the Garter, a distinction awarded by the sovereign himself. Unfortunately, only a few years later, Fastolf's repute was significantly tarnished after the teenage Joan of Arc succeeded in lifting the Siege of Orléans and sent the French troops in pursuit of their opponents. The English forces were routed at Patay and Fastolf fled the battle. He was accused of cowardice, and it was well over a decade before he was exonerated. He remained in France where he continued to serve as a military commander until 1440, when he returned home. He no doubt got to know the then-newly married Margaret and John around that time.

Fastolf succeeded in accumulating a substantial fortune during his lifetime. His marriage to Stephen Scrope's widowed mother made a significant contribution to this and Fastolf also benefitted from the income of the French estates that he was awarded in return for his service and from his investments in land in East Anglia and in property in London, including the Boar's Head tavern in Southwark. During his retirement in East Anglia, he spent much of his time transforming the manor house at Caister into a luxuriously furnished moated castle. As he got older, with an eye on the fate of his soul and his own posterity, Fastolf determined that much of his wealth should be used to establish at Caister Castle a chantry, a religious college for monks, priests and poor men, where prayers would be said for his soul in perpetuity. The Paston claim on Caister Castle would become the central focus of the conflicts over Fastolf's will. Fastolf's college never came into being and eventually much of his estate passed to Magdalen College, Oxford.

My own first visit to Caister Castle was in late summer. Heike and I drove there from Mautby, where we had been walking with our dogs: if one were to cross the fields and pass directly through the woods, Caister would be only a mile or so from Margaret's Mautby estate. Today the castle is known mainly for the extensive collection of vintage cars and motorbikes in its adjoining museum. Part of the more recent neighbouring Caister Hall has been turned into a small tearoom, boasting a framed and discoloured newspaper cutting with the headline 'LOCAL HERO FASTOLF'. Nevertheless, imposing remains of the edifice that Fastolf had built are still in situ. Parts of the pale pink, brick-built castle walls stand tall, with a gravelled path offering access in place of a drawbridge on the southwest side. Up in the corner to the left are two gargoyles, one with bulbous eyes offering a rather ominous welcome to guests, the other gazing across the water, green with algae and lined with reeds and spikes of rosebay willowherb. When we arrived, a couple of wildfowl had taken possession of the top of the circular great tower and were honking loudly and persistently. I was reminded of John III's one-time description of Caister Castle as so lightly defended that 'a goose may get it'.[9]

In Fastolf's and the Pastons' time the main entrance and drawbridge were located on the north or northeast side. A moat also originally divided the castle into two connected courtyards. Within the inner, residential, courtyard are rows of alcoves or boles built into the wall, in which traditional straw hives, known as skeps, would have been placed as winter habitation for the bees that supplied the castle with honey. Outside the castle there would have been gardens and fishponds, as well as a barge house. Fastolf's militaristic views are reflected in the defensive architecture. The northeast side is punctured with arrow slits, while the southwest has gunports, and the walls have machicolations or drop boxes from which stones, boiling water or burning torches could be thrown on the heads of attacking forces. Another tower protecting the ditch allowing access to the River Bure remains in place.

It can sometimes be difficult to imagine what the interior of such a ruin would have looked like in its heyday, but, fortunately, several inventories of Fastolf's capital and possessions at the time of his death have survived, at least one of which was carefully categorised and enumerated by John Paston himself.[10] Not all of this was kept at Caister or in his London residence: for reasons of security, Fastolf had left a considerable amount of money, gold and silverware at St Benet's Abbey, near Ludham. It is possible to derive from these inventories a strong sense of Caister's grand interior decorations, from the elegant tapestries and suits of armour and weapons adorning the walls in the more public rooms to the bedcovers, linen, feather mattresses and cushions in the private chambers. Even Fastolf's items of clothing are recorded in detail, as these too would have been of value for reuse or resale. With the help of these inventories, we can step inside Caister, and see it somewhat through the eyes of John Paston, as he set up camp in his late mentor's home for the Christmas season, ensuring that the administration of the estate, with which he was already so familiar, was running smoothly, talking to the servants and workers to ensure a smooth transfer of power, and taking stock of his new possessions.

In the lead-up to and throughout his Christmas stay at Caister, John worked and slept in its beautifully decorated rooms, and no doubt felt huge pride as the new owner, even if this were tinged with sorrow. Walls and beds were adorned with a variety of scenes, including Morris dancers, a noble lady holding a puppy, a giant with a bear's leg in its hand, and a wodewose, or wild man of the woods, carrying off a child. There were depictions of sieges and battles, shooting and hawking. One wall hanging portrayed a hunter turning on his own bloodhound. Others were devotional: the Assumption and Coronation of the Virgin and, appropriately enough at Christmas, a nativity scene, the adoration of the shepherds. In the great hall were crossbows, windlasses, battle axes, spears, a broad spear, lance, shield and even a target. In the garde-robe, that is a small storage cupboard, or possibly a toilet, John came across a collection of bows and arrows with swan feather fletchings. John and his men examined and noted down the contents of every room, from the vestments and furnishings in the chapel to the equipment in the bakery, brewery and kitchen, and the provisions stored in the larder.

Some items aren't mentioned in the inventories. Under Fastolf's literary patronage his highly educated secretary, William Worcester, wrote the *Boke of Noblesse*, addressed to Edward IV, which encouraged a martial approach to the defence of the realm, and Stephen Scrope translated Christine de Pizan's *Epistle of Othea*. There is no mention of a book collection in the later inventories, which only record the liturgical works kept in his chapel, but it seems likely he had his own library, and indeed a document exists from almost a decade prior to his death that catalogues his books, which were rather eccentrically stored in the 'stew' or bathhouse.[11]

But before John Paston was able to document his newly inherited wealth, he first had to organise Fastolf's funeral, and to ensure that it was fittingly elaborate. We can reconstruct what occurred from our knowledge of medieval death rituals and from the documentary evidence. Following his demise, Fastolf's corpse would have been washed and wrapped in a white shroud or winding sheet and embalmed with spices, herbs and wine before being laid in state at Caister Castle. Services would have been performed and prayers would have been said for his soul, starting with the Placebo, the office of Vespers on the eve of the funeral, and culminating in the Requiem Mass before the burial itself. Fastolf was laid to rest next to his wife in St Benet's Abbey. An eminent benefactor of the abbey, he had already paid for the building of the aisle in which his expensive tomb was located. Sadly, just as the plans for a college at Caister came to nothing, so, according to one of Fastolf's loyal servants, despite his generosity, the monks of St Benet's soon forgot their obligations to their former benefactor.[12]

St Benet's is situated on the banks of the Bure less than ten miles from Caister Castle, and Fastolf's body would have been transported there by barge. Today, access is still either by river or via a long, rutted, single-track lane between fields and farm buildings to a small car park, and from there on foot to the site itself. Although the abbey is remote and situated on farmland, it is a popular location, and when Heike and I visited on a warm August day there were a few people around although it was by no means crowded. The remnants of the abbey gatehouse, including the arch, are still standing, but somewhat bizarrely, an early eighteenth-century windmill has been built over it. Within the ruined mill it is possible to see the carvings of a knight fighting a lion on either side of the spandrels on the front entrance, although the lion's head is somewhat flattened. Inevitably, this decoration reminded me of the rhetorical question: 'Who painted the lion, tell me who?' uttered by Chaucer's Wife of Bath, alluding to the Aesopian fable of the man who shows a lion a depiction of a man killing a lion. The lion's cynical response, that if a lion had painted it the picture would be very different, is echoed by the Wife, as she castigates the misogynist clerical portrayal of women, and offers her own counter-perspective.[13] Presumably no such satire was intended in the decorative art of the gate at St Benet's.

Today, only fragments of the church and cloisters are still standing and Fastolf's grave has vanished. When we walked from the gatehouse to site of the former altar, a tractor was parked near the giant oak cross that was erected there in 1987. Recent visitors have hammered coins into the vertical beam, giving the appearance of spines. We sat on the bank, near the location of the wharf where the barge carrying Fastolf's remains would have docked, enjoying the commanding view of the gatehouse and mill as the river curves its way around. From the sheer size of the site, it is possible to imagine the grandeur of the funeral, with around 400 attendees dressed in mourning robes, followed by poor people, proceeding from the wharf side and through the abbey. Much of the actual organisation for this elaborate and lavish event was delegated to Fastolf's secretary, who unfortunately found himself paying for a large part of it out of his own pocket.[14] The mourners, led by John Paston who was accompanied by a large entourage, were attired in black. The abbey was decorated with heraldic and religious banners and pennants.

An illustration in a Book of Hours by an artist known as the Master of Sir John Fastolf[15] provides us with some visual insights into the service of the Mass of the Dead. This miniature depicts a coffin covered with a heraldic pall or mortcloth (in this case representing the white on red cross of the

Knights Hospitaller) within a structure for displaying the coffin known as a catafalque. The catafalque is adorned with crosses and lit candles. A priest reads the Office of the Dead from an open book, flanked by his tonsured brethren. Hooded mourners in black robes stand behind the coffin. This image has no direct connection with Fastolf or his funeral: the anonymous artist takes his name from another manuscript which Fastolf had commissioned him to illuminate.[16] Nevertheless, the illustration enables us to view the performance of the Mass for the Dead from a perspective akin to that of one of the attendees on the winter's day when Fastolf's body was committed to the ground and his soul commended to God. The funeral would then be followed by a great feast for the mourners and a meal for the poor. We don't know what role, if any at all, Margaret played in the preparations; medieval funerals were generally male affairs, and she would not have had a significant part to play in the ceremony. Nevertheless, as her Christmas Eve letter indicates, Margaret took charge behind the scenes at home.

While John remained in Caister after the funeral, busy with administering Fastolf's will and with assessing and securing his inheritance, Margaret prepared to celebrate Christmas with her family in their home in Norwich. Christmas in the 1400s was primarily a religious event, and one that was less significant than Easter. Advent, the lead-up to the Feast of the Nativity of Our Lord (Christmas Day), was traditionally a period of penitence and fasting, or at least abstinence. Margaret and her children and servants may well have attended Vespers on the evening of Christmas Eve, perhaps at St Peter Hungate, as well as the three masses on the Feast of the Nativity itself: at midnight, when Christ was born, at dawn and during the day. Christmastide itself lasted until at least Twelfth Night or Epiphany Eve on 5 January, Epiphany being the day when the Magi or Three Kings visited the baby Jesus. Sometimes it extended until Candlemas, the Feast of the Purification of the Blessed Virgin Mary almost a month later, on 2 February.

From Margaret's letter of Christmas Eve 1459 we know that the Christmas festivities at the Paston household in Norwich were to be suitably muted. Typically, Christmas would have involved the household being decorated with the foliage and berries of evergreens such as laurel, conifers, bay, ivy, holly and mistletoe. Tapers would be lit, and yule logs burnt. Presents might well have been exchanged during Christmastide, but not necessarily on Christmas Day itself. New Year gift giving was more common. Carols would be sung, such as those in John Audelay's sequence written for six days over Christmas, beginning with 'Welcome, Yule, in glad array' through to 'What tidings do you bring, messenger'.[17] But carolling was more active than it is today: the word 'carol' originally referred to a group of people singing *and* dancing in a circle. Despite the emphasis on religion and devotion, feasting and banqueting was nevertheless at the heart of Christmas. Goose might be served, or boar, venison, game birds and beef, along with pies, bread, cheeses, puddings and cakes, and wine and beer would accompany the food. Charitable sharing of food was also important, with gifts of pies and bread presented to the poor and needy.

The most famous literary account of medieval Christmastide is *Sir Gawain and the Green Knight*, an anonymous fourteenth-century alliterative romance written in the Northwest of England. While *Sir Gawain and the Green Knight* is set in a fantastic world of giants, trolls and wild men, it does provide us with a sense of how religious observance was combined with the merriment of the season. The poem is set in the reign of a youthful King Arthur, who, at its opening, is celebrating with his knights of the Round Table. There is great revelry at Camelot: jousting, carolling and fifteen days of eating, drinking, music and dancing, and on New Year's Eve, after mass, the knights and ladies of the court exchange gifts, and sit down for a great banquet. A year later, Sir Gawain finds himself arriving at the Castle of Sir Bertilak on Christmas Eve, where he joins a 'penitential' but plentiful meal of soups or stews and a variety of fish dishes with delicious sauces, and then enjoys three days of seasonal feasting and entertainment. At the heart of the poem are King Arthur's desire to hear a marvellous tale and a series of Christmas games, which in the world of the poem have potentially deadly consequences. In everyday life too, Christmas games, albeit of a less dangerous variety, were a very popular form of recreation.

For Margaret, the challenge of Christmas 1459 was to achieve a balance of celebration and sobriety. The house may well have remained undecorated, but Margaret would still have had to ensure that sufficient food was ready for the season's feasting. Indeed, her preparations would have already begun in October or November. In response to Margaret's request for advice about how the family should spend their time, Lady Morley instructed her that there should be 'no dressing up, nor harp nor lute playing, nor singing, nor any loud pastime'. Dressing up, in this context, would have referred to the putting on of costumes for a performance of some sort, quite possibly of a mummers' play, as these amateur local entertainments were often staged at Christmas. Dancing wasn't explicitly mentioned, presumably because it would require some sort of musical accompaniment, and so the fact that it was forbidden could be taken as read. Of course, these prohibitions confirm that such activities would normally be expected to take place. Several years later, Margaret's eldest son was to lament the loss of a man in his service, who for three years had performed for him in pageants or plays about St George and Robin Hood and the Sheriff of Nottingham.[18] Indeed a fragment of the Robin Hood play still exists that may well be the same one that John II's men performed.[19] The sparse dialogue in the text would have framed a series of improvised enactments of sporting competitions and fights. Instead of such boisterous revels, Margaret was advised that, following a death, the only appropriate amusements were much more sedentary: 'tables', chess and cards.

Board games were popular at the time among the higher social classes and backgammon and chess have a very long history. Tables refers to a version of backgammon played on a hinged board with 'men' or pieces and dice. The game of chess today reflects in part not only its medieval incarnation in terms of the rules, but also the hierarchical structure of medieval society in the naming of the pieces (King, Queen, Bishop, Knight, and Rook or Castle) and medieval warfare, with the pawns, representing the peasants and lower ranks of soldiers, leading the attack. In the absence of modern-day timers, dice were introduced to make the game faster, the numbers of pips dictating which piece to move. While tables and chess were restricted to two players, games of cards would have allowed more members of the household to take part. Fascinatingly, Margaret's letter includes one of the earliest recorded references to the playing of cards in England.[20] Margaret may have enjoyed an ancestral relative of whist, such as 'Triumph' which was certainly around by the sixteenth century, or she may have abstained entirely from the entertainments. Even though she had her family around her, she was keenly aware of John's absence. Indeed, her feelings for her husband far overshadowed her grief for Fastolf. Margaret urged John to return home as soon as he could, adding: 'I consider myself half a widow because you are not at home.'

9. 'THEY ACT AS IF THEY WERE EXPECTING A NEW WORLD'

....

7 January 1462 (Margaret to her husband)

....

Two years later, Margaret experienced a much more anxious Christmas. Early in January of 1462, Margaret wrote to John asking if he had received the correspondence that she sent on the Feast of St Thomas the Apostle on 21 December.[1] As this was traditionally the day when preparations for Christmas began and Margaret would no doubt have been coordinating the baking and cooking and other arrangements, it is a testimony to her devotion to John that she had taken time out on such a busy day to write to him. Margaret had hoped that this year her husband might join his family for at least some of the festive period: 'I truly believed you would have been home by Twelfth Night at the latest.' But John had not returned home at all, and Margaret had not received any messages from him, so she feared that something terrible had happened. She urged him to get in touch as soon as possible, because, as she puts it in her letter, 'my heart will never be at ease until I have news of you'.

Once again, Margaret found herself separated from her husband, but for very different reasons; her apprehension needs to be understood in terms of the wider political context. The outbreak of the Wars of the Roses in the mid-1450s intensified the factionalism and social unrest throughout the country, and Paston enemies were circling. Following the Lancastrian victory at the 2nd Battle of St Albans in February of 1461, for example, Margaret had written to her husband notifying him of a plot to ambush him hatched by their old foe John Heydon, and warning him that his life and property were at risk.[2] Alongside another adversary still threatening trouble was Heydon's associate, the courtier Sir Thomas Tuddenham. Like Heydon, Tuddenham had been a close ally of the late Duke of Suffolk, and he continued to serve the family. Very shortly afterwards, the Lancastrians were defeated at the Battle of Towton. Edward IV, the son of Richard, 3rd Duke of York and Cecily Neville, was crowned king. Margaret and John's eldest son entered royal service. Tuddenham was found guilty of treason and executed. Nevertheless, the disruption across the country continued, and John found himself caught up in the disputes over Fastolf's former properties, including Caister itself, which John Mowbray, 4th Duke of Norfolk, had recently tried to seize.

The concern for her husband that Margaret expresses in her letter of January 1462 was intensified by what was happening in her immediate locality. She was fearful of the criminality and social and political unrest which she had witnessed, and worried that there would be a rebellion: 'People around here grow rowdy ... [and there is] a very great fear of an uprising amongst the common people.' She also tells her husband that his absence had made matters worse for the tenants on his land because they were all the more vulnerable to attack: 'They say for certain that it is not well with you, and if it is not well with you they say that they are sure that those who want to wrong you will soon wrong them, and that makes them almost mad.'

Gathering rents owed on the Paston and Fastolf estates had become well-nigh impossible, and according to the assessment of the couple's eldest son, now a young man, 'those best able to pay, pay least'. In the chaos, established social norms, expectations and rules could be completely discarded, and most of the populace could do as they wished. As Margaret puts it, they 'act as if they were expecting a new world'. To her, it seemed like the end of times, with doomsday fast approaching.

Margaret recognised the need for some of sort of strong governance to be established in her locality, but she was far from optimistic that this would actually occur: 'May God in his holy mercy grant grace that there be a good and sensible regime established in this area in haste, because I never heard of so much robbery and manslaughter around here in such as short a time as there is now.' She reports rumours circulating that Edward IV's brother George, Duke of Clarence, accompanied by John de la Pole, 2nd Duke of Suffolk, would come to Norfolk to try to establish order by putting the rioters on trial. Unfortunately, this news caused further tension because no one had any confidence that justice would be served: 'People say that they would rather all go up together to the king and complain of such dishonest villains as they have been wronged by in the past than be complained about without reason and be hanged at their own doors.' Margaret observes to her husband in her letter that the Duke of Suffolk, and his mother, Alice Chaucer, the dowager duchess, are widely regarded as lawless and tyrannical: 'they say that all the traitors and extortionists of this district are maintained by them, and by those they can bribe', and that 'if the Duke of Suffolk comes there will be a malicious regime'.

Alice Chaucer was one of the Pastons' most intimidating opponents, and over time, Margaret developed a deep loathing of her. Alice was the only child of Geoffrey Chaucer's very successful son, Thomas. Around fifteen years older than Margaret, she married three times in all. It was following her last union, to William de la Pole, that she really came to the attention of the Paston family. Initially, the Duke and Duchess of Suffolk had been close to Henry VI and Margaret of Anjou, whose marriage Suffolk had negotiated. Alice and her husband had accompanied Margaret of Anjou on her journey from France to England, with Alice serving as her lady-in-wating. When William de la Pole was murdered in 1450 Alice found herself in a vulnerable situation, but she managed to survive a state trial that took place soon after, and for the next few years she fought to secure her own position and that of her son. Towards the end of the decade, the young duke married Elizabeth of York, sister of the soon-to-be Edward IV. Alice abandoned the Lancastrian side and subsequently even served as jailor to her former mistress, Margaret of Anjou. As her father's heir and a three-times widow, she accumulated considerable wealth during her lifetime, to which she added estates that she acquired herself. Indeed, as dowager duchess she was far better off than her own son, the current duke. After Fastolf's death, Alice and her son John set their sights on some of the estates to which the Pastons laid claim, including the manor of Cotton, which Alice's husband had sold to the old soldier and subsequently regretted. By the beginning of 1462, it was not just the wider populace who felt intimidated by Alice and her son: Margaret did too.

In Margaret's opinion, Alice Chaucer was both cunning and ambitious. Yet there was also a highly cultured side to her. She was a patron of the arts, adorned her home with beautiful textiles and furnishings, and possessed a large collection of books.[3] There is no record of Alice owning any of her grandfather's works, but her library did include a book by Christine de Pizan: *The Book of the City of Ladies*. It is easy to see the appeal of this utopian celebration of famous women's achievements to this highly intelligent, rich, powerful and apparently fearless aristocrat, and to imagine her reading it, either alone or with her female companions, in the great chamber that she had had decorated with tapestries depicting the legendary women warriors, the Amazons.

Alice Chaucer was also devout, as befitted her position in society. She and her third husband had been granted a royal licence to establish God's House at Ewelme in Oxfordshire, a chantry foundation with a school, a community of thirteen almsmen and two priests. Alice continued the project after her husband died. Although the Palace at Ewelme, the couple's main residence which they had constructed by extending the existing manor house, no longer stands in its entirety, the beautiful alms-houses and school are still in use to the present day, as is the Chapel of St John the Baptist within St Mary's Church where Alice is buried in a remarkable alabaster transi tomb; that is a monument that includes a sculpture of the skeleton or decaying body of the deceased and serves as a *memento mori*. Margaret Paston was to outlive her formidable and proud old enemy by almost ten years. Her animosity towards the duchess was such that she is unlikely to have shed any tears at her passing, or to have hoped to have been reconciled with her in heaven. At the beginning of 1462, however, Alice Chaucer was very much alive, and the Suffolks' worst depredations of Paston property were in the future.

Margaret's unease about the welfare of her husband in January of 1462 was intensified further by a recent personal misfortune. A couple of months previously, John had been thrown into the Fleet Prison in London for failing to respond to a royal summons. Margaret was greatly relieved when she received notification that he had been released after just a few days of imprisonment.[4] The men who on this occasion had complained to the King about John were the Duke of Norfolk and Sir John Howard, the High Sheriff of Norfolk and Suffolk. Margaret was able to pass on to her husband the good news that Howard had been incarcerated in his place, reassuring him that he still had many supporters in Norfolk. Shortly afterwards the Duke of Norfolk died, giving John some further respite on that front.

John's arrest in late 1461 proved to be only the first of a series of imprisonments. In the middle of the decade, because of challenges to his claim on Fastolf's estates, John was outlawed, and his subsequent confinements included one longer period of incarceration. The correspondence exchanged by Margaret and John at that time indicates that John sometimes experienced considerable despair and that Margaret quite rightly feared for his mental and physical health. From the evidence of her letters, it seems Margaret seldom, if ever, left Norfolk, but a few years after the anxious Christmas season of 1461–2, and after months of enforced separation, she sent her husband an encouraging note, reminding him to have faith that God would help him overcome all of his difficulties and promising to visit him in prison: 'If you think I might do any good in your business if I come up to see you, once I know your intentions, it will not be long before I am with you.'[5]

Margaret did make this journey to London and, in her wake, I made my own pilgrimage to the city, looking for the imprints of the buildings she saw and following the routes she may have taken. By chance rather than design, my trip coincided with the first day of Queen Elizabeth II's Platinum Jubilee celebrations in 2022, and I witnessed the Jubilee flypast over the city, a celebration of aerial prowess and pageantry that the Pastons would have understood and appreciated, even if the technology would have been unimaginable to them. But when Margaret was in the city, royal pomp and display couldn't have been further from her mind. Her husband's gaol was located just outside the walls of the city of London by Ludgate, a position which was convenient for the Inns of Court, the Courts of Chancery, Exchequer and Common Pleas and the Star Chamber. It was built on the east bank of the River Fleet and surrounded completely by water.[6] Its former site is at the southern end of modern-day Farringdon Street where towering glass office blocks and commercial buildings now enclose a pedestrian plaza. Standing in the middle of this concrete square, I felt that I could have been in any twenty-first-century city in the world. The oppressive ditches, waterways and ancient walls of Margaret and John's time have long since disappeared and been replaced by contemporary architecture, designed to give a sense of light and space amid the bustle of business and commerce.

The Fleet was first established at the end of the twelfth century and remained in operation for several hundred years. It had been destroyed in 1381, in Wat Tyler's Rebellion, but was rebuilt on the same site. It was mainly, but not exclusively, a prison for debtors. The Fleet was run for profit, so the wardenship was valuable, and passed down within a single family. At the time of John's imprisonments, the warden was a woman, Elizabeth Venour, poetically referred to by his second son, John III, as 'my fair mistress of the Fleet'.[7] On arrival at the Fleet, prisoners had to pay various admission fees, and also to pay for their board and lodging. Further fees were due when they were finally released. Prisoners could sometimes pay bail or purchase a licence to leave the prison, accompanied by an officer or 'baston', to conduct business. Even though, years later, Margaret and John's second son described the Fleet as 'a fair prison, but you have little liberty in there, because you have to appear when called',[8] prisoners enjoyed considerable freedom of movement within its walls and their activities were not usually closely scrutinised.

Medieval prisoners were accommodated according, in part, to their social status, and John found himself among men of a similar or a higher class to himself; women were housed in their own section. John would have had his own room, and shared a parlour and enjoyed better food and wine than the poorer inhabitants. Because medieval prisons were organised hierarchically, the various payments were graduated according to the rank and wealth of the prisoners and the comfort and liberties they would enjoy while locked up. John would have had to ensure his own welfare, for example by paying for any medical care he needed, something which would have been particularly necessary by the mid-1460s when his health deteriorated. If they could afford to, prisoners could be accompanied by their servants and John kept his man, Pamping, at his side. Even receiving visitors required a financial outlay. The Fleet was one of the most expensive prisons in London, so all of this would have amounted to a great deal of money, and John certainly felt the pinch.

While she was in London, Margaret received a letter from her second son, John III, which provides us with important information about other places in the metropolis she may have visited. John III asked his mother to collect some items he had ordered from 'the hosier with the crooked back next to the Black Friars gate within Ludgate', that is from a shop next to the gate of the Dominican friary that was situated just inside the western wall of the city.[9] While the monastery has vanished, its location is marked today by Blackfriars underground station and by the names of the streets: Blackfriars Lane, Church Entry and Friar Street. On the corner of St Andrew's Hill and Ireland Yard and across from the Cockpit pub, there is a memorial plaque commemorating Shakespeare's purchase in 1613 of a house in the former Blackfriars gatehouse. The gatehouse would have been just a few minutes' walk from the Fleet, and so would not have taken Margaret far out of her way. Wandering down the steep stairwells and the narrow and twisting alleyways around Carter Lane, making my way between high buildings, some of which were constructed after the Great Fire of London in 1666, it was not that hard to imagine the city as it was when Margaret went in search of John's stockings.

But John III didn't just want his mother to pick up his shopping, he also thought she should take some time to enjoy some devout tourism. He suggested she walk just four or five minutes further into the city to see the *Crux borealis* (northern cross), a 'rood' or crucifix at the north transept door of Old St Paul's, the Romanesque cathedral which preceded that built by Sir Christopher Wren, after it fell into disrepair and was severely damaged in the Great Fire. The *Crux borealis* was said to have been carved by Joseph of Arimathea and found miraculously floating in the Thames. The shrine of St Erkenwald, a seventh-century bishop of London, was another popular pilgrimage destination at the cathedral that Margaret may have visited, although John III doesn't mention it to her. While neither the Blackfriars Gate nor Old St Paul's were far from John's prison, the other holy place that he recommended was further afield: the Holy Rood on the wall of Bermondsey Abbey's main gatehouse.

Bermondsey Abbey was situated in Southwark across the River Thames from the Tower of London. The location of the Holy Rood of Bermondsey on the wall of the abbey gatehouse was a draw for pilgrims setting off from Southwark Cathedral to Canterbury Cathedral and the shrine of St Thomas Becket; it would have involved only a short detour from the main route, what is now the Old Kent Road. The walk to

Bermondsey from St Paul's Cathedral across London Bridge would take around three-quarters of an hour, so while, if she did take time out for this trip, Margaret could have gone on foot, she may have chosen instead to ride or to take a carriage.

In contrast to Southwark Cathedral, there are few physical remains of Bermondsey Abbey itself, but again the road names record the history of the area, and the layout of the streets made it possible for me to reconstruct in my mind's eye the shape, size and outline of the medieval buildings. Abbey Street in Bermondsey runs right through the site of the West Gate and church nave and choir. It is flanked on one side by the modern Bermondsey Square, which overlays the former inner or Great Gate and the abbey court, and on the other side by the grave-yard of St Mary Magdalen Bermondsey. This church formerly served the abbey's lay brothers but has been extensively rebuilt and remodelled over the centuries, so its medieval origins are indiscernible. The watchhouse on the corner of Abbey Street and Bermondsey Street, now a café, is nineteenth century not medieval, and is said to have been built to deter body snatchers from disinterring corpses to sell to anatomy students at Guy's and St Thomas's Hospitals.

The Holy Rood of Bermondsey that John III recommended seems to have been a copy of the famous early medieval *Volto Santo* [Holy Face] in the Cathedral of San Martino in Lucca, Tuscany. This wooden statue supposedly depicts a true likeness of Christ, carved by Nicodemus soon after the Resurrection. It is quite different to the more familiar depictions of the near-naked Man of Sorrows, suspended in suffering from the cross, pierced by his wounds. Instead, it depicts a larger-than-life-sized bearded Christ, wearing a crown and dressed in a long robe, standing erect with arms outstretched. Taken together, it is easy to see the appeal of both the Rood of the North Door and the Holy Rood of Bermondsey to a devout tourist in London, who would gladly have welcomed divine assistance in her affairs and in those of her husband. While it isn't certain that Margaret followed her son's recommendations and made these pilgrimages, it is likely that she didn't travel to London alone. John III's letter reveals that she was to be accompanied by her elder daughter, Margery, who had reached a marriageable age. John III even suggests that his sister should also go with her mother to the shrines to pray that she might find a suitable husband.

On Margaret's return from London in 1465, her husband thanked her 'for the great cheer that you gave me here, to my great cost and charge and labour',[10] and he asked Margaret to send him some worsted for doublets to keep him warm through 'this cold winter'. At the end of this already very lengthy letter he included some doggerel which he had written for their shared entertainment. No doubt, despite continuing to run his complex affairs from captivity, John still had time on his hands to put to creative use. The verses end:

> And look you be merry and take no thought,
> For this rhyme is cunningly wrought.
> My lord Percy and all this house
> Recommend them to you, dog, cat and mouse,
> And wish you had been here still,
> For they say you are a good girl.
> No more to you at this time,
> But God save him who made this rhyme.

The house of Percy in these lines refers to the Fleet. Following the death of his Lancastrian father, the Earl of Northumberland, at the Battle of Towton, Henry Percy was imprisoned there before being moved to the Tower of London. The word 'girl', although generally used to denote a young child of either sex, could also be applied to a young woman. Margaret was in her mid-40s at this time, so John is evidently applying the word affectionately. He goes on to sign off as 'your true and trusty husband'. Poignantly, this is the last letter from John to Margaret that we have.

Margaret replied a week later, promising to send the finest worsted she could obtain by Hallowmas, or All Saints' Day, and acknowledging 'the warm welcome you gave me and the amount you spent on me'.[11] Concerned that there was an element of reproach in John's letter she adds: 'You spent more than I wished you to, unless it pleased you to do so.' In a postscript, she urges him to sort out his affairs so that he can leave the Fleet quickly, because, as she had told him at the time of her visit, she did not trust some of the company which he was forced to keep there.[12] Margaret was a canny judge of character, and she believed that her husband could be at times too trusting. She was probably right. During this time of lawlessness and constantly shifting political allegiances, as described so evocatively by Margaret in her letter of January 1462, John found himself inextricably entangled in the conflicts over Fastolf's will and he struggled to know whom to trust. The series of imprisonments in the Fleet that began with his first short incarceration in the early 1460s were, in the middle of the decade, to prove the death of him.

10. 'MAY GOD MAKE A GOOD MAN OF YOU'

15 November 1463 (Margaret to her
eldest son, John II)

Despite the great affection and respect that Margaret and John showed each other throughout their marriage, relations between them were occasionally cool, with John evidently inclined to harbour grudges, and Margaret having to plead for his forgiveness, as is illustrated by the following example of one of her apologies: 'Upon my word of honour, I do not wish to do or say anything that should make you displeased with me, and if I have done I am sorry for it, and will make up for it.'[1] The first letter that we have from Margaret to her eldest son, John II, was written from Caister in the late winter of 1463.[2] In it, Margaret reproves him for causing a rift between herself and her husband after John II secretly departed from his post at the castle without their authorisation.

By this point, the Paston inheritance was being threatened on several fronts, with the probate hearing about Fastolf's will scheduled for the following January. John needed to remain in London and required his eldest son to support his mother and servants in ensuring that the estates were defended, and the rents collected. It is probable that John II had in fact left Caister for good reason, to join the King and the Yorkist forces following Margaret of Anjou's invasion of Northumberland in October. Margaret makes no mention of the political context, focusing instead on how she has been let down by his behaviour and observing: 'Your father thought, and still thinks, that I had agreed to you leaving and that makes me very sad.' Margaret's husband was concerned that she had taken their son's side against him, and this forced her into subterfuge: 'I dare not let him know about the last letter you wrote to me because he was very displeased with me at that time.' Margaret therefore instructs her son to write once again to his father seeking reconciliation.

Margaret takes the opportunity in her letter to give her son some advice on how to conduct himself towards his father in future, ordering him: 'In anything concerning your father that should be to his honour, profit or benefit to apply yourself and to do your best with all diligence to further it.' Her point is that it is imperative that the interests of the head of the family should always be furthered above all else. On no account should John II put himself first. Nevertheless, despite the friction that already existed between Margaret and her husband, Margaret continues to go behind her his back. Margaret is also concerned that her son can't handle his money. She warns him to be less of a spendthrift and to budget more carefully and tries to pry into his financial affairs without letting her husband know she is so doing.

John II was in his early twenties when he received this letter from his mother. Still in the service of Edward IV, he had recently reached the age of legal majority. Having been knighted at that time, he was now Sir John Paston. According to prevailing medieval views of the male lifecycle, childhood ended at the age of twelve, when adolescence began. A young man did not achieve full maturity until he was 30, by which age he would be expected to be more rational and less impulsive. Until he reached that age, no matter his role at court, John could expect to remain subject to the authority of his parents. His mother clearly regarded him as a brash youth who needed instruction and guidance; she signs off her letter with a benediction: 'May God protect you and make a good man of you.'

The tensions between John II and his parents had been building up for some time. In a letter written by John II to his father in the spring of 1462, he had tried to explain why he was so short of cash: 'May it please you to understand the great expense that I have daily travelling with the king, as the bearer of this can inform you, and how long I am likely to remain here ... and how I am charged to have my horse and harness ready and in hasty wise.'[3] He went on to remind his father that he was in service to the king, his master, and had to do his bidding, but that this was to his father's benefit as well as his own. Later in the same year, his younger brother John III pointed out to their father the extent of the necessary outlays he had in the household of the Duke of Norfolk: he urgently required new clothing as he only had his livery gown or uniform to wear, 'and we must wear it every day for the most part, and one gown without change will soon be done'.[4] The brothers were of the view that their father didn't understand how costly royal or aristocratic service was for them, or, for that matter, what demands it made of their time, and that sometimes they were caught between their conflicting duties to their masters and their father. They also considered him to be too frugal. Certainly, their father was not very diplomatic in his dealings with his immediate family or indeed people more generally. It is no wonder then that John II turned to his more judicious mother to act as mediator.

John II did not share his mother's sense of urgency about apologising to his father. Almost four months passed before he did as she asked, by which time he was back in Norfolk, where he was under strict instructions to remain. Clearly frustrated that he is forced to kick his heels in this way, he begs her: 'If there is any service that I can do, if it please you to command me, or if I can understand it, I will be as glad to do it as anything on earth, if it were something that might please you.'[5] In early May 1464, Edward IV was at Leicester preparing for a military expedition against the Lancastrians in Northumbria, and sent orders to both John I and John II to join him there, bringing 'as many persons defensively arrayed as they can, according to their rank', plus enough money to last for two months.[6] Margaret didn't want to risk angering her husband again by allowing their son to leave against his wishes, so she sought his permission to release John II, pointing out that their friends and supporters thought this was the appropriate action to take, and assuring him that his eldest son's conduct was much improved: 'As for his demeanour since you left, in good faith it has been very good and lowly, and diligent in the oversight of your servants and other things, which I hope you would have been pleased with, had you been at home.'

Margaret was firmly of the view that John II's punishment had been effective, and that his attitude towards his parents would improve henceforth. Unfortunately, that was not to be. Following further disagreements, John II was cast out of his father's house for a year, and all his parental support was withdrawn. Margaret's attempts to reconcile the pair resulted in an angry outburst from her husband, in which he characterised his eldest son as rude, reckless and lazy, comparing him to 'a drone amongst bees which labour to gather honey in the fields, and the drone does nothing except take his part of it'.[7] Margaret's pleas to her husband that he 'be a good father and show some fatherly feelings' proved unsuccessful.[8] His disillusionment led him to reflect upon his disappointed expectations of fatherhood: 'Every poor man who has brought up his children to the age of twelve years expects then to be helped and profited by his children, and every gentleman who has discretion expects that his kin and servants who live with him and at his cost should help him henceforth.'[9] John II simply could not seem to meet his father's standards and found himself repeatedly letting him down. There was little Margaret could do to change her husband's mind and, over time, she would come round to his way of thinking about their son.

Yet, while the main purpose of Margaret's letter of November 1463 may have been to attempt to dissipate the tensions within the family, she also took the opportunity to ask her eldest son to find out whether one of their servants, John Wykes, intended to marry a young woman called Jane Walsham.[10] Jane Walsham was evidently living at Caister at the time, no doubt also in service to the family, and Margaret considered herself responsible for her care. It was not the case on this occasion that Margaret was trying to arrange a political marriage. Rather, Jane had fallen in love. She insisted to Margaret that if she could not marry Wykes, she would remain single. Wykes had assured Jane that 'there was no woman in the world that he loved so much'. Margaret was clearly sceptical. Concerned that Wykes was playing fast and loose with the young woman's heart, she wanted her son to investigate the matter and if indeed Wykes was being insincere then she would look for an alternative match.

As it happened, Margaret's mind had already turned to thoughts of arranging marriages. Just a couple of days earlier, she had written to her husband telling him about an incident that had occurred on a recent shopping visit to Norwich. A relative of Elizabeth Clere's had met their adolescent daughter, Margery, at her grandmother Agnes's house. This man had had praised Margery as 'a fine young woman', and suggested a possible match to the son of Sir John Cley, the chamberlain of Cecily Neville, Duchess of York. Agnes very much approved of this suggestion if 'it could be arranged for less money than in the future'.[11] Nothing came of either of these proposed unions. Wykes, despite his lovemaking, had indeed not been serious in his intentions towards Jane, and Margery married beneath her in a love match which was to horrify her family. Jane, despite Margaret's attempts to protect her interests, ultimately fell victim of her own brother's greed: he sold her livelihood, and she was effectively coerced into marriage 'to a knave' or rogue.[12]

The economics and politics behind medieval marriage for the aristocracy and gentry class were then at odds with the ideals of romance, and all too often they went against the interests of women. While the marriage that Justice William and Agnes negotiated between Margaret and John was a success on anyone's terms, this was certainly not always the case, as Jane Walsham's fate illustrates. Women and men not infrequently found themselves united with someone for whom they felt little or nothing, or worse still, hated or feared. Divorce was generally only an option for very limited reasons, such as adultery, or because the marriage was not judged to be legitimate in the first place. And even though the consent of both parties was required, women could find themselves pressurised by their families or by social expectation. Indeed, a man could exploit for his own financial or sexual gain the need for a woman to protect her reputation. Unless a widow, a woman was expected to remain a virgin until her wedding night. If a man was determined to marry a woman regardless of any opposition, then he could turn to kidnapping to force the situation. Because the victim's honour would be effectively compromised by her capture, it would then be in the interests of her family to allow the marriage to go ahead.

Tellingly, the Latin noun *raptus* and Middle English 'rape' can mean both 'abduction' and 'rape' in the modern sense.[13] Archival evidence exists that the poet Geoffrey Chaucer was involved in some way in a *raptus* claim involving a woman called Cecily Chaumpaigne. As a result, the distinction, and the overlap, between these two senses of the word, and the possibility of other meanings entirely, has been discussed at length by critics and historians.[14] But, putting aside controversies over terminology, one thing that is clear is that, in the Middle Ages, rape and abduction were crimes of coercion and violence that were widespread at the time. Margaret's husband describes in one letter the kidnapping of Jane Boys, the widowed daughter-in-law of Lady Sibylle Boys.[15] According to his account, Jane Boys was 'ravished against her will'. She was tied to her horse and ridden away from her mother, who followed on foot as far as she could. Jane screamed oaths at her abductor and swore 'that she would never be wedded to that knave'. Nevertheless, Boys did subsequently marry her attacker. She doubtless had little choice, regardless of whether or not she was sexually violated. Occasionally, young men would also be abducted. At the age of twelve, Chaucer's own father was seized by an aunt in an unsuccessful attempt to unite him with her daughter. The motives behind such attacks were often pecuniary. At other times, the aim was to intimidate the target and their family, as was the case when Margaret had been threatened with kidnapping and imprisonment following the fall of Gresham.

Margaret intervened in one case of rape, in the sense of forced sexual intercourse. Her third son, Edmond, complained that his mother made him get rid of one of his servants, a man called Gregory, after he assaulted a young woman: 'It happened that he had a knave's lust, in plain terms, to swive [fuck] a quean; and so he did in the rabbit warren.'[16] As his language reveals, Edmond didn't take the assault seriously. He doesn't refer to it as rape or ravishment and he imputes blame to the victim by calling her a 'quean' which in this context has a derogatory meaning akin to 'whore' or 'slut'. Edmond records that when Gregory had finished his assault on the woman, he turned her over to two of Margaret's ploughmen who then 'had her all night in their stable'. From Edmond's account, Margaret's principal complaint was less the crime itself than its location: the attack may have taken place on her property. Gregory insisted that the violation had taken place elsewhere and that 'he had nothing to do with her [his victim] in my mother's place', but Margaret was not going to be hoodwinked. She held Gregory responsible for the wrongdoing and would not tolerate him remaining in the family's service. Edmond had no choice but to let him go, although he did try to convince one of his older brothers to take him on. While it may appear that Margaret showed little sympathy for the woman herself, the perspective that we have here is that of Edmond. Presumably, the young woman had made a complaint to Margaret about the attack, leading to her intervention, and for Margaret, focusing on the property violation may have been the most effective means of ridding her family of the rapist. As her involvement in the dalliance between Jane Walsham and Wykes also indicates, Margaret kept a firm control of her estates, her servants and workers, and sought to protect the reputation of the household and everyone within it.

The final section of Margaret's 1463 letter to John II is concerned with the health of his 'grey horse'. Margaret had sent the lame horse to the farrier, whose expertise extended beyond hoof care and shoeing horses to include looking after horses and caring for them when they were sick; effectively the farrier also took on the role of a veterinarian today. Unfortunately, the farrier had reported that the grey horse not only had splayed hooves, in other words that its toes pointed outwards, but 'his shoulder [was] torn from his body'. Perhaps John and his horse had taken a tumble or had a collision, or perhaps the horse had been injured in battle. Sadly, the prognosis for such an injury in an age before veterinary medicine was poor. According to the farrier, 'he shall never be any good for riding nor much good for plowing or pulling a cart'. Margaret was at a loss about what to do with the animal. John II hadn't just consigned his horse to his mother to attend to, he had also left behind his 'harness and gear' in the keeping of a good friend of his father, John Daubeney. But Daubeney could not tend to it because he didn't have the keys to the trunk. Of course, these items would need to be kept clean and dry, otherwise they would rust and rot, and Margaret warned her son: 'I believe it will deteriorate unless it is attended to soon.'

The horse was a utilitarian animal, central to medieval society, and it served several key functions. Before the invention of the train and the car, travelling on horseback or in a horse-drawn carriage or cart were the most common forms of land transport. Margaret herself would have travelled on horseback or in carriages. The horse was also vital to transporting goods, to agriculture and to warfare. Packhorses and sumpters carried their loads on their backs, often across difficult terrains, while carthorses and other drawing animals pulled ploughs and other farming equipment. The horse was an indicator of prestige, social status and wealth. A trained charger or war horse, whether a destrier (a tall horse ridden with armour) or a courser (a fast horse ridden without armour), would have been extremely valuable and would need very careful maintenance. Horses were also used for sport, whether for hunting or for riding in tournaments and jousts. Even a palfrey, a horse that was used simply for riding, or a jennet, a small horse which would often be favoured by women, was an asset to be looked after. From the farrier's summation, and Margaret's reference to a harness, which would be used to fasten the animal to a cart or plough, it is possible that John's grey horse was a rouncey, that is a general all-rounder that could be used for riding more generally as well in battle and might sometimes be employed in farm work. If this were the case, John may have kept it for one of his men to ride. He would have favoured more expensive beasts for his own use and entertainment. Only a couple of years later, John II participated in a royal joust at Eltham Palace in Greenwich, where he would surely have been riding a destrier.

The cultural and martial significance of the medieval horse is recognised in the literature of the time in the romances that celebrate all things chivalric and military. Some of the most well-known medieval literary descriptions of horses are found in *Sir Gawain and the Green Knight* in the descriptions of the Green Knight's charger and of Gawain's own mount, called Gringolet. The poem dwells on the elaborately decorated tack of the Green Knight's great courser, which matches the Knight's own dress:

> The pendants on his breast harness, the magnificent crupper, / the bridle studs, and all the metalwork were enamelled [green], / the stirrups that he stood on were the same colour / as were his saddlebows and his noble saddle skirts, / the green stones of which always gleamed and glinted.[17]

Gringolet is described in similar terms, save that he is attired in bright gleaming gold to complement Gawain's armour. These descriptions give us a sense of how much money could be spent by a courtier on a fully equipped horse, which would require its own protective gear or barding. A close emotional bond might develop between a medieval knight and his horse, as is illustrated by another English romance featuring Gawain: 'The Adventures of Arthur'. In this poem, Gawain's horse, here called Grissel or Grey, is killed during combat, and Gawain is overcome with such grief that he determines to avenge him. Gawain mourns the death of this 'dumb beast' as a comrade, friend or family member.[18]

While it is impossible to know what sort of bond existed between John II and his own chargers, his neglect of the horse and equipment that he had left behind for his mother to attend to was, in her mind, another indication of his moral failings. Indeed, Margaret's letter implies a connection between John II's neglect of his horse and his neglect of this family. She reminds him that his grandmother Agnes is expecting to hear from him, and pointedly suggests, that 'it would be well done if you were to send a letter to her saying how you are as hastily as you can'. Almost as an afterthought, she also instructs him that he should 'make much' of the messenger carrying the letter, the parson of Filby, a priest local to Mauby and Caister, and 'to give him a warm welcome'. Margaret no doubt anticipated that the reproaches contained within her missive, no matter how mildly expressed, would rile her eldest son, and cause him to lash out at the bearer.

11. 'CAPTAINESS'

....

10 May 1465 (Margaret to her husband)

....

The year 1465 saw an escalation in the disputes surrounding the Fastolf inheritance, which was now being challenged on several fronts. The urgency of the situation is reflected in the flurry of letters exchanged between Margaret and her husband at this juncture. The problems had been building up for some time. Sir William Yelverton, one of Fastolf's executors who opposed John, had tried to seize the manor of Cotton, some fifteen miles east of Bury St Edmunds. The probate hearing for Fastolf's will had begun the previous year. Now the Duke of Suffolk and his mother laid claim to the manors at Drayton and Hellesdon, which both neighboured the Duke's own manor at Costessey, just five miles northwest of Norwich. With her husband in London working on protecting the properties through legal channels, Margaret found herself once more in charge on the ground, leading the physical defence of the threatened Norfolk properties.

Sir John Fastolf built Drayton Lodge in the 1430s. Its ruins are still standing, and it has recently undergone repair and restoration work. The medieval lodge is a fortified house, built out of the same pale-pink brick as Caister Castle, with

137

slit or loophole windows and towers at each corner. Located at the southeast of the modern village, it is now semi-hidden by woodland, somewhat incongruously sharing its grounds with an early-twentieth-century building that has taken the name Drayton Old Lodge and a larger contemporary residential development. As I wandered around, I found it difficult to imagine the small medieval lodge as a highly contested site, overrun with men-at-arms determined to defend it from assault, but despite its unprepossessing size, it was strategically positioned above the River Wensum and the valley road.

Fastolf was also responsible for the construction of the hall and lodge at Hellesdon, the latter presumably resembling that at Drayton. Both these medieval buildings at Hellesdon have been lost: the current Manor House, situated near the river, dates to the Georgian period, while the building now called Hellesdon Lodge, with its neo-Gothic crenelated parapet, is nineteenth century. However, tucked away in the conservation village hidden behind the expansive modern housing and trading estates, the Church of St Mary still stands, with its distinctive lead spire and late medieval two-storey porch. Drayton is only one-and-a-half miles from Hellesdon, now a suburb of the city, and it is possible to walk between the villages by taking the first section of a trail that follows disused railway tracks. When my wife and I explored the area, we took a walk along the side of the Wensum, near the mill, watched anglers fly fishing, and spotted minnows and sticklebacks swimming in the clear shallows. This present-day tranquillity gives nothing away of the hostilities that Margaret, her supporters and her tenants had to face there in the summer and autumn of 1465.

On 10 May 1465, Margaret wrote what was one of several long letters from Hellesdon to John, updating him on events.[1] Margaret had installed herself there with the aim of collecting rents at Hellesdon and Drayton, and, if necessary, holding a manorial court at Drayton in order to exercise her jurisdiction over the lands and those who lived on them.[2] Margaret hoped her visible presence would reassure the tenants and assert Paston ownership of the properties. In the days preceding her arrival, one of Suffolk's men had seized a tenant's horse while he was out ploughing, and Margaret resolved to ensure it was returned to him. In turn, the tenants had seized two plough horses after Suffolk's men took their team onto the land at Drayton. This had only escalated the campaign of harassment of the Paston tenants. In retaliation, Suffolk's men had arrived at Hellesdon with over 160 men-at-arms; they proceeded to confiscate four horses. A standoff followed, with neither side willing to return the beasts that they had seized, and Suffolk's men threatening that if any of the Paston servants took anything from Drayton, 'even if it were only the value of a hen, then they would come to Hellesdon and there seize the value of an ox for it'.

Margaret's fears that Suffolk really did mean business were well grounded. In her letter of 10 May, she reports that 60 men had been stationed at Drayton Lodge the previous week, and that there were 'still sixteen or twenty people inside day and night'. Believing that Hellesdon was very much at risk of direct attack, she seeks John's advice about how best to protect it, and she offers her own recommendations. One possible course of action would be to encourage the affected tenants to pursue restitution through legal channels. But Margaret also tells her husband that, when she had gone in person to the Bishop of Norwich to complain about these threats and to seek his support, the Bishop had emphasised the importance of John's return: 'And he said to me ... that your presence should do more for them than a hundred men should in your absence, and your enemies would be afraid to act against you if you were at home and moving amongst them.' John's continued absence from his properties made them even more vulnerable.

Margaret once again seems fearless in the face of threats of physical violence, but the most remarkable feature of the letter of 10 May 1465 is how she describes herself. She reports that she will remain in situ at the hall at Hellesdon until she receives news from her husband, and that meanwhile she has charged her eldest son to guard Caister, 'because I would rather, if it pleased you, be captainess here than at Caister'. What exactly did she mean by this? The *Oxford English Dictionary* cites Margaret's letter as the first recorded usage of the term 'captainess' meaning 'A female captain or commander'.[3] In the context in which it appears, Margaret acknowledges her role as the commander of an armed militia, responsible for ensuring that the property is defended against attackers; a task that she had of course first assumed years earlier at Gresham.

Margaret knew of women who, in her own lifetime, had led battles and campaigns and even taken up arms. The most well-remembered medieval woman-of-arms today is Joan of Arc, the French heroine of the Hundred Years War. 'Jehanne la Pucelle' (Joan the Virgin), as she called herself, claimed divine authority for her martial ambitions, asserting that she was directed by visions of St Michael and other saints. Although she did not actually command the armies, and therefore was not a 'captainess' in that respect, she wore armour and carried her banner into battle, inspiring devotion and fortitude among the soldiers, while at the same time offering insightful advice on military tactics to those in charge. Following the coronation of the French King, Charles VII, at Reims Cathedral, at which Joan was present, Christine de Pizan wrote the *Ditié de Jehanne D'Arc* or *Song of Joan of Arc* in her honour. Writing at the peak of Joan's military successes, Christine celebrated Joan's victories as an intervention from heaven, and legitimised her activities by likening her to the Virgin Mary and to the prophets and leaders of the Old Testament.[4] Yet Joan's victories were to be short lived.

Joan was almost a decade older than Margaret, making Margaret around ten years old when Joan was executed. Nevertheless, Joan's fame, or rather, in England, her infamy, had spread quickly, and Margaret must have known about her exploits. She may well have heard stories about Joan directly from Sir John Fastolf, who would have had nothing positive to say about the woman whose military successes against the English at Orléans and in the Loire Campaign had so threatened his own good name. Joan's subsequent capture and condemnation as a heretic may have offered Fastolf some solace, but in the mid-1450s, just a quarter of a century after she was burned at the stake, an inquisition into her trial overturned the guilty verdict and Joan's reputation in France was restored. In England the populace remained unconvinced, and over a century and a half after her death, in *Henry VI, Part 1*, Shakespeare portrayed Joan as a would-be witch, who sought to conjure demons to assist her in battle.[5] It is unlikely, then, that Joan of Arc provided Margaret Paston with any sort of inspiration.

Closer to home was, of course, Margaret of Anjou. In contrast to Joan of Arc, Margaret of Anjou did have the authority to command her armies. She shared some of Joan's tactical abilities, but she too was constrained by the gender norms of the time from leading her troops directly into combat, and she often retired to the haven of a city or monastery when the fighting broke out. Even though the Paston political allegiances may have shifted to the Yorkists, and Margaret of Anjou's ill repute had spread throughout the country, Margaret Paston was certainly aware of her campaigns. Then there was Margaret's own enemy, Alice Chaucer, or 'my old lady of Suffolk', as John referred to her in a letter to his wife written in the summer of 1465,[6] whose manoeuvrings directly threated the Pastons' estates and tenants. In describing herself as a 'captainess', Margaret saw herself in part as a figurehead, standing in for her husband, reminding the Paston tenants of where their loyalties ought to lie.

Despite the very real threats on the ground, Margaret may well have felt safer in Hellesdon than Caister, and, not wishing to see a repeat of her traumatic experiences at Gresham where she was caught up in direct conflict, she now hoped to limit herself to a strategic role. If that were the case she was sadly disappointed. Having planned to remain in Hellesdon for only a couple of days, Margaret found herself forced to stay on for months, until, once again, she was evicted by force from a Paston property. Yet, even if she did not intend to don a jack or raise a crossbow, she was no less courageous or committed to the Paston cause, and it is equally possible that she simply felt that her eldest son, despite his manifest failings in his father's eyes, would be more able to offer an effective defence of Caister, the Pastons' most prized possession.

The disputes over the Paston properties were not only with hostile claimants outside the family; there were also inter-familial disagreements. In the final section of her letter of May 1465, Margaret advises her husband to settle a financial falling-out with his own mother, Agnes, not least because their wrangling has become the subject of gossip: 'In good faith, I hear much talk of the conduct between you and her.' Ever the mediator in her husband's quarrels with his family members, she tells him: 'I would be very glad, and so would many more of your friends, if things were different between you than they are, and if they were I believe you would have greater success in other business.' As always, Margaret holds back from criticising her husband directly or questioning his authority, but the implication is clear: the family troubles are at least partly of John's own making, and his lack of diplomacy only serves to exacerbate matters.

John's troubled relationship with Agnes had its roots in his conduct immediately after the death of his father, over twenty years previously. In a series of drafts of her own will, copied down shortly after her eldest son's death, Agnes gives her own account of what had happened. She claims that, on Justice William's deathbed, he had come to the realisation that he had made inadequate provision in his existing will for his two youngest sons: 'He had assigned ... so little that they would not be able to live on it unless they should till the land them-selves.'[7] Agnes records that William had then made an oral addendum in their favour, granting them the properties he had not explicitly assigned in his will, but that John, as his primary heir, refused to honour this: 'The said John Paston would not agree to this at all, asserting that by law the said manors ought to be his because my husband had not included them in his written will.'[8] What was worse, John had then gone behind her back and obtained the deeds, and had even spirited away his father's valuables that had been left for safe-keeping in Norwich Abbey. According to Agnes, after these events, 'my son John Paston never had any very kind words to say to me'.[9]

John was already dead by the time that Agnes put all of this down in a legal document, and this is significant. During his lifetime, she attempted to persuade her son to right these wrongs, but she also relied on his support and so had to tread gently to avoid alienating him completely. Even so, she did speak her mind on occasion. A wonderful letter survives from Agnes to John, which seems to have been written some months after Margaret's attempted mediation in the spring of 1465, while their quarrel was still ongoing. John had evidently asked his youngest brother, Clement, to step in and speak to their mother of his behalf. Agnes assures John that they can indeed be reconciled, and offers him an elaborate benediction on behalf of herself, her late husband and indeed the divine congregation: 'May that blessing that I begged your father to give you the last day that ever he spoke and the blessing of all saints under heaven and mine come to you all days and times.'[10] Nonetheless, her forgiveness is conditional, and is only granted 'provided that I find you kind and minded towards the well-being of your father's soul and for the welfare of your brothers'.

Agnes's disappointment in John at times somewhat uncannily anticipates John and Margaret's own frustrations with John II. This reveals as much about the unachievable level of parental expectations that extended across the Paston generations as it does about the moral and behavioural failings of their sons and heirs. Just as John felt his own eldest son was too easily distracted and had repeatedly failed to put first the interests of his immediate family, so, in her letter of 1465, Agnes reproves John, reminding him of his obligations to his late father and brothers, and urging him 'to have less to do in the world'. She goes on to recite a string of his father's favourite *communis sententia*, or moralistic and homiletic sayings: 'In little work lies much rest'; 'This world is but a thoroughfare and full of woe, and when we part from it, we take nothing with us except our good and bad deeds'; 'And no one knows how soon God will call him, and therefore it is good for every creature to be ready'; 'Whom God chastises, him He loves'. Agnes, apparently parroting Justice William's words, if to considerable effect, remains unyielding concerning her son's neglect of his responsibilities toward his kin, both the dead and the living.

John's own troubles with his mother contrast with the deep and enduring friendship that existed between Agnes and Margaret. For women of the gentry classes, it is no surprise that such a strong bond could be forged between mother-in-law and daughter-in-law. Mothers often assumed some of the responsibility for coordinating or negotiating the marriages of their children, just as Agnes had for John I, and it was not uncommon for them to have met the prospective spouses before their children did. Subsequently, a mother-in-law would often be the one to induct a new bride into her domestic and other household duties. Mother-in-law and daughter-in-law often worked side by side in the managing of their estates and the running of their households. They would share household tips, recipes and remedies. A mother-in-law could offer valuable care and advice before, during and after childbirth. The women would often attend church together.

Over the course of many years, Margaret must have spent as much, if not more, time in the company of Agnes than she did in that of her husband, and they were able to remain close despite all the family anger and resentment. It was, after all, to Agnes in Norwich that Margaret fled when she escaped Sustead after losing Gresham. Agnes was a woman who could hold her ground when she met with resistance, for example when she decided to reroute the road away from the manor house at Paston and found herself at the heart of a vicious dispute, from which she refused to back down. The villagers, furious at Agnes's high-handed behaviour, demolished the new wall that was being built to block the existing highway. In one confrontation that took place as Agnes left church following evensong, one of her neighbours cursed her publicly with the words: 'May all the devils of hell drag her soul to hell because of the road that she has made!'[11]

Despite her evident obstinance, Agnes proved to be a great support to Margaret and stood by her in times of family crisis. No matter how stubborn she was, Agnes was more than a mother-in-law to Margaret. She was also, for many years, her companion and confidante. When Agnes was in her seventies, she finally moved to London to live with her lawyer son William, who had by then made a good marriage to an aristocrat, Lady Anne Beaufort, daughter of Eleanor Beauchamp and Edmund Beaufort, 2nd Duke of Somerset. Agnes found herself living in spacious accommodation at Warwick's Inn near Newgate, but her health was in decline. In an unusual emotional outburst some ten years after the crises at Hellesdon and Drayton, and not long after Agnes's retirement to the city, Margaret wrote of Agnes: 'I wish she were in Norfolk, as well as ever I saw her, and as little ruled by her son as ever she was, and then I would hope that we all should fare the better because of her.'[12] These beautiful sentences form as fitting an epitaph as any for the irascible old lady.

Margaret's affection for her mother-in-law is palpable, as is her nostalgia for the years she and Agnes had spent as comrades-at-arms, figuratively speaking. In contrast, back in the spring of 1465, Margaret was experiencing dissatisfaction with her husband about the discord which had once again engulfed the family, and her frustration reveals itself in her final words to him in the letter: 'I pray that God will help you in all your business, and give you grace to have a good result in it soon, because this is too wearying a life to endure for you and all your people.'

Above left and above right: London, British Library, Add MS 43490, f.34r and f.34v. (Reproduced by permission of the British Library)

Supposed tomb of John Paston I, St Margaret's Church, Paston. (© Heike Bauer)

Above: Churchyard of St John the Baptist, Reedham. (© Heike Bauer)

Left: St Michael's Church, Stockton. (© Heike Bauer)

Oxnead Hall today. (© Heike Bauer)

Above: The site of Gresham manor. (© Heike Bauer)

Right: Walsingham Abbey ruins. (© Heike Bauer)

St Peter Hungate, Norwich. (© Heike Bauer)

Above and below: Katie Spragg, 'Doctrine of Signatures: Hair, 2021' and 'Doctrine of Signatures: Hands, 2021' in the Plants, Porcelain, People exhibition curated by Caroline Fisher in collaboration with Norwich International Youth Project. (Photographer Chris Roberts. Images courtesy of artist)

Norwich Cathedral.
(© Heike Bauer)

Right: 'The Paston House',
Elm Hill. (© Diane Watt)

Below left and below right:
Head bosses, St Peter Hungate.
(© Heike Bauer)

Above left: Paston impaled with Mautby, door of St Andrew's Hall, Norwich. (© Heike Bauer. Photographed with the permission of The Halls, Norwich)

Above right: Caister Castle ruins. (© Heike Bauer)

St Benet's Abbey ruins. (© Heike Bauer)

Drayton Lodge ruins. (© Heike Bauer)

The Parish Church of St Mary, Hellesdon. (© Heike Bauer)

Above: Bromholm
Priory ruins.
(© Heike Bauer)

Right: Photograph
of the ruined barn
or 'chapel' at Hall
Farm House, Mautby.
(Original photographer
unknown. Original
photograph from the
Church of St Peter
and St Paul, Mautby.
Reproduced with
permission)

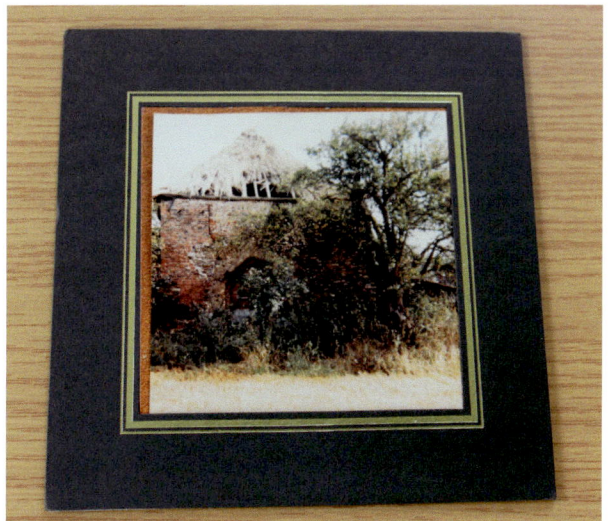

Above left: Masonry block recovered from the grounds of Hall Farm House. (© Heike Bauer)

Above right: Margaret Paston's memorial stone in the grounds of St Peter and St Paul, Mautby. (© Heike Bauer)

Church of St Peter and St Paul, Mautby. (© Heike Bauer)

Blo' Norton Hall, North West elevation, showing Virginia Woolf's room in the top left-hand corner. (© Heike Bauer)

12. 'THE COST AND THE TROUBLE ARE TOO HORRIBLE'

17 and 27 October 1465 (Margaret to her husband)

The conflict at Hellesdon continued to rumble on throughout the summer of 1465. Early in July, Margaret and her eldest son, supported by some 60 men armed with guns and other weapons, managed to face off a troop of the Duke of Suffolk's men.[1] Finally, Margaret acknowledges to her husband the strain these conflicts are placing on her physical and mental health. She tells him: 'What with sickness and trouble that I have had I am brought very low and weak.'[2] From our present-day perspective, we might be tempted to diagnose Margaret with depression and anxiety, but these conditions were not recognised in her own time; as in the case of Henry VI's mental breakdown, there was a condition known as melancholia which was understood in Antiquity and the Middle Ages to be a disorder of the humours.

Humourism was an ancient medical theory according to which the body was comprised of blood, phlegm, yellow bile and black bile, and imbalances of these fours humours resulted in ill health. Melancholia was believed to be caused by an excess of black bile and resulted in despondency alongside a range of other symptoms, including agitation, insomnia, digestive problems, nausea, loss of appetite and even delusions. The hugely influential tenth- to eleventh-century Persian physician and philosopher Avicenna, or Ibn Sina, described sufferers of the disease as experiencing an 'overflowing of thought and a constant melancholic anxiety'.[3] Melancholia was not in itself fatal (although it could result in suicidal thoughts), but circumstances were very challenging for Margaret and those around her became increasingly worried. John Russe, a former employee of Fastolf who now worked for the Pastons, wrote to John, urging him to find a solution to his various disputes because they were causing Margaret such a 'great heaviness' and he was concerned that they would 'shorten [her] days'.[4]

Unfortunately, John did not, or could not, heed this warning. In the autumn, by which time he was once again incarcerated, the situation reached another crisis point. Two letters from Margaret to her husband survive that were written in October 1465 – a month after her visit to the Fleet which had so succeeded in raising both their spirits. In the first of these, written in the middle of the month from their home in Norwich, Margaret describes terrible events that had taken place a couple of days earlier, presaged by the arrival in the city of the Duke of Suffolk himself, when he and his 500-strong force stopped en route for Hellesdon and Drayton. The Duke had summonsed the mayor and civic officers of the city and ordered them to flush out any Paston supporters and to detain them in their custody and have them punished.[5]

This was a terrifying turn of events for Margaret, with the Duke, claiming royal support, making such a public display of strength in the city which years earlier had offered her sanctuary following the loss of Gresham. The Duke faced no resistance from the civic officers of the city. A brass worker, one Robert Lovegold, was arrested and threatened with execution.

Lovegold had been with Margaret when she had previously been assaulted by the Duke's men, and she pleaded with her husband to ensure his release: 'He is a very true and loyal servant to you, and therefore I want him helped.'

The same morning the bailiff of Eye seized three Paston men at Hellesdon. Those captured included the cook, and the men were detained 'without a warrant or any authority of a justice of the peace' and the other servants and tenants who remained loyal to the family were threatened with imprisonment or death. Margaret reports that they are quickly losing their allies and that she has found herself almost completely isolated: 'I have no man to wait upon me at this time who will dare take sides except Little John.' Given that we know that some years later the Pastons had a Robin Hood play performed at Caister, it seems likely that this trustworthy servant's nickname alludes to the legendary heroic outlaw's right-hand man, as well as to his own height or bulk. Margaret complains that East Anglian gentlemen such as Sir John Heveningham and Sir John Wingfield are little more than the puppets of the Duke of Suffolk and his mother, too easily swayed by 'false shrews' and 'evil noise'. She dismisses Heveningham and Wingfield as 'dog bolts', worthless knaves, who will find themselves discredited in the future. The etymology of 'dog bolt' as a term of abuse is unclear, but the *Oxford English Dictionary* suggests that it refers to a blunt arrowhead, 'such as might be shot at a dog', of insufficient quality to be used in warfare. It is also found used in conjunction with 'cat bolt'.[6] Used in this context, Margaret suggests that these are men who could never be relied on in any sort of conflict.

Over the course of three days in mid-October, from the Monday to the Wednesday, the Duke's men destroyed the lodge and manor at Hellesdon. To Margaret's horror, on the night of the 16th, the bailiff of Eye and his men took the opportunity to requisition the family's belongings, loading them onto a cart and taking them away. Margaret promised to send John a complete catalogue of the stolen goods, or at least as full a list as she could recall, and these records still exist, not among the other letters and papers in the British Library, but in the Bodleian Library in Oxford.[7] They are exhaustive documents that, as is typical, itemise the purloined chattels according to their location – the buttery, brewery, kitchen, chamber, church and chantry. They enumerate the different kinds of sheep that have been taken and describe the obliteration of the warrens used for breeding rabbits and hares. The records thus provide a fascinating snapshot of the domestic economy at Hellesdon. They also list, by owner, the valuable and even exotic personal possessions that have been seized, and thus provide an unexpected and intimate glimpse into Margaret's own personal possessions. The items removed from Margaret's room included expensive embroidery threads of Venice, Genoa and (most expensive of all) damask gold, as well as silk and linen, and some black velvet fabric. There was also a kerchief made of Holland cloth, which was a fine linen imported from the Netherlands, and an ivory stopper for a glass container and a large ivory comb. From the evidence of the threads, we can reasonably assume that, like many women of her class, Margaret was a talented embroiderer, and that she spent many hours creating beautiful textiles for her home, family, friends and church. Margaret's comb may well have been elaborately carved on both sides, like a very beautiful fourteenth-century ivory comb, made in Paris in around 1320, which is now in the Victoria and Albert Museum in London.[8] The decorations on this comb comprise a series of scenes depicting a courting couple, so it may have been intended as a gift between lovers. Margaret's comb and glass container may have been part of an expensive *trousse de toilette*, or toiletry set, and could well have been gifts from her husband.

Margaret doesn't mention any of these precious objects in her letter to her husband, in which she refers to everything that has been lost simply as 'the featherbeds and all the stuff'. The inventories also start by enumerating the two featherbeds and all the pillows, bolsters, mattresses, curtains, coverlets, blankets, sheets and head sheets that had been taken. In referring to the loss of the featherbeds, it should be noted that Margaret is not primarily concerned with the bedstead or frame, but rather the furnishings and soft furnishings, although the inventory does mention the loss of two 'celures' and 'testers', that is the bed canopies and headboards.[9] In mentioning the featherbeds, Margaret is alluding specifically to a sack stuffed with plumage which would be placed on a straw litter or pallet to make it more comfortable; what we might today think of as the mattress (in the late medieval period, the term 'materas' might mean some sort of cover for sleeping under). The featherbeds deserved special mention because they were luxury items. In the medieval and early modern periods, elaborate beds and fine bedding were important signifiers of status, power and of course wealth, and they would have been some of the most expensive pieces of furniture in a large manor house. A century and a half later, when William Shakespeare bequeathed his second-best bed to his wife, Anne Hathaway, he was specifying that she should inherit an item of some considerable value. A wonderful example of a late-fifteenth-century bed is the 'Paradise Bed', the elaborately carved oak four-poster marriage bed of Henry VII and Elizabeth of York, which was rescued from destruction in 2010 and is now held in a private collection.[10]

Ten days after her previous letter, on 27 October, Margaret provides her husband with a much more detailed account of the attacks, which has led to crowds of sightseers arriving to view the devastation: 'I was at Hellesdon last Thursday and saw the place, and in good faith no one could imagine what a bad and horrible state it is in unless they saw it. Many people come every day out of curiosity, from both Norwich and other places, and say that it is a shame.'[11] The Duke of Suffolk's men had forced the Paston tenants at Drayton and Hellesdon to demolish the lodge and the manor house, and men from his estates stole what they could carry, including valuable metalwork, doors and gates, and destroyed what remained: 'They have hacked it apart in the most malicious manner.' Nor did they stop at vandalism and looting: having driven the priest out of the village church and seized everything that had been left there for safe keeping, the Duke's men 'stood on the high altar and ransacked the images'.

The desecration of Hellesdon church is perhaps the most shocking aspect of the whole affair. The sanctity of the church, and its inner sanctuary and most holy place, the consecrated altar, were violated in an act of iconoclasm, and its paintings and statues stolen, including, presumably, the crucifixes. Margaret asked her husband to ensure that some trustworthy men of the King should come to Hellesdon and view the devastation 'before any snows come' so that they could testify to it in court. For Margaret, who had retreated to Caister with a garrison of some 30 men employed to protect the family and building, the situation had become overwhelming, 'because the cost and trouble we have daily now, and shall have until things are different, are just too horrible'. She begs John to find a solution, encouraging him to seek the assistance of the Duke of Norfolk. After enquiring about his wellbeing and that of their sons, she ends with the valediction: 'God have you in his keeping and send us good tidings from you.' These are some of the last words we have that Margaret wrote to her husband. Margaret had no idea how prescient they were. A few months later, John died in London.

Here, in the months leading up to what was surely one of the most painful moments in Margaret's life, there is a frustrating gap in the archive. In the absence of any further correspondence between Margaret and John, we can only speculate about the events leading up to his death on 22 May 1466. The small handful of letters addressed to John that are datable to this seven-month period are not very revealing, but it does seem that once again he spent Advent and very probably Christmas in London, away from his family.[12] The family's troubles continued apace. In January 1466 Anthony Woodville, Lord Scales, seized Paston's property in Caister and Norwich. John was forcibly returned to the Fleet Prison early that year, but he was staying in lodgings in the Inns of Court when he passed away, with neither his wife nor any of his children by his side.[13] John was only 44 when his life ended. According to some views in the Middle Ages, old age began at 40, or thereabouts, although others regarded the onset of *senectus* as 60 or even later. There is nothing to suggest that, despite his ailments, Margaret regarded John as being anything other than in his prime. She may have had little or no warning that he had again fallen ill and that his health was rapidly deteriorating. Her attention was no doubt still diverted by the ongoing threats to their properties in Hellesdon, Drayton, Caister and even Norwich. John's death seems to have come as a complete shock: we simply don't know whether Margaret had the opportunity to send her husband a final, loving, message, and we have no idea how she reacted to the news of his sudden and untimely passing.

John Paston's death was a momentous event for the family. Suddenly his eldest son, John II, who had turned 24 the previous month, found himself to be the head of the family. First, there was a funeral to organise, and although it was ultimately John II's responsibility, Margaret would have been determined to ensure that this was a fittingly grand affair suitable for Fastolf's heir, on a scale that is quite difficult to comprehend today unless we consider the arrangements made following the death a reigning monarch.[14] The tents, banners, pennants and mourning dress had to be prepared, and arrangements made for the hearse. Then, after seven days during which John's body remained at the Inn where he had died, a torchlight cortege began to wind its way back to Norwich. This procession included a priest, a woman employed to tend to the corpse, and twelve poor men carrying the beacons. It took seven days to reach the city. Once in Norwich, John's remains lay in state overnight, surrounded by candles, at St Peter Hungate. There, children dressed in surplices crowded within and around the church, while 38 priests sang lamentations for his soul. Bells were rung at St Peter's and at St Stephen's in Norwich. The prioress of the Benedictine convent of Carrow attended in person, accompanied by a young woman.

From Norwich, the cortege, now expanded in size to include the Dominican, Franciscan, Augustinian and Carmelite friars of Norwich, made its way in the direction of the village of Paston, to Bromholm, the neighbouring Cluniac priory, for the interment. The funeral took place during Whitsun week, in early June. The atmosphere inside the church during the services was, quite literally, stifling: a glazier had to be employed to remove temporarily two panes of windows, 'to let out the reek of the torches at the dirge'. The funeral itself was followed by lavish banquets and extensive entertainments. With the event being conducted on such a grand scale, it was inevitable that not all those attending behaved appropriately. Bromholm hosted some of the guests, and the prior had to be recompensed afterwards for pewterware that had vanished and never been recovered. Even after the funeral was over, further memorial events had to be organised, including masses for John's soul and the purchase of a pardon from Rome, an indulgence for sins, as Margaret has it, 'for all our friends' souls'.

Visiting the scattered remains of Bromholm today, it takes some effort to imagine it hosting such a significant affair as John Paston's funeral. The priory is found on the outskirts of the windswept coastal village of Bacton, which Pesvner described as 'one of the prettiest in this part of Norfolk'.[15] Now, both Bacton and the village of Paston are dominated by the massive gas terminal complex that opened nearby in 1968, less than a decade after Pesvner was writing. Nevertheless, the priory is still in a rural setting, located on private land at Abbey Farm. The scale of the priory is indicated by the spread of the ruins across the fields that now occupy the site. Parts of the northern gatehouse, with its imposing flint-and-red-brick archway, are in place and provide access to the farm and its outbuildings; these abut some of the former priory buildings. It would be through this gate, no doubt, that the body would have been brought, and that Margaret and her family and guests at the funeral would have entered. There are fragments still standing of the chapter house, dormitory and refectory. Of the church itself, which was located at the centre of the priory buildings, only part of the north transept has not been destroyed. This is the most prominent of the ruins, easily viewable from the footpath that runs alongside the priory boundary. It stands square, with three upper windows and a doorway, an arch opening and part of a spiral staircase. At its bottom it has a Second World War pillbox built into it. The nave and aisle have almost completely vanished, and with them the glory of the interior in which John's grave was originally located. Of all the sites associated with Margaret that I have visited, Bromholm stands out for me as the most desolate and lonely. Gazing, one dull and grey afternoon with the threat of rain in the air, at the windswept and scattered remains of this once majestic complex, I had a strong sense of the grief and bewilderment that Margaret must have felt at her sudden and unexpected loss.

Yet, amid all the hubbub of the funeral, it is unlikely that Margaret had much time to grieve, and the full pain of her bereavement may only have been felt later, when everything quietened down. Or perhaps, given the grave effect of the family's troubles on her wellbeing in the months preceding John's death, the numbness gave way to an even more intense despondency. If so, Margaret preserved no record of her heartache. The first letter that we have from her from after John's death was written to their eldest son five months later; over twelve months after the sack of Hellesdon.[16] Margaret's status within the family had abruptly changed. She was no longer the wife of the head of the household, but subject instead to the authority of her son. But because John II was unmarried, she found herself assuming many of her former responsibilities, including, so it seems, providing guidance on legal, financial and property matters. The transition cannot have proven easy for her, especially because her concerns about John II's reliability remained. In this letter of October 1466, Margaret urges her son to keep an eye on her affairs, to warn her if any legal action is being taken against her, and to continue to pursue the Paston interests that she believed had killed his father: 'Progress your business now so that we may be at peace in the future, and do not give up now because of difficulty.' Probate still needed to be obtained, so that John's estate could be settled, and Margaret advises her son to proceed without incurring unnecessary charges. She is clearly worried that John II has failed to keep all his paperwork in order because she writes: 'I advise you always to be careful to guard your important documents wisely, so that they do not fall into the hands of those you would do you harm in future. Your father, may God absolve him, in his troubled period set greater store by his documents and deeds than he did by any of his moveable goods.' Margaret's words of instructions here are highly prescient. The survival of the Paston collection, and especially Margaret and John's own letters, long after all their other possessions have disappeared, and their most prized properties have been either reduced to ruins or radically redesigned, is no doubt owed to the weight the couple placed on preserving every scrap of written evidence they could. The importance to Margaret of maintaining a personal and familial archive did not diminish when she suddenly found herself a wealthy widow in control of her own property.

13. 'ONLY A BRETHEL'

Three years after the loss of her husband, Margaret had settled into a widowhood that was no less eventful and traumatic than her former life as a wife. While the disputes over Fastolf's will continued, an important and ongoing concern was to ensure that her children made advantageous matches. Of course, ultimately it was now John II who was responsible for his siblings. He remained unmarried but had recently begun negotiating his betrothal to a woman called Anne Haute, a cousin of Edward IV's queen, Elizabeth Woodville. This marriage, if it were to come off, would signal a very real rise in standing for the Paston family, whose gentry status had only recently been formally confirmed by the King. It was around this time that John II's uncle William married Lady Anne Beaufort. It looked like John II was also going to make an advantageous match. From the start, Margaret harboured reservations. In March 1469, she had warned John II against committing himself, 'because often haste brings regret, and when a man has made an agreement like that, he must keep it, he has no choice in the matter'.[1] The following month rumours had reached her that the couple were now engaged and Margaret reminded her son that if they were true, then he must honour the commitment.[2] It seems that Margaret was right to have her doubts, because the relationship soon ran into difficulties, and eventually the engagement was dissolved.

But in September 1469, another hasty marital commitment was causing Margaret great consternation: that between her elder daughter, Margery, and the family bailiff, Richard Calle. In this case, the problem was that the union was with a social inferior and had been formed against the wishes of the family. And, of course, it put paid to any sort of strategic marital alliance for Margery that might be useful for her brothers, politically as well as financially. Tensions had been building up in the family for some time. In the spring, Margaret had urged John II to find a place in service for Margery in a suitable aristocratic household, such as that of 'my lady of Oxford or with my lady of Bedford', that is of Margaret, Countess of Oxford, or Jacquetta de Luxembourg, Dowager Duchess of Bedford, wife of Sir Richard Woodville and mother of the present queen consort. She even offered to contribute towards the expense, 'because we are both tired of each other'.[3] Margaret did not explain further, but added, cryptically, that she would tell him more later when they met in person. Margaret did not want to put the circumstances down in writing, because she was all too aware that, if the letter fell into the wrong hands, news of the potential scandal could be used against the family.

Margaret's worries were justified. A month after Margaret had suggested removing Margery from her household, and out of the way of Richard Calle, Margery's second brother, John III, wrote an angry missive to his elder brother.[4] Margery and Richard had claimed that John III supported their relationship, a point which he vehemently denies in his letter, insisting that he knew nothing about it. On the contrary, he states categorically he would never agree to the wedding, even if his whole family, including his late father, were in support of it, because it goes against everything for which the family had striven. Richard Calle was no gentleman, or so John III implies, because his father was a Suffolk tradesman, a grocer to be precise. John III colourfully announces that marriage to Richard Calle would see his sister reduced to selling 'candle and mustard in Framlingham'. This statement is revealing about the family's real concerns. Framlingham was indeed Richard's hometown, and so it was not unlikely that if they stayed together the couple might move there, especially as Richard had by now been sent away to London by the family. But more importantly, its castle was the seat of the family's powerful opponent John de Mowbray, 4th Duke of Norfolk. If Margery had wanted to humiliate her family before their enemies, and cause her mother and brothers the greatest heartache, she could not have planned it better.

Clearly her family's disapproval did nothing to dissuade Margery from committing herself to the man of her choice. At some point in the spring or summer of 1469 she and Richard formalised their bond in a clandestine ceremony. The medieval church's position on secret marriages was complicated. Notionally, the church prohibited them and required that banns should be called three times prior to a wedding to ensure that any objections could be heard. The cornerstone of medieval marriage was consent. A promise to marry followed by sex between the couple would be understood as marriage, because consent was implied by the physical relations. An exchange of words of consent was also recognised as binding, without the presence of a priest or witnesses, the agreement of parents or legal guardians, or even consummation. Margery and Richard understood the system. They went ahead and exchanged their vows in private and then announced that they were married, much to the horror of the Paston clan.

Perhaps Margery and Richard were inspired by Edward IV's match with John II's prospective relative-by-marriage, Elizabeth Woodville, which was made just a few years earlier. Elizabeth had been married to Sir John Grey, and the couple had had two sons, but she found herself widowed in her mid-twenties, and, struggling to obtain the estate to which she was entitled, she petitioned the King in person. The couple subsequently married privately, but sometime afterwards the King was forced to acknowledge his wife publicly to put an end to negotiations for a union that would have proved diplomatically advantageous for the country. The news of this secret wedding brought widespread disapproval. The Renaissance historian Polydore Vergil claimed that the King had been swayed 'by blind affection, and not by rule of reason'.[5] Intriguingly, an even closer exemplar for Margery from among the aristocracy was Elizabeth's mother, Jacquetta, one of the women into whose service Margaret had suggested Margery should enter. As a member of the royal Luxembourg dynasty, Jacquetta's second marriage to Sir Richard Woodville, a mere knight who had been in service to her first husband, had proved scandalous in its own time.

Controversy dogged Jacquetta's life. Shortly after Richard Woodville's execution in August 1469, so around the same time as Margaret was attempting to block her daughter's marriage, Jacquetta was accused of witchcraft. Jacquetta was accused of making poppets, including images of the king and queen, in order to cast spells, and although it isn't clear what the purpose of her incantations was, they presumably favoured her royal daughter and son-in-law. These were serious allegations – Jacquetta's sister-in-law by her first marriage, Eleanor Cobham, Duchess of Gloucester, died in prison years earlier after being found guilty of 'treasonable necromancy' – but they were also almost certainly politically motivated. At the time when the charges were brought against Jaquetta, Edward IV was in prison, having been captured by Richard Neville, Earl of Warwick (the so-called 'Kingmaker'). Following the King's release she was completely exonerated. But while Margaret kept a weather eye on changes in the political landscape, she wasn't one to waste energy worrying that she had almost placed her daughter in the care of a woman who allegedly dabbled in sorcery. She had far more urgent matters to address.

We don't have any letters written by Margery herself, but we do have a single missive from Richard Calle, addressed to 'my own lady and mistress', that was sent at some point during the long summer months when the couple were forcibly kept apart.[6] Even though this letter includes the instruction that Margery should burn it, it was evidently intercepted and confiscated. Perhaps it never made it into Margery's hands. Or, as Richard suggests has occurred on previous occasions, Margery may have been pressurised into handing it over to her mother. Richard's letter describes the lengths to which Margaret, working with the family chaplain, Sir James Gloys, was prepared to go to break up the couple. Not content with spreading false rumours about Richard, or with cross-examining his servant and refusing him access to Margery, Margaret hatched an elaborate plan to get hold of the couple's correspondence. A servant was sent to Richard's intermediary with a ring, under the pretence that it was a love token from Margery, to trick him into handing over any letters or tokens he was carrying to Margery. Fortunately, on this occasion at least the deception was unsuccessful.

In his letter, Richard writes that he has heard that Margery has not yet told her family about the 'great bond of matrimony that is made between us', and he encourages her to do so because they refuse to believe him. He is sympathetic to her position and understands the pressure that her family are

putting on her but encourages her to hold to the promises
she has made him, insisting on the legitimacy of their union.
The phrasing of his letter is particularly striking, as it draws
on the words of marriage service, asserting that 'we that ought
out of right to be most together are most asunder'. Presumably
this sentence echoes the actual vows that Richard and Margery
had made to one another. Richard also avers that Margaret
and the rest of the family are in the wrong in the eyes of the
church, and even suggests that the family should be excom-
municated for trying to prevent rightful matrimony. Richard
was a highly intelligent, self-educated man, and this letter also
reveals him to be sensitive and very caring. It is easy to see why
Margery was willing to risk her place in her family to be with
him. Sometime after this letter was written, she finally faced up
to her mother and told her what she had done.

When it came to Margery and Richard's secret marriage,
although there was no fixed formula for the marriage vows,
it still mattered that the right words had been said. Margaret
was determined to have the marriage annulled by proving
that the promises that the couple had made were not valid.
In September, with her mother-in-law by her side, Margaret
demanded an audience with Walter Lyhert, Bishop of Norwich
to discuss the situation. She gives a very full account of what
happened in a letter to her eldest son, which was written on
the 10th or 11th of the month. Together the women asserted
that they did not accept that the two young people had made
a formal commitment, but rather that they both were still 'free
to choose' another spouse.[7] The Bishop was sympathetic, but
firm. He insisted that the only way he could get to the heart
of the matter was by interviewing Margery in person. The
Paston family had hoped to avoid this eventuality, presumably because they already knew what the outcome would be
if Margery were to be allowed to give her side of the story,

but there was nothing more that Margaret or Agnes could do to prevent it. Margery was summoned to the Bishop's court, where she was asked to give an account of herself. The Bishop reminded Margery of the importance of being guided by her family and encouraged her to reflect carefully before she spoke, but Margery would not be swayed: 'And she repeated what she had said and said that if those words did not make it sure, she said boldly she would make it surer still before she went from there. Because she said she believed in her conscience she was committed, whatever the words were.'

Margaret concludes her report of this interview by dismissing everything her daughter has said, stating: 'These foolish words grieve me and her grandmother as much as all the rest.' Yet, her description of the Bishop's examination reveals her daughter to be a resolute and unyielding young woman who refused to be cowed by clerical authority, just as she refused to be cowed by family pressure and threats of social censure. Margery was evidently cut from the same cloth as her mother and grandmother. As a result of this meeting, and his subsequent interrogation of Richard in which he confirmed Margery's account, the Bishop was eventually forced to conclude that Margery and Richard were indeed already wife and husband.

Margery was around 21 years old when she secretly married Richard Calle, who was more than ten years her senior. Up to this point, we have every reason to believe that she was a dutiful and deferential daughter, and her decision to marry for love and against the wishes of her family must have been very hurtful for her mother. Margaret responded to her daughter's disobedience in anger, by immediately disowning her and casting her out of her home. The Bishop sent Margery to stay in the household of a Norwich grocer, and sometime mayor, called Roger Best. It is probably mere coincidence that this civic worthy was of the same trade as Richard Calle's father. Margaret claims that he only took in Margery unwillingly and comments approvingly that 'he [Best] and his wife are of a serious disposition, and she will not be allowed to play the brethel there'. Later, Margery was moved to a convent, Blackborough Priory, about five miles from King's Lynn, where she was reunited with her husband.

It is worthwhile pausing on the word 'brethel' that Margaret applies to her recalcitrant daughter, because she uses it twice in this letter in the space of just a few lines. She goes on to urge her eldest son not to grieve too much over his sister's banishment: 'But remember, as I do, that in losing her we have lost in her only a brethel and so take it less to heart. Because if she had been virtuous, whatever she had been, things would not have been as bad as this.' 'Brethel' is defined in the *Middle English Dictionary* as meaning 'a worthless person, a wretch; a pauper'.[8] *The Oxford English Dictionary* provides a similar definition, adding 'contemptible' and 'good-for-nothing' for good measure.[9] But 'brethel' also had a very similar meaning to 'brothel' and the words share an etymology: both are descended from the word 'brethe', meaning 'to go to ruin'.[10] 'Wretch' then provides only a rather inadequate translation of 'brethel'. While it was only in the early modern period that 'brothel' took on the sense of a house from which sex workers operate, eventually replacing the medieval word 'stew', the word was also used in the sense of 'a lecherous person, a lecher, a harlot'.[11] In the context in which it appears, Margaret may well deliberately allude in sexualised as well as derogatory terms to her daughter's relationship, sinful and dishonourable as it was in her eyes, even if it was not, ultimately, judged by the ecclesiastical authorities to be illicit.

Margaret believed she would never be able to forgive her daughter. At the time she told John II that 'even if he [Calle] were to fall down dead at this hour, she would never be in my heart as she used to be'. We simply don't know if Margaret and her daughter were permanently estranged, or if some sort of reconciliation eventually took place. Just over a year later, Margaret, still furious, wrote to her eldest son: 'As for your sister, I can send you no good news about her. May God make her a good woman.'[12] But Richard Calle did return to his employment with the family, and the couple went on to have children together. Margery passed away a few years before her mother, only a decade or so after her marriage, when she was in her early thirties.

Margery's elopement coincided with a dreadful period in the Paston family fortunes. The previous month, the Duke of Norfolk had taken advantage of the national disruption caused by the revolt against Edward IV led by Richard, Earl of Warwick, which had resulted in a short period of imprisonment for the King. Amid this upheaval, Norfolk laid siege with a large army to Caister Castle. John III was stuck within the castle, valiantly trying to defend it with the support of a troop of servants and associates and four trustworthy and experienced soldiers whom his elder brother had employed specifically to guard and protect the property.[13] It seemed increasingly likely that Caister would be lost. A day or two after updating John II on the Bishop's interview with Margery and its fallout, Margaret wrote to him again, having heard terrible news that one of the family's most loyal supporters, John Daubeney, had been killed in the conflict, alongside her illegitimate cousin Osbern Berney.[14] In fact, there was only some truth in the rumours: Daubeney had indeed died after being shot by a crossbow, but Berney, although injured, had survived.

Sieges did not in fact play a significant role in the Wars of the Roses, although English commanders had gained considerable know-how in France in the Hundred Years War.[15] Siege warfare relied in part on blocking provisions from entering the fortress, and Margaret warns John II that food supplies in the castle are running low, and they have run out of both gunpowder and arrows. Usually, sieges avoided full-scale bombardments, relying instead on relentless but low-intensity attacks. Nevertheless, according to Margaret, the castle had already been damaged by the besieger's guns and a large-scale assault was planned for the following week. She reports that 'they have sent for guns to [King's] Lynn and other places beside the sea, so that with their great multitude of guns, with other firearms and equipment, no one will dare appear in that place'. Of course, intimidation was an important strategy, but Margaret did not want to take any risks. Negotiation was an equally important aspect of siege craft. Margaret is uncompromising in her instructions to her eldest son: 'Do not fail to get this done quickly, if you want to save their lives and to be esteemed in Norfolk, even if you should lose the best manor of all to secure their release. I would rather you lost the property than their lives.' Angry with John II for letting the situation escalate in this way, she urges him to accept the terms offered by the Duke of Norfolk, or else to seek the intervention of other powerful lords, even if that means giving up the castle.

Thankfully, John II was finally coming to the same conclusion as his mother: that negotiation with his enemy was the only option. He smuggled a letter into the castle, reassuring his younger brother that the Duke's council was already regretting its actions and 'they are charged on pain of their lives, that even though they get the place, they should not hurt one of you'.[16] John III had begun his career as a page in the household of Elizabeth Talbot, Duchess of Norfolk, with whom he enjoyed good relations, and he must have recognised the irony in the way that his former lord and master had shown him so little mercy. Finally, having been granted safe conduct out of the castle, John III and his men raised the white flag and surrendered.[17]

Some years after the siege, John II, who owned several books about statecraft and chivalry, must have purchased the newly published political and moral allegory entitled *The Game and Playe of the Chesse* because it is mentioned in his inventory of books.[18] This work figures the medieval social hierarchy (from the king and queen down to the pawns) in terms of the ancient game of strategy. It outlines the qualities of a knight in the following terms: 'A knight's virtue and might is only known by his fighting. And in his fighting, he does much harm, because in so far as his might extends into so many points [spaces], there are many risks in their fighting. And when they escape, they have the honour of the game.'[19] The disastrous end to the siege must have seemed like checkmate: the Pastons had lost Caister once and for all. Yet although John III had not succeeded in 'escaping', he certainly was not dishonoured by having given in. Trapped for several weeks within the stronghold, running out of food and ammunition and fearful that no reinforcements would arrive in time to relieve them, the decision to surrender was reasonable and respectable.[20] While the defeat at Caister was a blow, the Paston brothers refused to resign themselves to its loss. In the years after the siege, John III continued try to reach an agreement for the castle's return. A decade later, immediately after the Duke's death, the family were finally able to reclaim Caister, not by force, but by legal means. Margaret blamed the Fastolf inheritances for the many misfortunes that befell the family over the years. After hearing (false) rumours that her eldest son has been murdered by poison, she wrote to John III: 'I wish you had never known the land. It was the destruction of your father.'[21] Together, the twin losses of her daughter and of Caister Castle made 1469 an *annus horribilis* for Margaret.

14. 'REMEMBER WHAT TROUBLE I HAD'

....

6 July 1470 (Margaret to her second son,
John III)

....

Even after she was forced to accept the validity of her elder daughter's marriage, Margaret's worries concerning her children continued. Less than a year later, it was Margaret's younger daughter who was causing her mother consternation. Sometime following the death of her father, Anne had entered the household of Sir William Calthorpe to complete her education. We know that Anne had been placed there for at least fifteen months, because the previous April, shortly before the trouble with Margery started to come to a head, Margaret had asked John II to purchase some open-work fabric, from which fashionable neckerchiefs could be made for Anne, to be worn tucked into the front of the gown, 'because I am put to shame by the good lady she is with because she has none and I can get none in all this town'.[1] Appearances evidently continued to matter for Margaret, whether her own or her daughters'.

Sir William was a wealthy relative of Margaret. He held manors in Burnham Thorpe in the north of the county and Ludham, in what is now the Broads. Margaret was good

friends with his second wife, Lady Elizabeth, who, a few
years before Margaret's death, was to play an important role
in resolving a feud between Margaret's second son, John III,
and his uncle William.[2] But, back in the summer of 1470,
relations between the two families were put to the test after
Sir William contacted Margaret asking her to remove Anne
from his service. Margaret wrote a hasty missive to her second son seeking his assistance.[3] In it, she explains that she is
puzzled by Sir William's request. Sir William has claimed that
he is struggling to collect his rents and therefore intends to
economise by reducing his household. He has also said that
Anne was 'growing tall' and it is time that Margaret finds her
a husband. Margaret is unconvinced that these are his real
reasons and fears that Anne is effectively being expelled due to
her misbehaviour: 'Either she has displeased him or else he has
caught her out in some wrongdoing.'

The prospect of having Anne return home evidently filled
Margaret with dread. She tells her son: 'With me she will only
waste her time, and unless she is willing to be better occupied, she will often annoy me and cause me great anxiety.'
Margaret's estrangement from Margery did not immediately
bring her closer to Anne. If anything, it made her less tolerant
of any perceived wilfulness or misdemeanours. Margaret's
emotional distance from her daughter is not untypical of the
period; it is reminiscent of her mother-in-law Agnes's vio-
lently expressed frustration at having her daughter Elizabeth
still in her home rather than married and living elsewhere.
Once a daughter reached adulthood, if she remained single
for any period, she would very quickly be perceived as a
financial burden and cause of worry. In contrast, a daughter-
in-law entering the family, so long as she had been chosen by
them or at least met their social and financial expectations,
might well become a close friend and ally, as Margaret was

for Agnes. Of course, it was perfectly possible for mothers and daughters to forge deep and lasting relationships with one another, but the years after a girl reached a marriageable age could evidently become very tense. In some desperation, Margaret asks John III to sound out a prospective suitor for his sister in London: 'Do your share to help her on in a way that will be to your credit and mine.'

In the same letter, Margaret remarks to John III, 'remember what trouble I had with your sister'; words which were to prove prophetic. Like Margery, Anne also fell in love with an unsuitable older man in service to her family. In this case, the person in question was John Pamping, a retainer who had remained at her father's side in the Fleet Prison and had risked his life in the siege of Caister. His willingness to sacrifice himself for the family did not make him any more worthy as a prospective son-in-law, and the Pastons were determined to block this relationship before it was too late. The situation blew up the year after Anne left the Calthorpes, and Margaret took immediate action and had Pamping sent away. Just a few months later, the family began negotiating her marriage to William Yelverton, the grandson of a Norfolk judge who, along with the other executors, had disputed Fastolf's will and her father's inheritance of Caister. This was a political match, aimed to reconcile two families that had become enemies. Margaret wrote to her elder son outlining exactly what Anne's settlement would be and how much she personally would contribute to the couple's finances: 'She shall have as her jointure his mother's property after the death of her and her husband, and I am to pay £10 a year for her and her husband's livelihood until £100 are paid.'[4] Margaret was determined that this marriage should go ahead and was unwilling to consider other prospective suitors. John II was also getting impatient, resenting the fact that he still had to provide financially for this sister: 'I will provide for her ... even though she is not my daughter.'[5]

Unfortunately, Margaret's wrangling did not prove sufficient, and the match stalled, to the consternation of both brothers. John II reported that the future was uncertain: 'As for Yelverton, he said but late that he would have her [Anne] if she had her money, and otherwise not.'[6] To complicate matters further, Anne had been taken ill, but John III's main concern was that her 'old love for Pamping should not renew'. To ensure that this did not happen, he dismissed him from his employment, while keeping a weather eye open for alternative husbands for this sister. Five years after the negotiations with Yelverton had commenced, Anne was still at home with Margaret, no doubt to Margaret's continued chagrin, but shortly afterwards the marriage did finally go ahead. As is the case with her sister Margery, we have no letters from Anne to give us insight into her feelings and thoughts about being a pawn in the Paston game.

Yet, although we don't have any of Anne's letters, we can glean some insight into her character and interests from her reading, which reveals her to be an educated and cultured young woman, who, while she may have had feelings for the family servant, evidently also enjoyed social contact with her brothers' more distinguished connections. Writing in 1472, when the negotiations over Anne's marriage to William Yelverton were still in the early stages, John Paston III mentioned to his elder brother that Anne had lent to the Earl of Arran her own copy of *The Siege of Thebes*, a work by the prolific Suffolk monk and poet John Lydgate (who enjoyed the patronage of Alice Chaucer, among others).[7] John III held Thomas Boyd, Earl of Arran, in exceptionally high regard, extolling him as 'the most courteous, gentlest, wisest, kindest, most sociable, noble, generous and most bounteous knight ... one of the lightest, most

agile, most well-spoken, best archer, most devout, most per-
fect and truest to his lady of all the knights that ever I was
acquainted with'. He recommended his elder brother also get
to know Boyd, going so far as to add, 'would to God my lady
liked me as well as I do him and his knightly disposition'.
While John II may have been a little in love with Boyd himself,
he wasn't suggesting him as a possible match for Anne; Boyd
was already married to Princess Mary of Scotland.

What was it about *The Siege of Thebes* that would have
appealed to Anne? In terms of the narrative itself Lydgate frames
his work as the last of *The Canterbury Tales*, claiming that he
had joined the pilgrims on their return journey to London and
been convinced by the Host to join their story-telling compe-
tition. Lydgate's subject matter is the power struggle between
Oedipus's sons Eteocles and Polynices and the Theban civil
war, and he thus covers the legendary events leading up to
those described in Chaucer's 'Knight's Tale'.[8] His moralising
chivalric history also addresses matters of love, albeit often in
critical terms, and Anne might have found within it some loose
parallels with her own situation. Perhaps she saw something
of the bravery of John Pamping, the recent hero of Caister, in
the character of the injured Tydeus, married to a daughter of
King Adrastus of Argos. Equally she may have identified with
the awe-struck daughter of King Lycurgus, who nursed Tydeus
back to health.

But while some speculation about women's literary interests
can be productive, we should be wary of making reductive
assumptions about how and why women read specific texts.
While Anne was apparently not socially ambitious (otherwise
she wouldn't have fallen for a servant), it is just as likely that
Anne's ownership of this work indicates something of her
cultural aspirations. Lydgate's poem had been written some
half a century earlier and initially circulated among the courtly

elite; only more recently had it reached a wider readership. That Anne had refined tastes was presumably confirmed in John III's mind by the fact that she passed the work on to such a distinguished aristocrat as Boyd. From John III's letter, it is evident that the family knew about Anne's reading and approved of it. They certainly weren't worried that her head was being turned by unsuitable books.

Despite her frustrated early love for Pamping, it appears that Anne was happy enough to settle with the husband her family had chosen for her, but early on in her marriage she lost a baby. Her brother Edmond wrote: 'My sister is delivered, and the child passed to God, may He send us His grace.'[9] We cannot tell from this brief remark whether Anne miscarried or suffered a stillbirth, whether her baby died due to complications during labour, or whether he or she died shortly after being born. Difficult births, miscarriages and stillbirths were common occurrences, and medieval medical manuals such as the compendium known as *The Trotula*, which circulated in England at this time, provided advice on pain remedies for use during labour, guidance on performing caesarean sections, and advice about how to remove a foetus that had died *in utero* while preserving the life of the mother, as well as information on induced abortions. While historians have for some time studied pregnancy and birth, it is only recently that they have begun to turn their attention to women's experiences of infertility and of gestation that does not result in a live birth.[10] One reason for this is that much of the remaining evidence is sparce and is mainly restricted to legal, religious and medical sources, which offer largely negative representations. Arguably, the situation has not changed that much in the present day, and a veil of silence continues to overlay many women's sufferings regarding infertility and peri- and neonatal mortality. The very language we still use to describe these occurrences – 'miscarriage' and 'spontaneous abortion' – has negative connotations of misconduct, misbehaviour and failure.[11]

Tellingly, the Middle English word 'abortif' or 'abortive' can refer to a premature or stillborn child, and, in very disablist terms, to 'one who is born deformed, a monster'.[12] This offensive equivalence was rooted in medieval theology. Birth 'flaws' were common, but infant disabilities and other perceived 'irregularities', such as multiple births, were still considered divine punishment for the sins of the parents, and especially the mother. The late-twelfth-century Middle English text *Hali Meiðhad* or *A Letter on Virginity* warns women against conception, observing that if a mother gives birth to a baby with 'one of its limbs missing or has some kind of defect, it is a grief to her and shame to all its family, a reproach for malicious tongues, and the talk of everyone'.[13] In Marie de France's lay 'Le Fresne' [The Ash Tree], a woman claims that the reason another woman has given birth to twins is because she slept with two men. The first woman then gives birth to twins herself and, fearing for her own reputation, abandons one of them.[14]

Stillbirths were often blamed on sex during pregnancy, or on other aspects of the mother's behaviour, although there was some understanding that women's physical makeup or inadequate care during pregnancy might be factors. Premature births and stillbirths were seen to be especially problematic because, according to the Augustinian doctrine of original sin, everyone is born in a sinful state, and so the salvation of infants who die before baptism was seen to be in jeopardy. The point of 'ensoulment', when the soul entered the foetus, coincided with the quickening, therefore the loss of a foetus after that time was a serious spiritual matter. In the later Middle Ages, it was believed that unbaptised infants entered limbo, a sort of midway between heaven and hell, and midwives were therefore permitted to perform emergency baptisms in the absence of a priest. Pregnancies which did not reach full term or result in the birth of a live baby were therefore often a source of shame for the parents, especially the mothers, and women, if they spoke of them at all, for the most part did not make any permanent record of what had happened. Families too tended not to dwell on such matters.

We don't have any letters from Margaret from this period in Anne's life – it is possible that her own health was such that she no longer felt able to correspond in writing – so we have no insight into how she responded to Anne's loss or whether she offered any support. Yet, with infant mortality rates so high, it is extremely likely that Margaret too would have been through a similar experience. Certainly, in a letter written some quarter of a century earlier, a pregnant Margaret wrote to her husband: 'I beg you that if you have another son that you will let it be named Harry in remembrance of your brother Harry.'[15] There are no other records of Agnes and Justice William having had a son called Harry, indicating that he probably died in infancy. Nor are there any records of Margaret and John ever having had a son with that name. It seems then likely either that at the time Margaret gave birth to a daughter rather than a son (Anne herself), or that this child also did not survive. As there is also a gap of several years in Margaret's correspondence after that letter, we can only surmise.

According to the *Letter on Virginity*, even a child born healthy would be a worry to its mother because 'fear of its loss is born along with it, for she is never without fear lest it should come to harm'.[16] In Anne's time, every parent might expect to lose at least one child. Indeed, in England, this pattern continued until well into the twentieth century. In the Middle Ages, at least one in five children died in early infancy, comparable to the number of women who died giving birth. An analysis of infant burials excavated from the medieval cemetery of Wharram Percy in Yorkshire shows very high levels of still-births and neonatal deaths.[17] In 2014 an excavation took place on the site of a modern extension at the Church of St Peter and St Paul in Margaret's home village of Mautby. A significant number of graves were uncovered in the process, including those of three newly born infants. While only a few of the graves were medieval, there were several children and infants among them.[18]

Despite the frequency of miscarriages and stillbirths, the high levels of infant mortality, and the silences around them, there is every reason to believe that the loss of a child before, during or after birth affected the parents, and especially the mothers, in much the same way as it does today. Stillborn babies were not supposed to be buried in consecrated ground, but this was not strictly enforced, especially in rural areas, as the Wharram Percy evidence confirms. The question of the heavenly status of infants is at the heart of the Middle English dream poem, *Pearl*, which describes a man's visionary encounter with an uncannily familiar maiden, whom he describes as closer to him 'than aunt or niece' and who is often identified as his deceased two-year-old daughter.[19] *Pearl* is profoundly religious in subject matter and the maiden and the dreamer debate issues such as the power of divine grace. But the poem is also a very moving examination of grief and mourning and reflects the depth of suffering felt by those who have experienced the death of a child. It offers reassurances to parents that they will be reunited in Paradise.

That the Paston family mourned the deaths of their infant children is illustrated very vividly by the recent identification of a memorial brass of a child, somewhat hidden away in the church of St Michael and All Angels, Oxnead.[20] The brass reads: 'Here lies Anna, daughter of John Paston Knight, on whose soul God have mercy, Amen.' This is in fact the only fifteenth-century brass for a member of the Paston family still to exist in the present day. It is likely that this Anna Paston was Anne's niece, a daughter of her second brother, John III, who eventually inherited his grandmother Agnes's former home at Oxnead, alongside the other properties, when he became head of the family following his elder brother's death. While it isn't possible to date the memorial brass with any precision, and no indication is given on it of Anna's age, evidence from the Paston letters themselves suggest that she lived sometime between 1483 and 1495 and that she may have been around three years old or younger when she died. If Anna were named after Anne, then Anne may have been one of her godmothers, and she would have also felt this loss keenly. It is quite possible that Margaret, who died in 1484, never knew this granddaughter.

From all this evidence, then, it seems reasonable to surmise that even though it was not unusual that the Yelvertons' baby had 'passed to God', the parents would have been deeply affected by its passing. It seems possible that Anne never had any other children. Anne is mentioned in Margaret's will but there are no bequests to any Yelverton grandchildren, which suggests that either there were none at that time, or that they too had died in infancy. While the catastrophe that Margaret feared of Anne proving as unruly as her sister and making her own unsuitable union was averted, Anne's married life may nevertheless have been marked by sadness. Like stillbirths, the absence of children in a family was seen as a source of shame and blamed on the mother, and, if Anne and her husband did not have any surviving children, she is likely to have experienced guilt as well as sorrow. She died only a decade after her mother, when she was around 40 years old, and her husband passed away a few years later at the turn of the sixteenth century.

15. 'RATHER A GOOD SECULAR MAN THAN A FOOLISH PRIEST'

....

18 January 1473 (Margaret to her chaplain,
Sir James Gloys)

....

While Margaret was worrying about the inappropriate or unwise romantic relationships being formed by her eldest son and two daughters, she was also giving some thought to the education and careers of her youngest sons, especially the second-youngest, Walter. In a letter to her chaplain, Sir James Gloys, written early in 1473, Margaret discusses her hopes and fears for Walter, who is about to embark on his studies at the University of Oxford.[1] Margaret writes to ask the priest to accompany Walter to Oxford, instructing him to purchase a horse in Cambridge to transport Walter's luggage if a faster carrier is unavailable. She requests that he ensure that Walter is settled and is 'put in good and serious order' because he is so dear to her. Margaret confides to Gloys that she 'would be reluctant to lose' Walter because she hopes 'to have more joy of him' than she has had of his elder brothers.

Walter may well have been Margaret's favourite son, but she was concerned about the company he was keeping. In this letter, she complains to Gloys about his friendship with Robert Holler, the son of a family connection, Thomas Holler of Moulton in Norfolk, who, back in 1460, was one of the jurors in the inquisition into Fastolf's property. Along with Margaret's husband, John, Holler was named as executor of the will of her uncle John Berney, and he and John had shared responsibility for John Berney's illegitimate son, Osbert, while he remained a minor. Margaret expresses the hope that Walter will make more appropriate acquaintances during his student life: 'I wish Walter to be associated with someone better than Holler's son, where he is going.' Margaret also has an immediate grievance. It seems that Holler's son had been entrusted with some letters to Margaret that she had not received, and she doesn't know whether to blame the son or the father. At the same time, she does not want to get involved in any unpleasantness with Robert's father Thomas, 'because he is a countryman and a neighbour'.

Margaret's main concern in this letter is nevertheless the welfare and future of Walter. She even asks Gloys, who, she believes, already knows her mind, to write a letter of guidance to Walter on her behalf. She tells Gloys to relay to Walter that 'as long as he does well, learns well, and is of good conduct and attitude, he shall not lack anything that I can help with, provided that he needs it'. Somewhat ironically (given Gloys' profession) she wants Gloys to advise him to take his time before deciding to join the church: 'And ask him not to be too hasty to be bound by holy orders until he is 24 years old or more, even if he is advised otherwise; for often haste brings regret.' Margaret concludes: 'I would rather he were a good secular man than a foolish priest.'

Margaret's words here are revealing not only about her anxieties about this new stage in her son's life, but also about her letter-writing practice. There are other examples of Margaret effectively delegating the writing of her letters to someone else, rather than dictating them directly to whoever was acting as her scribe, and this must have been a fairly common practice. In fact, the term secretary might be more accurate than scribe when it comes to correspondence because, in the fifteenth century, the word had the primary meaning of 'one entrusted with private or confidential matters, a confidant; a trusted servant or counselor'.[2] Margaret chose men in whom she could confide and on whom she felt she could rely to act as her secretaries. These included her own sons, as well as Gloys himself, who also wrote letters and documents for her husband. Gloys was responsible for writing all or part of some twenty of Margaret's letters, most but not all of them after her husband's death. It is timely therefore to remember that Margaret's voice as we encounter it in her letters is always mediated by her scribes, and perhaps more extensively than is immediately apparent. Margaret entrusted Gloys to provide appropriate and effective advice to Walter and even to speak on her behalf.

Sir James Gloys was one of the most loyal servants of the Paston family. He made his dramatic entrance into Margaret's letters 25 years earlier, in 1448, when a minor quarrel erupted into violence. In May of that year, Margaret and her mother-in-law were insulted in the street by a Paston opponent, John Wymondham or Wyndham, who assaulted Gloys, and threatened to kill him.[3] Margaret proves herself to be an accomplished storyteller when she recounts these events. She records that the furore broke out in the street while she and Agnes were attending mass in the parish church at the very moment 'of the elevation of the Host', the climactic moment at the conclusion of the Eucharistic Prayer when the priest raises the sacramental bread for the congregation to see. This is significant. Christian miracles cluster around the Eucharist, and it was widely believed that those who viewed the elevation of the Host would be protected from dying suddenly and unprepared. Margaret implies, then, that, unlike their opponents, she and Agnes had God on their side, while at the same time she conveys the potentially life-threatening nature of the attack. Perhaps, without divine intervention, they and their supporters would have been killed.

Margaret also captures the lively verbal exchange between the two parties after Gloys rudely refused to doff his hat as he passed Wymondham and his cronies: 'Cover thy head!', 'So I will, for thee', 'Will thou do so, knave?' The use of 'thee' and 'thou' rather than 'you' was extremely offensive, suggesting familiarity with the person addressed or, in this case, inferiority in status. The encounter escalated, with daggers drawn, rocks thrown and a sword and spear fetched. Insults were traded. Gloys was called a 'thief' and Wymondham a 'churl' or peasant, and when Agnes and Margaret intervened, drawn out of the church by the furore, they were called 'strong whores'.

In his outrage, Wymondham denigrated the Paston family itself, apparently alluding to its lowly origins. The word 'Gimingham', the village from which Justice William's grandfather originated, can just be made out in the manuscript of this letter, apparently added above the line (as if Margaret has corrected her scribe after the letter has been read back to her).[4] At this point, a hole in the letter means it is impossible to be entirely sure what Wymondham said, but it is likely that he responded in kind to Gloys' insult. Did Margaret's husband, the recipient of this letter, rip the offensive word out of the page after reading it? Nor did the violence end there. While Margaret and Agnes went to seek the assistance of the prior of Norwich, Gloys and one of Agnes's servants were assaulted with a sword, and threats were made against John himself. Margaret warned her husband in a postscript to this letter that he was not safe even in London: 'I know well he will not attack you heroically, but I believe he will set upon you or some of your men, like a thief.'

The outspoken and hot-headed young priest that we encounter in 1448 is not so very different from the irascible and cantankerous elderly man who features in the later correspondence. Following John Paston's early demise, Margaret found herself increasingly isolated. In 1470, an ageing Agnes travelled to London with her son William, and soon settled there permanently, much to the annoyance of the family who suspected that William was seeking to gain control of her wealth. After Agnes's departure, Margaret became more and more reliant on Gloys for company and advice. Close relations between women and their spiritual directors were certainly not uncommon in the later Middle Ages. This was especially the case, perhaps, for nuns and anchoresses, but it was also true of pious lay women. The Norfolk visionary Margery Kempe describes at length the importance of priestly approbation, and the difficulties she faced when her confessors and other priests disapproved of her often boisterous and flamboyant piety, and she too turned to her son and to clerics to write and indeed to read for her. Unfortunately, it seems that Margaret's sons felt that they were being pushed out by Gloys, which led to friction within the household.

In the early winter of 1471, Margaret complained to her second son about his elder brother's suspicions that Gloys had an undue influence on her thinking, which was exacerbating the rift between them:

> It is the death of me to think about it. It seems to me from your brother's letter that he thinks I am told by some of those around me to do and say what I have before now, but upon my word he suspects wrongly ... And when I have revealed my opinion to a certain person whom perhaps he also suspects, they have consoled me more that I could have by any thought in my own mind.[5]

Although Margaret does not name Gloys in this passage, it is clear that he is the 'certain person' alluded to here. Margaret is insistent that she can think for herself: 'I do not need to be told any such thing. I work things out in my own mind, and understand enough, or too much.'

In July 1472, the summer before Walter set off for Oxford, matters came to a head. Writing to his elder brother, John Paston III vividly described the tension at home. According to his account, Margaret was deliberately provoking arguments with him and with her middle son Edmond, to get them to leave her house. Almost every evening the two brothers found themselves in trouble; nothing they could do was acceptable to Margaret. This culminated in a clash with Gloys, which Margaret witnessed. Edmond describes the exchange in colourful language: 'We fell out before my mother with "Thou proud priest" and "Thou proud squire", my mother taking his part, so I have almost shat the boat at my mother's house.'[6] What was worse, Margaret had announced that she would make an inventory of all her property in order to write her will, and was holding this threat over his head: 'In this anger between Sir James and me she has promised me that my part shall be nought; what yours shall be I cannot say.' In a subsequent letter, in which he describes his mother's growing distrust of John II ('my mother weeps and takes on marvellously'), John III also complains that Gloys is always 'chopping' at him in front of his mother to incite her displeasure and to provoke him to anger but his own strategy is to respond calmly, smiling and saying, 'It is good hearing these old tales.'[7]

In the same letter, John III mentions that Gloys has been appointed parson of St Andrew's Church, Stokesby, which was in the gift of one of Margaret's relatives. This was a significant move for Gloys. The position would provide him with accommodation and an income. But Gloys had no intention of leaving Margaret's side. Stokesby is just over three miles from Mautby, so only an hour's brisk walk. Margaret had already resolved to retire from Norwich to Mautby and, in her letter of 18 January 1473, she mentions that she very much likes her 'dwelling place and the district' in which she finds herself, that she is well cared for, and that she is looking forward to the arrival of the summer 'and the fair weather'. In other words, three months after the news of Gloys' benefice broke, Margaret had already made her move to live near his new residence. Margaret, it seems, could not bear to be without her beloved priest. In the same letter, she urges Gloys that if he does decide to accompany Walter to Oxford, then he should come to visit her immediately on his return, or, alternatively, if there is time, before Walter's departure. Unfortunately, by the end of November of the same year, Sir James Gloys had died. Margaret had lost her closest ally, and her sons saw this turn of events for the opportunity it was. John II wrote to John III: 'Beware from henceforth that no such fellow creep in between you and her.'[8]

When Walter began his studies in 1473, he matriculated at one of the oldest universities in the world. The University of Oxford has its origins as far back as the eleventh century, although its foundation date is unknown, unlike the University of Cambridge, which was founded in 1209 and granted its royal charter first in 1231. Medieval European universities were first created to educate the clergy. They were therefore the preserve of men, and this continued to be the case for many more centuries. The first women who formally matriculated at Oxford did so as late as 1920. St Benet's Hall was the last Oxford residence to admit women, which it did in 2016.

As Margaret's letter to Gloys indicates, by the time Walter went to university, higher education was not simply the preserve of the priesthood – his father, who had studied at Cambridge, trained in the law – but Walter was considering taking the cloth. This was an age when scholasticism, a learning method that emphasised dialectical reasoning, dominated the medieval university system, and Latin was the language of education. Walter would have studied the liberal arts, which began with the trivium, an introductory course in grammar, logic and rhetoric. This led at Master's level to the quadrivium, the study of maths, astronomy, music and geometry. From there, if he wanted to progress further, he could have specialised in theology, law or medicine. Walter's initial focus, therefore, would have been on the study of language and its application, and on analytical thinking and what we now think of as philosophy. Like most students over the centuries, he would have attended lectures and studied books.

Attending university was the privilege of those with an education whose kin had money to pay for their studies, but inevitably tensions within the families or changing circumstances led to some students struggling to support themselves. In the earliest of Walter's small collection of letters, all of which date to his time in Oxford, he writes to his mother with an account of his expenses that need paying, explaining that he has borrowed money from his tutor, Edmund Alyard.[9] Walter, or rather his family, had to find money to pay the equivalent of tuition fees as well as board and lodging, clothes and even a horse. He received an exhibition from the Bishop of Norwich, but this did not fully support him. Books were expensive because they were still mainly copied by hand. The printing press, which rendered them more affordable, would only be introduced into the city five years after Walter's arrival, when Theodoric Rood set up his press in the High Street.[10]

The university was organised initially around monastic halls, followed by secular academic halls and, from the thirteenth century, colleges, which were first established as student residences. Nevertheless, some students still took lodgings in town. Chaucer's 'The Miller's Tale' is set in Oxford, and features a scholar called Nicholas who rents a room from a carpenter and his young wife. Chaucer provides a vivid inventory of its contents, which included his books, his astrolabe (an astronomical instrument), the counting stones for his abacus, and a psaltery (a stringed instrument, a type of zither). After 1410, students were required to live in approved accommodation. Walter would have stayed with a small number of other students and tutors in a shared chamber with partitioned-off space for private study.

The imprint of the medieval university is still visible in the centre of Oxford today with its late Gothic or Perpendicular architecture. Walter's studies coincided with the 'great period of college building' which had begun a century before his arrival and continued to the Reformation.[11] Established in the thirteenth century, Balliol, University and Merton are the oldest of the colleges. While Balliol famously has a nineteenth-century façade, chapel and hall, its earliest surviving buildings, which are found in the front quad, date to the fifteenth century. University College moved site and its current buildings are mainly early modern or later. Merton's Mob Quadrangle, which incorporates the treasury, sacristy and library, is the earliest quadrangle in the university. It was built between the late thirteenth and late fourteenth centuries. The chapel also dates to the late thirteenth century. Merton College Library lays claim to being the oldest academic library that has remained in continuous use, and stepping into the Upper Library, with its wooden panelling, rows of bays and fourteenth-century stained-glass windows, is particularly evocative.

By Walter's day, seven more of today's Oxford colleges were in existence. The most recent was Magdalen College, founded in 1458. One of the medieval academic halls, St Edmund Hall, survives as a college, and another, Hart Hall, evolved into what is Hertford College. One medieval monastic hall, Blackfriars, was refounded in the early twentieth century. Work began on the Divinity School, one of the first purpose-built university buildings, in the 1420s and it was used for lectures and examinations. Following the death of Humphrey of Lancaster, 1st Duke of Gloucester, in 1447, and his bequest of 281 books to the university, construction began on a second floor to house this library, and this was still ongoing while Walter was a student. Prior to its completion, the main library was housed in a building erected next to the Church of St Mary the Virgin, where Congregation, the university's sovereign body, also met.

But, of course, there was more to life than studying for many students, even though the university tried to prevent them from drinking in alehouses. Some public houses in Oxford that have their origins the Middle Ages remain, such as the Crown, the Turf Tavern and the Bear Inn. Whether Walter frequented any hostelries is impossible to know, but as Chaucer's 'Miller's Tale' reveals, students in the late Middle Ages could be easily distracted from their education by opportunities for sex, mischief and cruel pranks. From her letter, Margaret is clearly anxious that his new acquaintances will lead Walter astray. Relations between town and gown in Oxford had long been hostile. This tension had reached its climax in the St Scholastica's Day riot in 1355, when two students drinking in an inn called the Swindlestock Tavern on Carfax in the city centre got into a violent dispute with an innkeeper over the quality of the wine they had been served. The fight spread beyond the inn and escalated into a riot that lasted three days. Over 90 people were killed, two-thirds of them from the university. The enmity continued in the centuries that followed, and Margaret may well have been aware of this, adding to her worries about her favourite son.

Walter would have been around seventeen when he arrived at the university. He makes one of his first appearances in the Paston collection, although he is not named, in a letter written a couple of years earlier, in the plague year of 1471, in which John II describes the horror of what he called 'the most universal death', and advised the family to move out of Norfolk into the countryside: 'For God's sake, ensure my mother takes care of my young brothers, so that they are not in a place where sickness is reigning, nor entertain themselves with any other people who go around where there is any sickness.'[12] A year later, John III mentions that young Walter, fortunately still fit and well, has borrowed a book from John II: 'The proud, peevish, and evil disposed priest to us all, Sir James, said that you commanded him to deliver *The Book of the Seven Sages* to my brother Walter, and he has it.'[13] *The Book of the Seven Sages* was a misogynist storytelling collection that was very popular in medieval Europe. The frame narrative begins with wife of the Roman Emperor attempting to seduce her stepson and then falsely accusing him, and many of the tales focus on the wickedness of women. This tells us that Walter was not just reading edifying scholarly texts. Walter evidently got on much better with Gloys than his brothers did, and the priest may well have inspired him in his first choice of career and persuaded him of the benefits of a celibate lifestyle.

Walter was a diligent enough student and completed his degree six years after he had started it. The small cluster of letters from and concerning Walter that survive from 1479 allow us insight into the final stages of his university studies and the continuing influence of his mother over his choice of profession. In February of that year, when Walter was still a student, Dr William Pickenham, a church lawyer, chancellor of the diocese of Norwich and archdeacon of Suffolk, wrote an uncomfortable letter to Margaret informing her that Walter was not yet qualified to be presented as a priest.[14] The logical next step for Walter would have been for him to join one of the minor orders of the church, in this case the evocatively named exorcists, but, as Pickenham observed, Walter had not yet been ordained. Whereas today the term 'exorcist' conjures up the idea of a priest battling with a case of demonic possession, in the Middle Ages, exorcists, or benets, as they were known, had a far less dramatic role; they were simply responsible for performing ceremonies prior to baptism. At only 23, Walter was still too young and inexperienced. Although not named in this letter, Margaret had a specific benefice in mind for Walter: the church of St Peter and St Paul in her own village of Mautby, where Walter had inherited land from his father. Margaret obviously wanted to advance Walter's career, and to keep him close to her, but in the process, she risked making a fool of herself, or worse, because as Pickenham pointed out, her proposal was illegal and 'neither goodly nor godly'. Margaret ultimately, if grudgingly, accepted these arguments. Only a year later, her plans for Walter having come to nothing, she presented Thomas Heveningham to the position.

A month after Pickenham's letter, Margaret received a letter from Walter's tutor, Edmund Alyard. This reveals that, between them, Margaret and Alyard had now decided that Walter should change direction and follow his father into the law.[15] Walter's brother Edmond had also considered joining the legal profession, and had briefly been a member of Staple Inn, before changing his mind. Margaret was keen to have Walter back home with her in Mautby for a few weeks, so Alyard recommended that he graduate from the Faculty of Arts at midsummer and commence his legal studies in the Michaelmas term. Two months later, Walter was preparing for his inception, when he would formally take his degree, and he once again had to approach his family, in this case John II as the head of the household, for financial help.

Unfortunately, the costs of the educating the youngest of the Paston sons was mounting. At this time their brother William was completing his studies at Eton College in Windsor, which had been founded by Henry VI four decades previously, and Margaret had already informed John II that she was unwilling to contribute further to the young man's 'board and his school hire'.[16] Walter's frustration over his financial situation is clear in the sarcasm of the closing lines of his letter: 'And if you don't know what this term "inceptor", means, Master Edmund, who was my supervisor at Oxford, the bearer hereof, can tell you, or else any other graduate.'[17]

Walter also passed on news that would be a great disappointment to Margaret. He no longer planned to return home in the summer, because he wanted to attend an important event later in the year: the University of Oxford was to award Lionel Woodville, the brother of the Queen, an honorary degree (the first recorded), a doctorate in Canon Law. The following year Woodville would be named Chancellor of the University. Walter graduated as planned in June and celebrated with a feast a couple of days later. Catherine, Lady Harcourt, a relative of the Duke of Suffolk, had promised Walter a gift of venison but unfortunately it did not materialise; nevertheless all Walter's guests enjoyed the meal. John Paston III had written to enquire of Walter the exact time that he would proceed, in the hope that he could attend. The two brothers were especially close. But, as Walter explained, his message had gone astray, and John III missed the event.[18]

Within two months of graduating as a Bachelor of Arts, Walter was dead. Having fallen severely ill in Oxford, he was brought home to Norwich to receive care. Realising that he was not going to recover, Walter drafted his will on 18 August.[19] He named Edmund Alyard and John III his executors. The will is revealing about Walter's Oxford network and family relations.

He gifts his gowns, cloaks and bolsters to a small group of scholars and students, including Alyard and Robert Holler. Walter's friendship with Robert Holler, despite his mother's disapproval, had evidently continued to flourish throughout the intervening years. Walter also leaves a gown to one Robert Holland, whom he describes as his 'spiritual son'. Alyard is to inherit Walter's remaining Oxford possessions and to pay his university debts. Walter bequeaths his estate in Mautby to his brother Edmond, sister Anne and John III's wife. He leaves his remaining land to John III, with the proviso that if John III inherits his father's estates it should pass to Edmond. John II isn't mentioned, but as his father's main heir and as head of the household that is unsurprising. Nor is his sister Margery, although she may have predeceased Walter. It is somewhat odd that his younger brother William is omitted; perhaps the two did not get on.

Three days after the will was drafted, Edmond wrote to John III: 'Sure tidings have come to Norwich that my grandmother is deceased, God forgive her. My uncle had a message yesterday that she would not escape, and today came another when we were at mass for my brother Walter, may God forgive him.'[20] This was the same letter in which Edmond passed on the news that Anne had given birth but that her baby had died. By the end of the year John II would also be dead. The deaths of Walter, Agnes and John II occurred in the last major plague years of the century: around 20 per cent of the population was wiped out in this wave. Walter, his grandmother and brother likely fell victim to this pestilence. Margaret would surely have been by Walter's bedside, if her health allowed it, or perhaps one of her children had to share the devastating news of his demise. At his own request, Walter was buried before the altar of St John the Baptist in the Church of St Peter Hungate in Norwich, the parish church which his parents had paid to restore. With his passing, Margaret was more alone than ever.

16. 'IT IS TOO FAR TO THE CHURCH AND I AM UNWELL'

....

28 January 1475 (Margaret to her two eldest sons)

....

By January 1475, Margaret was fully settled in Mautby Hall. The current house at Mautby is postmedieval, but from her own accounts and from the evidence of surviving Norfolk residences from the period, we can get a sense of what the medieval manor house would have looked like and how it was built and improved. In the early 1460s, Margaret and John's close friend William Lomnor rebuilt Mannington Hall in Norfolk in a style that reflected the fashions of the time. John was invited to visit while the work was taking place so he would have seen this at first hand. He was also asked to supply some wood from his nearby estate for the construction.[1] The moated manor house that Lomnor built still stands proud today, having been in the possession of the Walpole family since the eighteenth century. After the destruction of Gresham and before they settled in Norwich, Margaret and John considered Mautby Hall as a possible main residence and Margaret oversaw a plan of renovations there. While Mautby was not remodelled so extensively as Mannington, important improvements were nevertheless made.

The progress of the work at Mautby, back in the 1450s, proved frustratingly slow, at least in part due to the weather. Margaret had to warn her husband that, while the thatcher's work on the roof of the main hall was satisfactorily completed, 'it is not likely any more will be built this year except the gables of the chamber and the chapel windows … As for the little house that you wrote to me about, my uncle and Sir Thomas say it would be better for you not to have workmen in it until winter is over. The masons gave up a fortnight after I went there.'[2] John was keen to have the work advanced, even during the harshest months, but, without either himself or Margaret in residence, this proved an impossibility. From these accounts, it seems that the medieval manor house at Mautby was a traditional timber-framed build, rather than brick and flint, with a roof thatched with reeds, and new gables, chimneys and windows added. While the installation of chimneys does not seem so remarkable today, it is an indication of the ambition in Margaret's plan of modernisation; domestic chimneys did not become commonplace until the sixteenth and seventeenth centuries.

Another surviving house that might provide a better idea of the appearance of the medieval hall than Mannington is the Old Vicarage in Methwold, a village 50 miles west of Mautby, on the edge of the fens, between Downham Market and Thetford. The timber framing dates to the late fifteenth century and, like Mautby, the house was originally thatched. The Old Vicarage is also jettied, in other words the upper floor projects beyond lower one, and it has a particularly striking ornamented external chimney which climbs up the middle of the gable. Whatever its external appearance, like other manors of the time, Mautby Hall was more of a complex than simply a house, with not only the chapel and great chamber mentioned by Margaret, but also, typically, a main hall, buttery for storage of provisions and a solar, usually on the upper floor, which provided the private accommodation for the family. There would be a dairy, bakehouse, brewhouse and stables, and gardens with fruit trees and beehives, and, as is still the case, it would have been surrounded by farmland for animal husbandry and crop growing.[3]

Further evidence of the appearance of Mautby Hall, and especially its interior, is found in Margaret's will, and the same document provides information about its furnishings. Margaret mentions a parlour at the Hall and describes its green wall hanging and canopied and curtained feather bed.[4] Margaret may well have spent many of her days in this room and slept in it at night. The parlour had a 'brass chafer to set by the fire and a chafer for coals', that is a vessel for heating water or food and one for heating the room. Margaret also lists an embroidery or tapestry depicting Alexander the Great hanging over a bed in the Great Chamber or main bedroom, and a white travel bed in the 'little chamber'. The Alexander hanging is particularly interesting. The history of Alexander the Great was a popular topic, as seen, for example, in two mid-fifteenth-century tapestries in the Villa del Principe in Genoa.[5] The first depicts the heroism of Alexander's youth, culminating in his coronation. The second details Alexander successfully besieging and conquering a city, and depicts a medieval legend taken from *The Alexander Romance* where, in order to see the entire world, the hero descended to the bottom of the sea and up into the sky, raised on a chair drawn by flying griffins lured heavenwards by skewers of meat. The griffin was of course the heraldic symbol of the Paston family, and it is tempting to speculate that Margaret's tapestry may have included this scene, reflecting perhaps that she and her husband identified in some lesser way with Alexander's triumphs. While Margaret would have spent some of her time on needlework, her domestic tapestries and hangings would have been produced by professional embroiderers either in London or on the continent. Arras, Tournai and Brussels were centres of tapestry in the fifteenth century, but England too was well known for its embroidery.

Although neither the medieval hall nor its contents have survived, the grazing marshes of Mautby and Caister Castle remain. In Margaret's time, they were rich in salt pans and provided a much-needed supply of reeds for thatch and construction, as well as for other uses such as basket and pen making. Nearby Mautby Decoy, a pool for trapping waterfowl, may have been located on a site where peat was formerly cut. Pickerhill Holme Dyke, the stream cutting across the marsh from the Bure to Caister Castle, had been widened by Fastolf initially to enable the transport of building materials to the castle, and evidence of brickworks was found in the area in the twentieth century.[6] When I first visited Mautby marsh, Heike and I walked with the dogs out from Great Yarmouth, along the river where cattle were grazing on the banks, past farms, ditches and drainage mills, across a landscape that, despite its changes across the centuries, surely still resembles that which was familiar to Margaret. Now, however, there is far less visible human industry and activity than would have been typical in Margaret's time.

Margaret wrote two letters from Mautby Hall on 28 January 1475. The first was to her eldest son.[7] It is mainly concerned with financial matters, including the selling price of grain, the repayment of an outstanding debt to the Clere family by her brother-in-law, William, and the sale of Sporle Wood, an ancient woodland that still exists in the Breckland district of Norfolk, albeit as a fraction of its former size. Well-maintained woodlands were a vital aspect of the rural economy, but, since the death of Margaret's husband, Sporle had suffered neglect and proved difficult to lease. John II was planning to dispose of a potential asset, but in its current state it was a drain on his resources, and the family's finances were already stretched.

Three years earlier, Margaret had complained to John II that she had recently heard rumours, 'that I am likely to have little good from Mautby, if the Duke of Norfolk still has possession of Caister'.[8] The waterways that connected Caister to Mautby ran through Margaret's land, with a ditch passing close to the hall itself. The proximity of Mautby to Caister, 'the fairest flower in our garland' as Margaret called it, which had previously been advantageous, now placed her home in a vulnerable position, and indeed Margaret did suffer from a night raid by Norfolk's men, who stole sheep and shot at one of her tenants. In the 1460s the family also struggled to find tenants for the home farm at Mautby because it proved unprofitable, and Margaret worried that the estate cottages were in a state of disrepair. Nevertheless, despite these ongoing concerns about money, Margaret initially felt that it would be a mistake for John II to sell Sporle because, as she observed, 'your father, may God rest his soul, cherished in every manner his woods'.[9] By early 1475 her opinion had changed. Unfortunately, so had the political situation. Edward IV was planning an expedition to France and funding it by raising taxes. Margaret complains in her letter that whereas previously she could have sold Sporle to a 'chapman' or merchant, now no one will consider purchasing it.

In the same letter to John II of January 1475, Margaret thanks him for some flasks he had sent her and promises that she will be as good a 'huswyff' or 'housewife' for him as she is for herself. What Margaret meant by this was that she would take good care running her son's household and his estates, striking the best bargains and financial deals on his behalf. The word 'housewife' had been previously used by John II in relation to Sporle Wood: John II promised his brother John III that if he could raise more than 200 marks on its sale then 'I should say you are a good housewife'.[10] In early 1475, John II was incapacitated by injuries to his eye and his leg, and so Margaret's intervention was necessary. Margaret advises him: 'If God will not allow you to have health, thank him for that and endure it patiently, and come back home to me, and we shall live together as God will give us grace to do.' John II still did not have a wife to whom he could turn for support and Margaret had her own opinion on this topic. She recommends that he end his on-off engagement with Anne Haute once and for all because 'I believe you could do better'.

Margaret's letter to John II does not simply focus on financial and practical matters. She also mentions the sale of books from the estate of the late James Gloys. Margaret writes:

> Regarding the books belonging to Sir James that you wanted, the best and finest of them all has been claimed, and it is not in his inventory. I shall try to get it for you if I can. The price of all the other books besides that is 20s 6d. I am sending you a list of them. If you approve of their price and you want them, send me word.

To get a sense of the value of these books, the cost is the equivalent to more than a month's wages for a skilled craftsman. John II was less than enthusiastic. He replied plaintively: 'As for the books that were Sir James's, God rest his soul, I think it best if they remain with you until I can speak with you myself. My mind is now not most upon books.'[11] John II was writing from Calais, where both he and John III were stationed, after being pardoned for their parts in the Battle of Barnet four years previously. John assured his mother that his health was improving but was clearly preoccupied by his mounting debts.

John's avowed lack of interest in expanding his library is untypical of him; he usually leapt on opportunities to add to his collection. At some point in 1475 or shortly thereafter, he made a rough catalogue of the books in his own library.[12] Among these, some religious books are listed, including a life of St Christopher and a 'red book', which was made up of several texts, most of them devotional. The 'red book' cannot have been the prized book belonging to Gloys that Margaret mentions because John II specifies that he obtained it from someone else. Nevertheless, the existence of the volume within John II's library suggests that he, or someone in his family, was interested in spiritual treatises and poems.

We know from notes that he made in his library inventory that John II borrowed and lent books. Occasionally he made generous presents of them. A case in point is a manuscript now held in the British Library, which, like John's 'red book', is a collection of moral and devotional works; the lives of three women saints, Katherine, Margaret and Anne, are found within it. Ultraviolet light reveals that it is inscribed, 'This is the book of dame Anne Wingfield of Harling' and it is likely that it was made specifically for her, sometime around 1460.[13] Anne Wingfield, or Anne Harling as she was then, was the niece of Sir John Fastolf. She became his ward after her father's demise. Anne was a wealthy heiress and following the death of her first husband, the Paston family hoped, in vain as it transpired, that she might marry one of their sons, probably John II. The volume may then have been a courtship gift from John II to Anne. Anne shared John II's love of books and had her own collection. Despite the unsuccessful marriage alliance, the friendship between the couple continued and there is a reference to her in John II's library catalogue. Unfortunately, John's book inventory has been burnt along the edge, making it difficult to read, but it appears that John II's copy of Chaucer's

Troilus and Criseyde also ended up in her possession, because he notes '*Ibi ego vidi*' [I saw it there].

It is possible that, like the volume he may have gifted to Anne Wingfield, John II's 'red book' was bought by him with another reader in mind, perhaps even his mother Margaret. If this were the case, then it is possible Margaret had her eye on the volume from Gloys' library for herself as much as for her son. But, regardless of whether Margaret did have a personal interest in any of the books in her son's library, she occasionally did help him to obtain volumes that he desired for the collection. As well as offering to buy the books in Gloys' estate on his behalf, she assisted him with the production of a manuscript commonly known as 'Sir John Paston's Great Book', which is now held in the British Library.[14] Judging from the other works that we know he owned, this compendium of heraldic and chivalric material was much closer to John Paston II's own interests than the 'red book' or any other religious work.

The second letter that Margaret wrote from Mautby on the same day in January 1475 is revealing about the importance of religious devotion to Margaret at this stage of her life.[15] The letter is addressed to John III and deals with some of the same issues as the first: specifically, the debt owed to the Cleres and the failure of John II and his uncle to ensure it is fully repaid. Margaret is frustrated that John II has not been communicating with her and asks his brother to prod him into action and keep her informed about what is going on. Margaret reiterates her concerns about John II's health, but her anxiety focuses primarily on her distrust of her brother-in-law, William, and in particular his influence over Agnes and attempts to have Oxnead Hall legally transferred into his name. In this letter, Margaret additionally mentions a more personal matter. She asks John III to write to the Bishop of Norwich to obtain the licence required for mass to be celebrated in the domestic chapel at Mautby Hall, 'because it is too far to the church and I am unwell'.

As Margaret struggled with her health, she found herself unable to undertake the mile-long walk from the hall to the Church of St Peter and St Paul. Besides, as Margaret goes on to point out in this letter, the priest was 'often absent'. Non-residential and part-time priests became an increasing problem across the country in the decades before the Reformation, and evidently the current rector, who had been presented by Margaret's husband a year before he passed away, was not meeting the spiritual needs of the locality. After the death of Sir James Gloys, Margaret wanted to find someone to fill his absence. In her letter, she asks John III to expedite her request for the licence, 'because of all sorts of misfortunes that have happened to me and mine'. It is then no surprise that just a few years later she tried to put her beloved son Walter forward for the Mautby benefice. Fortunately, the priest who was appointed instead seems to have been a perfectly satisfactory choice: Walter's brother Edmond calls him 'the good parson of Mautby'.[16]

The chapel at Mautby became increasingly important to Margaret as she grew older and less mobile. A domestic chapel or oratory played a crucial role in the late medieval manorial household; it was where the family and servants gathered for their divine offices and prayers.[17] It would usually be located near to or adjoining the hall itself. As with medieval churches, the east end of a domestic chapel would likely be dominated by a large tracery window, and Margaret may have followed this design in her renovations.[18] During the Middle Ages, most domestic chapels would be situated on the first floor, but by the fifteenth century a ground-floor location was increasingly common.

Margaret would have paid for ecclesiastical utensils, furniture and altar cloths for furnishing the chapel as well as robes for the priest. As well as leaving gifts of her primer and mass book in her will, she bequeathed chasubles (outer clerical vestments worn for the celebration of the mass), and orbs (symbols of authority) as well a silver pyx (a container for the consecrated host), and two altar cruets (small jugs for the wine or water) and her altar cloths. The cloths may have included a frontal depicting the crucifixion, the Virgin Mary or the saints. There is a fine example of such a decorated frontal, produced in England in the second half of the fourteenth century, in the Dumbarton Oaks Collection in Washington DC. It portrays St Lawrence and St Margaret of Antioch in silver-gilt and coloured thread against a backdrop of red velvet.[19] While it is less likely that Margaret would have been responsible for creating the wall hangings in the hall itself, she may well have taken the time to produce ecclesiastical embroideries such as this for her private chapel.

In her renovations of the chapel at Mautby Hall, Margaret may have been inspired by the activities of her mother-in-law Agnes, who, shortly after the death of Justice William, had had the manorial chapel at Paston either built or reworked. Agnes wrote to one of her sons about her ambitious plans, telling him to 'say to your brother John it would be well done to think of Stanstead Church', that is the Church of St James in Agnes's manor of Stanstead, near Sudbury in Suffolk.[20] The chapel at Mautby Hall must also have been a substantial structure given the presence of a chapel chamber. Margaret left to one of the executors of her will 'my whole little white bed in my chapel chamber at Mautby, with the featherbed that is now in the said chapel, with a pair of blankets, a pair of sheets, and a pillow of down'. The chapel chamber would usually be where the family chaplain resided, but Margaret's use of the possessive personal pronoun in relation to the 'little white bed' may indicate that, in the absence of a resident chaplain, she also slept in that room in her final years.

Intriguingly, as I was writing this book, I came across evidence suggesting that, as recently the late 1970s, Margaret's chapel was still standing, albeit in a ramshackle state. The circumstances leading up to this discovery were unlikely enough; this was no archival breakthrough. In the summer of 2022, I returned to Mautby to give a talk about Margaret in the Church of St Peter and St Paul, organised by the Paston Footprints project. When I arrived, the outside of the church was still decorated with bunting for Queen Elizabeth II's Jubilee celebrations. A busy bric-à-brac stall was in operation at the west end of the church, and the pews were filling up. Information panels from the Finding Paston Footprints: 400 Years of Norfolk Life exhibition, which had been hosted the previous year at Norwich Records Office, were somewhat precariously arranged around the nave, with one even balanced on the tomb of a Knight Templar. My lecture, delivered somewhat incongruously from the eagle lectern, seemed to be well received, and was followed by coffee and cakes and a raffle. A few days later, when I was back in Surrey, I received an intriguing message via social media that mentioned some photos kept in the church of a derelict barn in the grounds of what is now Hall Farm House. This barn, known in the village as the 'chapel', was, according to local knowledge, the building where Margaret had worshipped in her later years, a building which I had thought had been demolished long ago, along with the medieval manor house.

I couldn't find any reports on this barn and it wasn't mentioned by Pesvner or in any of the other publications that I had read about Mautby history. Curious and not a little perplexed, I emailed the church wardens, who kindly sent me copies of pictures of what turned out to be a thatched structure built of stone and patched up with modern brick and corrugated iron. Two of the photos showed what appeared to be either a low arched window or doorway set in a stone wall below the remains of the rotted timber roof frame. Others indicated bricked-up arched doorways. Supporting evidence comes from a local historian, Sam Howard, who was so fascinated by Margaret Paston that he insisted he should be buried in the village churchyard as close to her grave as possible. Sam Howard's reminiscences of Mautby were published in the 1990s, and he stated that the 'chapel' at the hall had been used as a cow shed since the late nineteenth century, and that it was demolished in 1979 by its then owner, Norfolk County Council, because it was structurally unsound.[21]

Could these photos really reveal that the remains of the chapel at the medieval manor house at Mautby had somehow survived over centuries, incorporated into an agricultural structure that had become dilapidated over time? There are certainly precedents for this sort of change of usage. For instance, about an hour's drive southwest from Mautby is the former Chapel of St Mary in New Buckenham, constructed in the twelfth century and then, three centuries later, after the parish church was built, converted into the private chapel of the castle. At this point large windows were inserted, reminiscent perhaps of the sort of improvements Margaret made to her own chapel. The Chapel of St Mary was subsequently transformed into a barn in the mid-sixteenth century; it is now a holiday cottage.

Through my newly made contacts in the village, I got in touch with the current owners of Hall Farm House, Emma-Jane and Mark Siddell, who kindly invited me to visit. My wife and I returned to Mautby, where we also met with Ian Hinton, chair of the Norfolk Historic Buildings Group, and James Mindham, the digital artist responsible for the 3-D historical reconstructions on the Paston Footprints website. James brought along his drone for an aerial view, and we took a walk around the grounds. Eventually, following a much-needed cup of tea in the kitchen, and with the aid of a historic map provided by Mark, a hand-drawn map that I had been given by a contact from the village and the directions of a neighbouring farmer, we succeeded in locating the site of the former barn or cow shed. Now occupied by some poultry runs and used as a space for storing old building materials, and grown over with trees, there seemed little to see, either on the ground or from the drone.

Yet, after looking more carefully, I did spot something that seemed out of place, propping open the door of one of the coops: a block of fine, smooth, dressed and carved stone with a hole running through it. Mark confirmed that he had dug it up from the ground in the vicinity. I showed it to Ian, who agreed that it looked medieval and suggested that it might be part of a pillar piscina (a basin with a drain for washing the vessels of the Mass) or the shaft of a sedilia (a series of usually three seats for the priest). It was in remarkably pristine condition which seemed out of keeping with the evident state of the building prior to its demolition. After our visit, James produced a 3-D model generated from the photographic and site evidence. Based on this reconstructive work, James posited that the blocked archways indicate a screen passage from the main hall rather than a chapel. Certainly, there is no indication of a great east window, or of any tracery. All that can be concluded with any certainty at this stage and without excavation is that there were some remains of the medieval manor buildings still standing towards the end of the twentieth century. But taken together, the provocative clues – the old photographs, local lore and communal memory, and that single tantalising block of masonry – still suggest to me that this now lost building may indeed have been the chapel that had proved so important to Margaret as her health declined.

17. 'THE MARRIAGE OF MY COUSIN, MARGERY'

....

11 June 1477 (Margaret to Dame Elizabeth Brews)

....

By 1477, Margaret was keen to see at least some of her children married off to appropriate spouses. Margery was a lost cause, but sometime in the spring or early summer Anne finally married William Yelverton. John II was pursuing a formal release from his engagement to Anne Haute. Margaret's youngest sons were in service, at university and at school. And a match had been found for John III: a kinswoman called Margery Brews. Margaret found herself deeply involved in the somewhat protracted negotiations which, by the summer, had almost completely broken down. The marriage settlement was, not untypically, the sticking point. John III blamed Margery's father, Sir Thomas Brews, for being miserly. Sir Thomas, in turn, felt that John II, who as head of the household was responsible for his siblings' marital agreements, was making unreasonable financial demands, and that if he were to give in to them, Margery, her prospective husband and her sisters would all be disadvantaged in the longer term. Margaret intervened to resolve the impasse, writing from Mautby to Margery's mother, Dame Elizabeth Brews, on 11 June to arrange an urgent meeting with her and her husband at one of their residences, Stinton Hall, in the village of Salle.[1] This is one of the very few letters exchanged between women that survive in the Paston collection and it is testimony to the crucial role women had in matters of domestic diplomacy.

Margaret opens her letter to Dame Elizabeth by reminding her of the many frank conversations they have had about the union of John III and Margery, about which she confesses, 'I have been as glad, and now lately as sorry, as ever I was about any marriage in my life.' Margaret insists that if the three parents meet together, they will able to get to the bottom of what has caused this rift and 'with your and my help and advice together we will find some way to stop it breaking off'. She observes that, given how far the arrangements have proceeded, ending the betrothal will bring dishonour to both families. Initially Margaret claims, disingenuously, that she does not know what – or who – is responsible for preventing the wedding from going ahead, but then she goes on to acknowledge that money is at the root of it: 'As far as my son is concerned, he intends to do well by my cousin Margery and not so well by himself.'

Margaret entrusts the delivery of this reconciliatory letter to her new son-in-law, William Yelverton, who is expected to return with news of when she might be expected at Stinton. Margaret ends by asking Dame Elizabeth to pass on her regards to Sir Thomas, and to 'my cousin Margery, to whom I expected I could have given another name before now'. In suggesting that she had hoped that she would already be addressing Margery as her daughter-in-law, Margaret echoes a memorable signature used by Dame Elizabeth Brews in an earlier letter: 'By your cousin ... [who] by God's Grace shall be called otherwise.'[2]

To understand why Margaret was so determined that this wedding should go ahead, we must go back to the earlier stages in its planning. Most importantly, all parties saw the advantage in this match, not least John Paston II, even though he was not fully in support of his mother's generosity towards his younger brother. Back in March, he wrote to Margaret in favour of bringing the arrangements for the potentially 'wealthy and convenient marriage' to a successful conclusion.[3] But it seems that financial gain was not the only or even the main factor at play. John II enumerates the many positive aspects of the union, including 'her [Margery's] person, her youth, and the stock that she comes from', as well as, crucially, 'the love on both sides'. This was then a love match as well as an arranged marriage (the one did not preclude the other), and judging from the characters of her parents, he is convinced that 'the maid should be virtuous and good'. John II observes that Margery's parents think highly of both their daughter and his brother, and fully endorse the relationship. Perhaps John II felt the need to reassure his mother, and himself, that John III had not succumbed to an unsuitable infatuation.

Despite the financial wrangling between the Paston and Brews families, John II's evaluation of the situation is confirmed by one of the letters that Dame Elizabeth wrote to her prospective son-in-law around this time.[4] In it, she ends a discussion of the finances with the announcement: 'But, if we come to an agreement, I will give you a greater treasure, that is an intelligent gentlewoman, and even though I say it myself, a good and a virtuous one.' Dame Elizabeth stresses that she is reluctant to part with her daughter, 'because if I were to take money for her, I would not give her away for £1,000', but that she is willing to do so because of the high regard in which she holds John III, despite his lack of riches: 'But cousin, I trust you so much that I would think her well bestowed on you even if you were worth much more.'

The praise Dame Elizabeth bestows upon Margery contrasts strikingly with Agnes Paston's attitude towards Margaret's sister-in-law Elizabeth and Margaret's outspoken condemnation of her own elder daughter. Dame Elizabeth's letter, with its commendation of her daughter's acute mind as well as her modest character and disposition, provides an all-too-rare recorded example of a medieval mother's appreciation of the cerebral attributes of her female offspring. Fortunately, Margaret agreed with this evaluation.

In this case we have, rather unusually, direct access to the prospective bride's thoughts on the marriage. In February 1477, Margery Brews sent two letters to John III. These further substantiate John II's judgement of the situation: Margery Brews was very much in love with John III, and her feelings were reciprocated. The difficulties the couple faced were not due to a lack of commitment on either part. Together, the letters can lay claim to being the first Valentine missives in English we know of that were written and sent. Indeed, one of the letters is written partly in rhyming couplets and very much from the heart:[5]

> And if you command me to remain true wherever I go,
> Indeed, I will use all my might you to love and never no mo.
> And if my friends say that I do amiss, they shall not stop me for to do
> My heart commands me ever more to love you
> Truly above all earthly thing.
> And if they be never so angry, I trust in shall be better in time coming.

The association of the Feast of the early Roman martyr St Valentine with love emerged in Europe in the later Middle Ages. The Christian Feast of St Valentine in mid-February replaced a pagan Roman festival, Lupercalia, which was associated with fertility and purification. But it was only in the late fourteenth century that the Feast of St Valentine gained romantic connotations. Chaucer's poem *The Parlement of Foules*, which may have been written to celebrate the betrothal of Richard II to Anne of Bohemia in 1381, makes the first known reference to 'Saint Valentine's day' as a day for lovers, or as Chaucer writes: 'When every fowl comes there to choose his mate.'[6] There is some dispute about whether Chaucer actually meant 3 May, the date of Richard and Anne's engagement, rather than 14 February, on the grounds that this was the feast of another St Valentine, a former bishop of Genoa, but almost a century later the February date for celebrating the occasion prevailed. On 9 February 1477, Dame Elizabeth sent an invitation to John III to visit, reminding him in terms highly reminiscent of Chaucer's poem that 'on Friday is Saint Valentine's Day, and every bird chooses himself a mate'.[7]

If Dame Elizabeth found her match-making inspiration in Chaucer's work, Margery was more influenced by his disciple John Lydgate, who composed several Valentine poems, albeit religious in subject matter. Margery's, in contrast, are entirely secular, which is what makes them so original. In her first Valentine letter to John III, Margery portrays herself as a wounded lover who is suffering in the absence of her 'dearly beloved Valentine'. She confesses: 'If it pleases you to hear how I am, I am not in good health in body nor in heart, nor will be until I hear from you.' Yet while Margery does not quote directly from Lydgate's poetry, one couplet in her letter resonates with lines from his hagiographical work, *The Life of St Margaret*.[8] Lydgate's poem in honour of this saint may have had a personal significance for Margery as it did for her mother. St Margaret was also Margery's namesake, the name

'Margery' being derived from 'Margaret'. Doubtless, Margery hoped John III would recognise the allusion.

The Valentine verses Margery penned for John III were not the frivolous or naïve declarations of affection that they might appear to be at first glance. Rather, Margery utilised them to convince John III that the marriage should go ahead, despite her father's apparent lack of generosity. In her second Valentine letter of February 1477, which is more formal and contains no verse, Margery tells John III she will be the 'happiest one alive if only the business might come to fruition', and if it comes to nothing, 'then I will be even sorrier and full of sadness'.[9] But while Margery expresses the hope that her 'good, faithful and loving Valentine' will accept her 'poor person', she also insists that she will accede to his decision, even if it is not in her favour, 'on condition that I may be your faithful lover and petitioner for the duration of my life'. Margery, like her future mother-in-law Margaret, and like her own mother, Dame Elizabeth, understood the importance of tact. She recognised the importance of reassuring John III about her feelings for him, while not challenging his authority.

Ultimately, the decision about whether they would marry had to be John III's, and his alone. Nevertheless, Margery did all she could to ensure that the wedding would take place. When Dame Elizabeth Brews wrote to John III in the same month, she complained that he had broached the subject of the marriage with Margery before the agreement had been finalised, and in so doing, 'you have made her such an advocate for you that I can never have rest night nor day because of her entreating and appealing to bring the said business to its accomplishment'.[10] Like Margery, Dame Elizabeth encouraged John III to persist, if in more forceful terms, reminding him that 'it is only a feeble oak that is cut down at a first stroke'.

One question that Margaret's letter to Dame Elizabeth Brews on 11 June raises is the extent to which John III was involved in its composition. By the end of the month, John III was himself at Stinton Hall with the Brews family. From there he wrote to his mother, 30-or-so miles away in Mautby, with the text of two letters that his mother should send to Salle in her own name, the first to Dame Elizabeth, and the second to John III himself.[11] He asks her that she should follow his wording but have the correspondence copied 'in some other man's hand' so that Dame Elizabeth will not recognise the writing and realise who is really behind it.

The content, tone and voice of these letters, written by John III on behalf of his mother, is fascinating. The letter to Dame Elizabeth addresses the issue of the marriage settlement delicately, shifting any blame away from herself and from John III, who is 'wont to tell me no untruths'. Rather, any fault on the Paston side lies with John III's elder brother, who failed to follow Margaret's wishes. John III even has 'Margaret' make a heartfelt appeal to Dame Elizabeth: 'But, madam, you are a mother as well as I,' reminding her that she has other children whom she must treat with equal generosity, or they will resent her for giving John III 'so much and them so little'. This proviso seems to be a riposte to the earlier assertion by Sir Thomas Brews that he 'would be very loath to bestow so much on one daughter that her other sisters would fare the worse'.[12] The second draft letter, which John III addresses to himself, is intended to be shown to the Brews family, and it urges his immediate return to Mautby. In this letter, he has 'Margaret' warn him that he will lose her support in future if he doesn't follow her advice. He also has 'Margaret' express her sympathy for Margery Brews: if the arrangements fall through, 'I would be as sorry for her as for any gentlewoman living'.

It is only the context in which these two drafts appear that reveals them to be John III's own compositions, written in Margaret's name, but without any input from her. John is effectively ventriloquising his own mother to further his own interests. Is this something that he and his brothers did regularly? While Margaret entrusted Sir James Gloys to write a letter to Walter on her behalf, did she have the same confidence in her sons? It seems feasible, given that even the writing of very personal letters was sometimes entirely delegated to those who acted as scribes. Even in the production of literary texts, collaboration was much more common than we may realise, it was usual for scribes to intervene in the texts which they were copying, and the connection between authorship and original composition that is considered so important today was far less clear. Indeed, many medieval texts, such as *Sir Gawain and the Green Knight*, are anonymous, and sometimes authors had works attributed to them which they certainly didn't write, for example the apocryphal *Tale of Gamelyn*, which appears as one of Chaucer's poems in early manuscripts of *The Canterbury Tales*. We have no way of knowing whether Margaret ultimately decided to have these letters copied and sent, and *if* she did, whether she followed the wording, exonerating John III so completely as it does, or had them edited and emended. The tone of both of John III's drafts is after all quite different from Margaret's own earlier letter to Dame Elizabeth, which demonstrates far more subtle negotiation skills. Margaret was fully behind the marriage, but that does not mean that she allowed herself to be easily manipulated by her son and she might simply have ignored his instructions all together.

Although writers from Chaucer through to de Pizan, Lydgate, Shakespeare and beyond produced Valentine's poetry, the widespread sending of mass-produced Valentine verses and cards only began in the nineteenth century, with the creation of national postal services and stamps; the fashion of sending anonymous missives dates to the same period. Margery Brews' Valentine letters were the product of a very different context, in a period when modern ideas of privacy were only beginning to emerge. What might seem, on the surface, to be a highly intimate exchange between Margery and John III was no such thing. To understand these letters fully, rather than being considered in isolation, they need to be located within this flurry of correspondence from the first half of 1477 that involves the heads of both families, John II and Sir Thomas Brews, and the lovers' mothers, Margaret and Dame Elizabeth.

There was also a fifth, more surprising, figure involved in the marriage negotiations: Thomas Kela, an evidently highly trusted servant in the Brews household. Despite instructing John III not to allow anyone else to see her correspondence, Margery had, perforce, to share her intimate love poetry with Thomas Kela, in whose hand both her Valentine letters are written. Margery, like her future mother-in-law, may well have been unable to write. Or perhaps she simply felt that employing a secretary would in no way compromise the confidentiality and highly personal nature of her communications. Certainly, Sir Thomas Brews and Dame Elizabeth also relied on Kela to act as their scribes in this matter. More unexpectedly, in February 1477, Thomas Kela also wrote directly to John III, urging him to agree to the terms offered by the Brews family.[13] Like John II and Dame Elizabeth, his letter emphasises Margery's ardour for John III, because, as he observes, she has told him about it directly. Kela also quotes from one of Dame Elizabeth's own letters: 'And I heard my lady say that it was a feeble oak that was cut down at the first stroke.'

Did Thomas Kela simply copy out the Brews family letters, either from rough drafts or from dictation, or was he more involved in their composition? He may well have given his employers and their daughter advice and counsel regarding their correspondence. He was involved from the early stages of the marriage negotiations and clearly served as intermediary between the two families. But while it may at first seem unlikely that he did so without his master and mistress's permission, there is reason to think that he was actively recruited as a go-between by John III to further his interests. In his own letter, Kela reminds John III that he, Kela, has made an oath of loyalty: 'As I promised you, I am your man and you shall have my good will in word and deed.' Kela's position in the Brews family was not dissimilar to that which had been enjoyed by Sir James Gloys in Margaret's household, and John III was determined to get his own way, even if that involved a little scheming and deception. Whether or not his mother was complicit in or even encouraged his Machiavellian manoeuvres is unclear.

John Paston III was in his early thirties when he became engaged to Margery. Margery would have been somewhere in her twenties at the time. John III already had an illegitimate son, Jack, who was around the same age as John III's brother William, and whom Margaret had helped care for when he was a child. Because Jack was already fifteen or sixteen years old at the time of John III's marriage, Margery did not have to worry about his upbringing. John III was a courtier and a soldier. A few years after the twenty-year-old John III entered the household of the Duke of Norfolk, he, along with his elder brother, joined the entourage of Margaret of York, sister of Edward IV, when she travelled to Bruges to marry. Having led the defence of Caister, he fought alongside his brother at the Battle of Barnet where he was injured, shot through the lower arm with an arrow. According to his elder brother, writing ten years before the betrothal, John III was a 'personable' or presentable, even handsome man.[14] At the time John III had been considering marrying a neighbour of the Brews family in Salle: a daughter of Sir Geoffrey and Anne Boleyn, and great-aunt of Henry VIII's future queen.

Life at court seems to have come more naturally to John III than to his elder brother, who as a young man was criticised by his family because he lacked the self-assurance to advance in such a competitive environment. From the outset, John III was more confident and assertive. He was also more discerning than his father had been, and he was attentive to Margaret's advice not to trust too much 'in the promises of lords'.[15] He was fully aware of his vulnerability in such treacherous times, quoting to his brother the proverbial verses: 'But Fortune with her smiling countenance strange / Of all our purpose may make a sudden change.'[16]

Appropriately enough for a courtier, John III thought of himself as a wordsmith. Among his draft documents is a poem: 'My right good lord, most knightly gentle knight', addressed to an anonymous superior, perhaps the Earl of Oxford.[17] The speaker in the poem, evidently John III himself, apologises for this unsolicited correspondence and explains why he is sending it. One verse reads:

For when I count and make a reckoning
Between my life, my death, and my desire,
My life, alas, it serves no thing,
Since with your parting departs my pleasure.
Wishing your presence sets me on fire,
But then your absence makes my heart so cold,
That for the pain I don't know where to hold.

The description of the languishing retainer, metaphorically dying for love, is indistinguishable from that of an abandoned paramour, which is precisely the point of the homosocial and homoerotic language of the court, where the oaths men made to their masters were as much a commitment as their marriage vows. Love letters from John III to other women have survived. One secret missive was addressed to 'my own fair Mistress Anne' whom he praised for her ability to read English.[18] Another, written shortly before John III and Margery began their courtship, was to an unnamed woman whom he had not yet even met in person. In this he promised his devotion and obedience, begging the recipient to ease his 'poor heart that sometime was under my rule, which now is at yours'.[19] Whether addressing a man or a woman, John III was adept in his use of the language of service and Margery recognised this. When she sent him her own Valentine verses, she acknowledged their common interest in poetry.

John III and Margery's union lasted less than twenty years – Margery died in 1495 – but it remained a happy one. Like her mother-in-law before her, Margery lived for a time in Norwich, and she also resided at Caister. She seems to have been a doting mother. Around four years into the marriage, Margery wrote to John III from Norwich complaining that neither she nor his mother had heard from him, and reassuring him that his mother was well 'and all your babies are too'.[20] In their time together, the couple had several children, but, like their daughter Anna, their eldest son, Christopher, who was born a year after they married, died in infancy. At the time of this letter from Margery to John III these losses were still in the future. Margery adds a postscript asking her husband to send for her if he plans to remain in London much longer, 'because it seems to me a long time since I lay in your arms'.

In another letter, written around the same time, Margery addresses her husband as 'my own sweetheart';[21] clearly her feelings for him remained as strong as ever. As her correspondence reveals, Margery readily assumed business and domestic responsibilities that had been previously undertaken by Margaret, and demonstrated similar capabilities, even offering to intercede on her husband's behalf with the Duchess of Norfolk, after being advised that 'one word of a woman would do more than the words of twenty men'. Margaret in turn valued Margery's contribution to the family and, evidently, her piety: it was to Margery that Margaret bequeathed her own mass book, silver pyx, cruets and altar cloths. Margaret never regretted the lengths to which she went to secure Margery as a wife for John III.

18. 'AS LONG AS I LIVE'

27 May 1478 and 4 February 1482
(Margaret to her eldest son, and Margaret's will)

Margaret's last extant letter was written to her eldest son, from Mautby, when she was in her late fifties.[1] It dates to a year prior to the deaths of Agnes, Walter and John II. Once again, this letter is concerned with John II's responsibilities as his father's heir. The relationship between Margaret and John II was marred throughout Margaret's widowhood by her son's failure to erect a suitable memorial for his late father at Bromholm Priory. For many years, Margaret had complained that it was a dishonour to the family and a cause of gossip in the neighbourhood that the grave remained unmarked. Despite John II's promise to construct a fitting monument, as the letter of 1478 reveals, the matter remained unresolved, and Margaret feared that he would instead squander the money needed for the project: 'Letting you know that I sent you the cloth of gold by Wheatley, ordering you not to sell it for any other reason than the completion of your father's tomb, and to send me word in writing.'

Margaret goes on to observe in this letter that other families in the area have made generous contributions to the priory

223

church: 'My cousin Clere goes to so much expense at Bromholm as will come to £100 on lecterns in the quire and other places, and Heydon likewise.' There is certainly a strong element of neighbourly rivalry at play here. Elizabeth Clere plans to spend on the church furnishings several times the value of Margaret's cloth of gold. Once again Margaret is concerned about the dishonour that is brought to the family 'to see him [her husband] lie as he does'.

The cloth of gold in question is mentioned in several letters exchanged between Margaret and her two eldest sons. A cloth of gold is a piece of expensive fabric, such as silk, brocaded with gold thread. It is distinguished by its raised design, which is woven into the fabric rather than embroidered on it. Its use in revels and memorials signalled wealth and power. John II had purchased the Paston cloth of gold some years before Margaret's letter of 1478, very possibly at the time of John I's extravagant funeral. Immediately after the death of John de Mowbray, 4th Duke of Norfolk, in 1476, John II was reminded of its existence by a similar cloth draped over the Duke's hearse, and he asked if Margaret could lay her hands on it.[2] Although Margaret was reluctant to part with it, she agreed then that the cloth should be sold, but was insistent that her sons should make sure they receive a good price.[3]

Some of this precious fabric would have been used to cover John I's coffin, like the pall of patterned red and gold depicted by the fifteenth-century French manuscript illuminator Jean Fouquet in a miniature imagining his patron's funeral in *The Hours of Étienne Chevalier*.[4] Some beautiful English palls from the fifteenth and early sixteenth centuries have survived. The Fayrey Pall, which dates to between 1470 and 1530, and is now in the Victoria and Albert Museum, has a centre panel of patterned cloth of gold, with red velvet fabric woven with gold thread, and embroidered sides.[5] Another, possibly later, example of a cloth of gold central panel is the Fishmongers' Pall, still held by the Worshipful Company of Fishmongers.[6] The Paston cloth of gold was much longer than either of these because John II mentions selling twelve yards (or almost eleven metres), and so, even if a pall were made from it, he must also have originally intended to use much of it for other purposes, not necessarily funereal.[7] Cloth of gold was often used for ecclesiastical vestments, and by royalty and the aristocracy. In the mid-1460s John II rode on the king's side in a tournament at Eltham Palace, so it is possible that he also used the fabric at that or another event at court, or when he and his brother travelled to Bruges in the retinue of the king's sister. In the summer of 1520, when Henry VIII met with François I of France for a festival celebrating their friendship, the meeting and the site came to be known as the Field of the Cloth of Gold because so much of the sumptuous fabric was on display in the tents and garments.

The sale of the cloth of gold took longer than expected, with potential buyers losing interest and backing out. Nevertheless, by the spring of 1478, John II was confident that the market for such luxurious fabric was buoyant because at that time Edward IV was commissioning copes and other vestments for the collegiate church of St Mary and All Saints at Fotheringhay in Northamptonshire, where the body of his father, Richard of York, had been reinterred a couple of years previously.[8] John II was in negotiations with a vestment maker, and even though he would still make a considerable loss on the sale, he was confident that by Michaelmas the tomb would finally be complete, and so grand that 'there shall be none like it in Norfolk'. Margaret was not taken in by John II's easy reassurances. He already owed her a great deal of money, and had generally shown himself to be untrustworthy in financial matters. In her response to his confident promises, she reminds him that she has had to pay twenty marks to redeem the gold cloth which apparently had been pawned; this was well over a year's salary for a skilled craftsman. She warns him that 'if you sell it for any other purpose, then on my word of honour I shall never trust you as long as I live'.

Margaret's letter of May 1478 also addresses her son's ongoing land dealings. She advises John II against alienating Elizabeth Clere's son Robert, whom she describes as 'a man of substance and honour', stating, 'I would like each of you to help each other, and live as relatives and friends.' She also encourages him in his attempts to reclaim Hellesdon and Drayton. She has heard that he is doing well at court and enjoys the favour of the King. This brings her to the second piece of business in her letter. Margaret has heard rumours that once again John II has plans to marry, and on this occasion his prospective bride is 'a close relation of the Queen', and so Margaret takes the opportunity to provide her son with some sound advice.

Margaret acknowledges that she does not know the actual identity of the woman in question, but she recognises that the intended union must be purely strategic: 'But if it should be that your land comes back due to your marriage, and is settled in peace, out of respect for God do not abandon it.' This would not, then, be a marriage like that of his brother, John III, which was based on mutual attraction and affection. It would simply be the means to an end: the restoration of Paston property, and also, as Margaret goes on to make clear, the provision of a Paston heir. Margaret – not unreasonably, given John II's protracted entanglement with Anne Haute, whom we might recall was herself a cousin of Edward IV's queen, Elizabeth Woodville – is clearly apprehensive that her son will rush into yet another relationship to which he will be unable to commit himself in the longer term. She adds the proviso that he should only progress with his plans 'if you can find it in your heart to love her, and if she is such a one by whom you can have children. Otherwise, on my word of honour, I would rather you never married in your life.' With her second son now married, and his first child on the way, Margaret felt that she could speak her mind and tell John II outright that he might be better off remaining single.

One of the difficulties Margaret faced with John II was that his ambitions and his emotions seem to have been at odds with one another. While the idea of an advantageous marriage appealed to him, not unusually for a man for his rank, he looked elsewhere for affection and sex. Two letters from lovers of John II have survived in the collection, and they are, in their different ways, revealing about his personal conduct towards women who lacked high social standing or wealth. The first letter was written in the 1460s, when John II was still in his twenties, and his father was still alive.[9] We don't know anything about its author, Cecily Daune, beyond what we can surmise from her letter.

Cecily Daune wrote to John II having heard inaccurate rumours that he was to marry a daughter of Lady Eleanor Beauchamp, the widow of Edmund Beaufort, 2nd Duke of Somerset (it was of course John II's uncle William who wed her daughter, Lady Anne Beaufort). Cecily warns John II against making a hasty union, implying that she has undisclosed information that, if he were privy to it, might make him reconsider. She insists that she is not trying to stand in his way and that she only has his best interests at heart: 'But I shall do and pray to God every day to send you such a person to be your mate in his world who will respect and faithfully and genuinely love you above all other creatures on this earth. Because that is the most excellent riches in the world, I believe.' Her views on the institution of marriage are outlined in terms of which Margaret herself would approve: 'Because worldly goods are transitory and marriage lasts for the term of one's life, which for some people is a very long time.' Unlike Margaret, Cecily expresses herself to John II plaintively, apologising if her intrusion into his affairs is unwelcome.

What is most striking about Cecily's letter is that despite its familiarity and intimacy, there is evidently a significant class divide between writer and addressee. Although it appears that she could write her own name (she signs the letter herself), and therefore had some education, Cecily describes herself not as a friend and equal but as an impoverished inferior, dependent on his gifts for her survival. She complains that winter is coming and that the only clothes she has are those that he has given her. She asks him to have a gown made for her, using the word 'livery' in this context to reveal that she was literally, rather than just metaphorically, his servant. John II had exploited his position in having an affair with a woman who was in his employ, and who may not, ultimately, have felt she had much choice but to go along with it, knowing all the while that the relationship could only ever be transient.

The second love message to John II was written in March 1478, just a couple of months before Margaret's final letter to her son. It is shorter than Cecily's and suggests considerable intrigue.[10] The writer identifies herself as Constance Reynyforth, and she describes her plans for a secret assignation with him. Constance was staying with her cousin in Cobham, either in Surrey or in Kent, and thus unable, without subterfuge, to meet with John II as they had previously arranged. She asks John II to send one of his men to collect her, without revealing who he is, 'and I shall provide a letter in the name of my uncle, which he shall deliver to my cousin as if he were my uncle's messenger, and by this means I will come at your request'. Again, we don't know much more about the identity of John's lover. Constance is far less deferential to John II than

Cecily, and she is evidently not a servant, so she is presumably somewhat nearer him in terms of her social standing. She may even have been educated well enough to write the letter herself. Given its substance she presumably would have if she were able.

It isn't clear whether Margaret knew about John II's affairs, and more specifically whether, in the spring and early summer of 1478, she was aware of his involvement with Constance Reynyforth. Given that she had taken at least some responsibility for Jack, the illegitimate son of John III, she must have accepted that, except for Walter and his younger brother William, her sons were having relationships with women out of wedlock. She was no doubt oblivious or indifferent to the double standards that meant her daughters did not have similar freedom regarding their sexual partners. Margaret found out about Constance Reynyforth soon enough, because sometime the following year Constance gave birth to John II's child, a daughter also called Constance. Indeed, it is possible that Constance was already pregnant in the summer of 1478, when John II was rumoured to be looking for another woman at court to marry.

While Constance's birth isn't discussed directly in the Paston correspondence, John II evidently told his family about it. It would have been important to John II to acknowledge publicly his paternity of the little girl. In so doing, he could establish his control over her upbringing and her future marriage. Eighteen months later, on 6 November 1479, John III wrote to John II about negotiations concerning their brother Edmond's marriage to a young widow, and he mentions an illegitimate son of Edmond's.[11] The boy's mother was a married woman, Mistress Dixon, and her husband brought up the infant, who took his name, as his own lawful offspring. Consequently, when the stepfather died, Edmond was unable automatically to take over the boy's wardship, which had been claimed by the crown. John II would not want to risk something similar happening to his daughter. At the same time, John chose not to marry her mother. If he had done so, according to English inheritance law, in the absence of a legitimate male heir, on his death little Constance, rather than his brother, John III, would automatically have become heir to the Paston fortune.

John III's letter of November 1479 is the one that includes a distressing postscript concerning the severity of the plague in Norwich, where many of his neighbours were dying, and where he was trapped with family and servants with nowhere safe to which they might escape. It is possible that in alluding to his children, his 'young folks' as he calls them, John is including the infant Constance. Certainly, it is likely that he and his wife, Margery, took in John II's child and brought her up alongside her cousins.[12] It isn't clear what happened to her mother. Constance Reynyforth may have died in childbirth or shortly thereafter, or perhaps her uncle or other family banished her in disgrace to a convent.

John III's letter of November 1479 was the last he was to send to his elder brother, because it was that same month that John II succumbed to the plague in London. John III was devastated by his brother's sudden death. He rode to London immediately, with the intention of bringing home his body, along with that of his recently deceased grandmother. He was frustrated in that attempt and struggled to attend to his business in the city, complaining to his mother: 'I have much more to write, but my empty head will not let me remember it.'[13] Margaret's reaction to the loss of her eldest son is unrecorded, but she did remember his daughter Constance in her will.

Margaret's letter of May 1478 was written at a point when she still exerted her matriarchal influence over the extended Paston family. Although it is the last of her correspondence to have survived, it was not the last document she had drawn up and it may not have been the last letter that she wrote. Still the need for her to write surely diminished in the years that followed. After John II's death, his brother John III became head of the household. John III's wife, Margery, took over many of the duties of her mother-in-law regarding the Paston estates and Paston business. Given Margaret's great trust in her daughter-in-law's abilities, she must have been relieved to pass on her responsibilities to this capable woman. Margaret, who had by now lost three of her children – Margery, Walter and John II – as well as Agnes and Sir James Gloys, retreated into her isolated retirement at Mautby, where she became increasingly incapacitated by illness. Her world closed in on her. In February 1482 she drew up her will, informing her daughter-in-law Margery that she believed her end was approaching, and of her planned bequests to her surviving children and servants, and asking her to ensure that her husband honoured them.[14]

Margaret's remaining immediate family members were key benefactors.[15] Edmond, now married, his wife, Katherine, and their son, Robert, are mentioned first and are left specified items, as well as an annuity for their lifetimes. Among their other gifts, Robert is to inherit Margaret's herd of swans. Anne is left an array of household furnishings and ornaments, as well as Margaret's primer, and the marriage money owed to Anne and her husband is to be paid to them. Later in the will, almost as an afterthought, Anne is also left £10. Among his other bequests, William is left 100 marks to be given to him when he comes of age, or to be used for the purchase of land or of a ward for him to marry. Edmond, William and Anne are also left 'the residue of the stuff in my household'. John III and his wife Margery are mentioned after William. Their first child, Christopher, must have already died when the will was drawn up, but 100 marks are left to each of their two other children for when they come of age. John II's daughter Constance is left a sum of ten marks, to be given to her when she is twenty, while Margery's son John Calle is left £20 to come to him when he reaches the age of 24.

What is clear from this will is that Margaret gave considerable thought to her bequests, as she includes more personal items alongside money, household goods and valuable ornamental treasures such as ornate standing cups. The will also reveals a hierarchy of status and favour. John III's children each receive more than the Calles' eldest child, who in turn receives more than John II's illegitimate daughter. That the breach between Margaret and her elder daughter was not fully resolved by the time of the latter's death, and that distance remains between the families, is indicated by the fact that John Calle's two younger brothers are to receive nothing unless the eldest passes away before he has received his inheritance. Anne, on the other hand, is treated generously. The need to find a wife for William once he reaches maturity is clearly an outstanding concern. A more distant family member who is named, and then only much later in the will, is Margaret's cousin, Osbern Berney, who assisted in the defence of Caister.

Following the close family members, Margaret's will lists her bequests to her godchildren, servants and executors. To her servant Agnes Swan, a valued companion during her last years at Mautby, Margaret leaves, as well as her ornamental black girdle and twenty shillings in cash, a gown of musterdevillers and black fur. This grey woollen robe with its black trim and accessories, which would have been worn by Margaret in her later widowhood, contrasts starkly with the bright blue or red dress that, over four decades earlier, Agnes Paston had asked Justice William to buy Margaret for her wedding. Margaret also specifies in her will that her household at Mautby is only to be dissolved six months after her death, presumably to allow her servants the opportunity to find positions elsewhere.

Margaret's bequests don't just tell us about the people who, at the end of her life, mattered to her most, they also tell us about the places that mattered. Margaret leaves goods to pay for repairs to the churches on her estates, including All Saints, Gresham, and money for her tenants. Restoration work is to be undertaken at St John the Baptist in Reedham. Norwich benefits significantly more than Great Yarmouth, despite the proximity of the latter to Mautby. Churches, the cathedral, the friaries and the recluses in the city are all beneficiaries, including an unnamed anchoress at Conesford, likely Dame Elizabeth Scott, a successor to Julian of Norwich. Alms are to be distributed to the poor inhabitants of the Hospital of St Giles, to lepers at the city gates, and to every household in the parish of St Peter Hungate. Prayers are to be recited, diriges chanted and masses celebrated.

At the heart of these services of remembrance is, of course, her funeral at the church of St Peter and St Paul, Mautby. Margaret's hearse is to be accompanied by twelve men, dressed in white hooded gowns. The colour white for mourning dress was popular among late medieval queens on the continent and signifies purity and rebirth. Each of these hooded mourners is to carry a torch, and tapers will burn around the hearse during and after the funeral service. According to the customs of medieval Christianity, Margaret's yearday, the anniversary of her death, will be celebrated with a religious office or service for twelve years. Instructions are given for requiem masses for herself and her parents, her husband and his ancestors. A candle is to burn on her grave for the next seven years.

But most important of all, in the will, are the detailed directions concerning Margaret's burial. Margaret specifies that she is to be placed in the south aisle of the church of

St Peter and St Paul, 'before the image of Our Lady', where her ancestors rest. This aisle is to receive a new roof, its walls are to be rebuilt, and the windows leaded and glazed. Margaret had been planning the new aisle at Mautby for at least a decade before she wrote her will, and she is resolute that her heirs will see the work done.[16] She is equally determined that, unlike her neglected husband, she should have an appropriate sepulchre. Her will stipulates that, within a year of her death, a marble slab should be placed over her grave.

Unfortunately, the south aisle on the church was demolished during or after the Reformation. Only the outline of the blocked arcade is visible from inside the church, and the faint outline of the foundations of the aisle can, in dry weather, be detected in the grass. Facing the church, this runs from a buttress on the right to beyond the porch on the left. The image of the Virgin Mary, whether a carved statue, painted icon or stained-glass depiction, is long gone. Although its likely site is now marked by an engraved memorial stone, installed just a few years ago, with grass and dandelions already encroaching on its edges, Margaret's tomb has also vanished, having been razed to the ground with the aisle in which it stood. Nevertheless, the instructions in Margaret's will enable us to envisage it. The marble slab is to be set with escutcheons, or shields, displaying the coats of arms of her ancestors and of her husband.

As she approaches her death, Margaret's status as a Paston widow is less significant to her than her own heritage. Her final instructions read: 'In the midst of the said stone I will have an escutcheon set of the Mautby's arms alone, and under the same, these words written: "In God is my trust."' Around the edges, the marble tomb is to be inscribed with the words, 'Here lies Margaret Paston, late the wife of John Paston, daughter and heir of John Mautby, squire' and, after the date of her death, 'on whose soul God have mercy'.

EPILOGUE

B lo' Norton Hall is a timber-framed, gabled and moated Elizabethan great house located deep in the East Anglian countryside, near the border between South Norfolk and Suffolk, around eight miles from Diss. This is where Virginia Woolf and her sister, Vanessa, stayed with family and friends in August 1906. The hall and its moat have medieval origins, but the house was rebuilt and extended in the sixteenth century, as its leaded bay windows, fireplaces and carved wooden hall screen testify. It still stands in its own estate, with, on its south and west sides, beautiful gardens: a parterre of box and bay, a pond, topiary and roses trained up its pink and brick walls. The estate and farm buildings lie to the east. Next to the abandoned and derelict kennels that formerly housed the hunting hounds is a recently resurfaced tennis court. The hall itself, until recently once again let out as a rather exalted holiday home, is furnished with antiques and paintings.

That so much of the historic building has been preserved is largely due to one person, Prince Frederick Duleep Singh, a son of the exiled last Maharajah of the Sikh Empire, who took out the lease on it three years after Woolf's visit and lived there until his death in the 1920s.[1] He was a keen archaeologist and conservationist, who not only resisted any modernisation of

Blo' Norton Hall (including the installation of electricity), but, as a member of the Society for the Protection of Ancient Buildings, helped prevent the demolition of a number of historical structures, including St Peter Hungate Church in Norwich, the same church that Margaret and her husband paid to have restored, and the church where Margaret's beloved son Walter was buried.

When I stay at Blo' Norton in a mild and sunny early spring, it is in one of the converted barns rather than the house itself. There are maintenance staff but no other visitors, so it feels like we have the estate to ourselves. The sense of isolation from the modern world is remarkable, with little passing traffic and the sound of birdsong only occasionally being disturbed by dogs barking on the neighbouring farms and the crack of automated bird scarers in the surrounding fields. We see roe deer, muntjac, herons and hares, lots of hares, and listen to the sound of woodpeckers and pheasants, and, in the evening, the call of the tawny owls in the treeline and, much closer, the screech of a barn owl nesting in a nearby hollowed-out tree. We enjoy the swathes of snowdrops, aconites and early daffodils in the grounds of the hall.

Half a mile away, towards Thelnetham Windmill, is a network of fens running along the Little Ouse that are regenerating, gradually returning to the condition they would have been in prior to the Second World War. We take our dogs to walk along the muddy paths and board walks that crisscross the wetland as the mist burns off in the morning sun. In many respects, the countryside seems to have changed little since Woolf's visit. In her diary, Woolf describes her exploration by foot of 'this strange, grey green, undulating, dreaming, philosophising & remembering land'.[2] Yet at that time, navigating one's way through the wetlands was more challenging than it is today, and she complains that 'though a walk in the fen has a singular charm, it is not to be undertaken as a way of getting to places'.[3]

'The Journal of Mistress Joan Martyn', the 'beautiful brilliant' tale that Woolf wrote while she stayed at Blo' Norton Hall, is set in the relatively close vicinity, somewhere on the road between Norwich and East Harling.[4] The story opens with Rosamond Merridew, Woolf's fictional historian of late medieval land tenure, a single and childfree scholar in her mid-forties who spends her days on the hunt for as-yet-undiscovered sources. Merridew shares Woolf's enchantment with the quotidian existence of men and women from the past, people whose lives she encounters in the margins of her research and seeks to bring to life again in her writing. Indeed, Merridew reflects on the criticism she has received for straying too close to the creative realm of the author; imagination has its place 'but it should be allowed to claim no relationship with the sterner art of the Historian'.[5]

A spontaneous detour on her return journey from a research trip in Norfolk leads Merridew to 'one of those humble little old Halls, then, which survive almost untouched, & practically unknown for centuries & centuries, because they are too insignificant to be pulled down or rebuilt; & their owners are too poor to be ambitious'. Martyn's Hall shares many of the features of Blo' Norton Hall, including the wooded approach and the shape of the building, 'built like the letter E with the middle notch smoothed out of it'.[6]

Martyn's Hall, like Blo' Norton, is far less grand than Oxnead, where many of the Paston letters were discovered in the eighteenth century by Blomefield, but it is here, in Woolf's story, that Merridew comes upon the late-fifteenth-century diary of a young Norfolk woman that forms its second part. If Merridew the scholar is one alter ego of Woolf the writer, then Joan Martyn is another. Although the narrative voice of this half of the story seems much younger, we are told that the diary was written when the unmarried Joan was 25 years old, almost the same age as Woolf when she was writing the story. Joan's journal offers the unique perspective of an unmarried, educated and literate young woman, living happily at home with her parents, who is encouraged in her writing by her father (as Woolf herself was). Although indebted to the Paston correspondence in many of its details, Joan's story imaginatively fills the gap in the historical record left by the absence of any correspondence from women such as Margaret's sister-in-law Elizabeth prior to her marriages, or from Margaret's daughters Margery and Anne. It also offers a far more positive portrayal of the life of an unmarried daughter.

Particularly arresting is the portrayal of Joan's mother in the journal, inspired by Woolf's reading of the letters of Margaret Paston. The nostalgia and mourning encapsulated in this part of the narrative anticipate the memorialisation of Woolf's late mother, Julia Stephen, in her subsequent work, most famously in the depiction of Mrs Ramsay in her 1927 novel *To the Lighthouse*; indeed, the 'journal' is a paean to motherhood. The entries begin with Joan's mother closing the gates to the hall on a cold January evening, shutting out the world and its threats, and providing safety and comfort to the family and servants within. But Joan's arcadian existence is threatened by plans for her marriage, which she initially resists: 'So that I might continue in this country which I love, and might live on close to my mother, I would take less than my right both of wealth & of land.'[7] The diary ends before Joan's marriage takes place, with a visit with her father to the local church, and Joan's reflections on the tombs of her ancestors. And indeed, from the frame narrative, we already know that this marriage will never take place, and that Joan is fated to die just a few years later.

Like my reading of Margaret Paston's letters, my reading of Virginia Woolf's 'The Journal of Mistress Joan Martyn' is inevitably inflected by my own experience, causing me to reflect further upon my identification with Woolf's writing and with the losses and desires that drive it. Once again, I am reminded of my mother's absence. While Margaret Paston's position in society was so very much more exalted than my mother's, I recognise in Rosamond Merridew's descriptions of the stolid Mr and Mrs Martyn something of my impressions of my mother's parents, even though I never knew my grandfather and by the time I was born my grandmother was already in her late sixties. I am particularly struck that Merridew says of Mrs Martyn, 'she looked like a housekeeper'.[8] In fact, prior to her marriage to my grandfather, my already-widowed grandmother had been employed as housekeeper on his farm.

I also find in Woolf's portrayal of Martyn's Hall, 'the dignified little house', echoes of my mother's childhood home, Earby Hall in Newsham, ten miles or so from Richmond in North Yorkshire. Earby Hall is not a building that has been passed down through generations of my family. Rather it was part of the farm which my grandfather and his older brother, Tom, took over when they sought a larger landholding in the years after Tom's return from fighting in the First World War. Earby, as my mother called it, dates back in parts to the seventeenth century, and was used in the eighteenth and nineteenth centuries as a boarding school akin to the notorious Dotheboys Hall of Charles Dickens's *Nicholas Nickleby*, which is set in nearby Greta Bridge. My mother recalled that initials were carved on the walls of a former classroom, by then a cowshed, and that her aunt had once found a boy's suit and other possessions hidden under the floorboards. Her aunt promptly burned them, despite my mother's protestations.

Like Blo' Norton at the time of Woolf's visit, Earby had not yet had electricity installed when my mother first lived there, but despite the privations, and its haunting past, she found it an enchanting place in which to grow up. While I have never set foot in Earby Hall itself (although one of my aunts continued to live in the farm cottage with her family throughout my childhood), its furniture and furnishings were very familiar to me. I recall as a small child sleeping in the featherbed, or feather tick as my mother sometimes called it, that had been brought from Earby, on my grandparents' retirement to their new home in Barnard Castle. It had been my parents' when they first married, before they moved to the west coast of Scotland, where I was born, and had a house of their own. I have vivid sensory impressions of this bed, which was a delight to climb into with its deep, soft mattress, but which, by the morning, was flat and hard, and required considerable effort to plump back up.

After her years in Scotland, when we children had all left home, my mother returned to the landscape of her childhood. She inherited from Uncle Tom a house called Greystones, situated in a hamlet a few miles from Earby, near the border with County Durham. Like Margaret Paston in preparation for her retirement at Mautby, my mother set about a renovation project, which in the case of Greystones primarily meant replacing the windows with double glazing and installing central heating and a modern kitchen. Greystones has a field adjoining its large garden. A small plantation when Uncle Tom bought it, he cleared it to make a paddock for his horse, because he had never learnt to drive. My mother set about filling it once again with trees, to enable the wildlife to flourish. She lived there for almost 30 years, initially with my father, and then, after she was widowed, on her own, keeping an eye on her family from a distance. Sadly, my brother predeceased her, just a few months before she herself passed away.

Unlike Margaret, my mother did not make extensive plans for her own funeral and left only the sketchiest of instructions from which my sister and I had to work. As a result, we squabbled over many of the details, and indeed struggled to agree even on some of the most basic facts that had to be recorded on her death certificate. One detail which we both agreed upon when arranging the funeral was that her coffin should be made of Swaledale wool, in acknowledgement of her childhood on the farm and love of nature and animals. There were to be no candles or memorial masses or hooded mourners for my mother; hers was just a simple funeral with traditional hymns, attended by family, friends and neighbours. It was held at the crematorium chapel in the beautiful Victorian West Cemetery in Darlington. Nor was there to be an elaborate tomb. My mother's ashes were scattered in her garden, alongside those of my father and brother and near the grave of our family dog. In her memory, I adopted an oak tree near the old Cascade Bridge in the Yorkshire Sculpture Park.

Remembering my mother's passing brings me back again to Margaret Paston and Virginia Woolf. Woolf found a way through her mourning by writing about the past, and I have stumbled upon similar consolation. I think of the arcs of the lives of these two women, born so many centuries apart. Margaret's, as we know it, began with her marriage, and ended after almost two decades of widowhood in Mautby, north of the Bure. Virginia's spans from her childhood through to her premature death. A couple of years ago, while I was writing this book, I made the pilgrimage to Monk's House in Rodmell, where Woolf was living with her husband when she ended her own life, and we retraced her last walk down to the Sussex Ouse. I now notice the tragic irony that in her diary entries for her visit to Blo' Norton, the youthful Woolf records losing her footing when she tried to jump across the Norfolk tributary that shares its name.[9] I am inevitably reminded by association of the Ouse flowing through York, and then of the Tees in Barnard Castle, and the Swale in Richmond where my mother went to school, and of the Yare and the Bure where Margaret was born and died. Haunted by dead women, if not by their rivers, I recognise that it is finally time to give up their ghosts.

I make a promise to myself to revisit Monk's House and the Ouse, and pick up two stones, one for Margaret Paston and one for my mother. I will take Margaret's to Mautby, to place on the site of her grave. The other I will keep.

SELECT BIBLIOGRAPHY

1. Editions and Translations

Barber, Richard, ed., *The Pastons: A Family in the Wars of the Roses* (Woodbridge, Suffolk: Boydell Press, 1993).

Davis, Norman, ed., *The Paston Letters: A Selection in Modern Spelling* (Oxford: Oxford University Press, 1983).

Davis, Norman (vols 1 and 2) and Richard Beadle and Colin Richmond (vol. 3), eds, *Paston Letters and Papers of the Fifteenth Century*, Early English Text Society S.S. 20–22 (Oxford: Oxford University Press, 2004–5).

Gairdner, John, ed., *The Paston Letters, A.D. 1422–1509*, 6 vols (London: Chatto and Windus, 1904).

Virgoe, Roger, ed., *Private Life in the Fifteenth Century: Illustrated Letters of the Paston Family* (London: Macmillan, 1989).

Watt, Diane, trans. and ed., *The Paston Women: Selected Letters* (Cambridge: D.S. Brewer, 2004).

2. Secondary Sources

Barron, Caroline, 'Who were the Pastons?', *Journal of the Society of Archivists* 4 (1972): 530–5.

Bennett, H.S., *The Pastons and their England*, 2nd edn (Cambridge: Cambridge University Press, 1932).

Bosse, Roberta Bux, 'Female Sexual Behavior in the Late Middle Ages: Ideal and Actual,' *Fifteenth-Century Studies* 10 (1984): 15–37.

Castor, Helen, *Blood and Roses: The Paston Family in the Fifteenth Century* (London: Faber and Faber, 2004).

Clayton, Jane, 'Elizabeth Clere and Marriage between the Clere and Paston Families in the Late Fifteenth Century', *Notes and Queries* 66.2 (2019): 214–16.

Clayton, M. J. [Jane], 'Looking for Anna: The Search for Anne Paston,' *Norfolk Archaeology* 48.2 (2019): 218–223.

Clayton, Jane, 'Discovering Constance: Reconstructing the Life of the Illegitimate Daughter of John Paston II,' *Medieval Feminist Forum: A Journal of Gender and* Sexuality 56.2 (2021): 93–124.

Dalrymple, Roger, 'Reaction, Consolation and Redress in the Letters of the Paston Women' in *Early Modern Women's Letter Writing, 1450–1700*, ed. James Daybell (Basingstoke: Palgrave, 2001), pp.16–28.

Daybell, James, 'Medieval Women's Letters, 1350–1500' in *The History of British Women's Writing, 700–1500*, eds Liz Herbert McAvoy and Diane Watt (Basingstoke: Palgrave, 2012), pp.178–86.

Dockray, Keith, 'Why Did Fifteenth-Century English Gentry Marry?: The Pastons, Plumptons, and Stonors Reconsidered' in *Gentry and Lesser Nobility in Late Medieval Europe*, ed. Michael Jones (Gloucester: Alan Sutton, 1986), pp.61–80.

Ferrante, Joan M., *To the Glory of Her Sex: Women's Roles in the Composition of Medieval Texts* (Bloomington, Indiana: Indiana University Press, 1997).

Finke, Laurie A., *Women's Writing in English: Medieval England* (London: Longman, 1999).

Gies, Frances, and Joseph Gies, *A Medieval Family: The Pastons of Fifteenth-Century England* (New York: HarperCollins, 1998).

Harding, Wendy, 'Medieval Women's Unwritten Discourse on Motherhood: A Reading of Two Fifteenth-Century Texts,' *Women's Studies* 21 (1992): 197–209.

Haskell, Ann S., 'The Paston Women on Marriage in Fifteenth-Century England,' *Viator* 4 (1973): 459–71.

Howard, Samuel R., *Mautby Remembrance: A Personal Observation of the Medieval Villages* (Hemsby, Norfolk: Desne, 1996).

Knowles, David, 'The Religion of the Pastons,' *Downside Review* 42 (1924): 143–63.

Krug, Rebecca, *Reading Families: Women's Literate Practice in Late Medieval England* (Ithaca: Cornell University Press, 2002).

Maddern, Philippa, 'Honour among the Pastons: Gender and Integrity in Fifteenth-Century English Provincial Society,' *Journal of Medieval History* 14 (1988): 357–71.

Moss, Rachel E., *Fatherhood and its Representations in Middle English Texts* (Cambridge: D.S. Brewer, 2013).

Price, Vicki Kay, '"I shall send yw money to by such stufe as I wull haue": The Paston Shoppers' in *Women's Literary Cultures in the Global Middle Ages: Speaking Internationally*, eds Kathryn Loveridge, Liz Herbert McAvoy, Sue Niebrzydowski and Vicki Kay Price (Cambridge: D.S. Brewer, 2023), pp.277–92.

Richardson, Malcolm, 'Women, Commerce, and Rhetoric in Medieval England' in *Listening to Their Voices: The Rhetorical Activities of Historical Women*, ed. Molly Meijer Wertheimer (Columbia: University of South Carolina Press, 1997), pp.133–49.

Richmond, Colin, 'The Paston's Revisited: Marriage and Family in Fifteenth-Century England,' *Bulletin of the Institute of Historical Research* 58 (1985): 25–36.

Richmond, Colin, *The Paston Family in the Fifteenth-Century: The First Phase* (Cambridge: Cambridge University Press, 1990).

Richmond, Colin, *The Paston Family in the Fifteenth Century: Fastolf's Will* (Cambridge: Cambridge University Press, 1996).

Richmond, Colin, *The Paston Family in the Fifteenth-Century: Endings* (Manchester: Manchester University Press, 2000).

Richmond, Colin, 'Elizabeth Clere: Friend of the Pastons' in *Medieval Women: Texts and Contexts in Late Medieval Britain, Essays for Felicity Riddy*, eds Jocelyn Wogan-Browne, Rosalynn Voaden, Arlyn Diamond, Ann Hutchison, Carol M. Meale and Lesley Johnson (Turnhout: Brepols, 2000), pp.251–73.

Rosenthal, Joel T., 'Looking for Grandmother: The Pastons and their Counterparts in Late Medieval England' in *Medieval Mothering*, eds John Carmi Parsons and Bonnie Wheeler (New York: Garland, 1996), pp.259–77.

Rosenthal, Joel T., *Telling Tales: Sources and Narration in Late Medieval England* (University Park, Pennsylvania: The Pennsylvania State University Press, 2003).

Rosenthal, Joel T., *Margaret Paston's Piety* (Basingstoke: Palgrave, 2010).

Stiller, Nikki, *Eve's Orphans: Mothers and Daughters in Medieval English Literature* (Westport, Connecticut: Greenwood Press, 1980).

Stoker, David, '"Innumerable Letters of Good Consequence in History"': The Discovery and First Publication of the Paston Letters', *The Library* 17 (1995): 107–55.

Tarvers, Josephine Koster, 'In a Woman's Hand? The Question of Medieval Women's Holograph Letters,' *Post-Script* 13 (1996): 89–100.

Watt, Diane, '"No Writing for Writing's Sake": The Language of Service and Household Rhetoric in the Letters of the Paston Women' in *Dear Sister: Medieval Women and the Epistolary Genre*, eds Karen Cherewatuk and Ulrike

Wiethaus (Philadelphia: University of Pennsylvania Press, 1993), pp.122–38.

Watt, Diane, *Medieval Women's Writing: Works by and for Women, 1100–1500* (Cambridge: Polity Press, 2007).

Whitaker, Elaine E., 'Reading the Paston Letters Medically,' *English Language Notes* 31 (1993): 19–27.

Woolf, Virginia, 'The Pastons and Chaucer' in *The Common Reader*, 1st series (London: Hogarth Press, 1925), pp.13–38.

NOTES

Author's Note

1. London, British Library, Add MS 43488, Add MS 43489, Add MS 43490, Add MS 43491, and Add MS 33597.
2. David Stoker, '"Innumerable Letters of Good Consequence in History": The Discovery and First Publication of the Paston Letters,' *The Library*, 17.2 (1995): 107–55.
3. London, British Library, Add MS 43490, f.34r–v.

Introduction

1. *The Paston Letters and Papers of the Fifteenth Century*, 3 vols, ed. Norman Davis (vols 1 and 2) and Richard Beadle and Colin Richmond (vol. 3), Early English Text Society S.S. 20–22 (Oxford: Oxford University Press, 2004–05); *The Paston Women: Selected Letters*, ed. and trans. Diane Watt (London: D. S. Brewer, 2004). All references are to these editions, abbreviated *PL* Davis, *PL* Beadle and Richmond, and *SL* Watt, unless otherwise stated. Citations are by letter number.
2. Virginia Woolf, *A Room of One's Own* and *Three Guineas*, ed. Morag Shiach (Oxford: Oxford University Press, 1998), p.116.
3. *The Paston letters, A.D. 1422–1509*, ed. James Gairdner, 4 vols (Westminster: Archibald Constable and Co, 1900).

4. Sotheby's London, *English Literature, History, Children's Books and Illustrations*, 14 July 2011, Auction Catalogue, Lot 117, available online at https://www.sothebys.com/en/auctions/ecatalogue/2011/english-literature-history-childrens-books-illustrations-l11404/lot.117.html. I am grateful to the current private owner who kindly answered my questions about the volume and to Dr Philip W. Errington for putting us in contact.
5. *The Letters of Virginia Woolf: The Flight of the Mind, 1888–1912*, eds Nigel Nicolson and Joanne Trautmann (London: Hogarth Press, 1975), vol. 1, no.248.
6. *The Letters of Virginia Woolf*, eds Nicolson and Trautmann, vol.1, no.249.
7. Susan M. Squier and Louise A. DeSalvo, 'Virginia Woolf's "The Journal of Mistress Joan Martyn,"' *Twentieth Century Literature* 25.3/4 (1979): 237–69.
8. Virginia Woolf, 'The Pastons and Chaucer,' in *The Common Reader* (Harmondsworth: Penguin, 1938), pp.12–31.
9. Woolf, 'The Journal of Mistress Joan Martyn,' p.252.
10. Woolf, 'The Pastons and Chaucer,' p.20.
11. See *Poems and Carols (Oxford, Bodleian Library MS Douce 302) by John the Blind Audelay*, ed. Susanna Greer Fein (Kalamazoo, MI: TEAMS/Western Michigan, 2009), no.38.
12. Nikolaus Pevsner, *The Buildings of England: Northeast Norfolk and Norwich* (Harmondsworth: Penguin, 1962), p.298n.
13. Pevsner, *Northeast Norfolk and Norwich*, p.298n.

Chapter 1

1. For the Berney family tree, see *British History Online*, 'Walsham Hundred: Reedham' at https://www.british-history.ac.uk/topographical-hist-norfolk/vol11/pp121-132#fnn12.

2. *PL* Davis 230.
3. *PL* Davis 13; *SL* Watt 1.
4. *Middle English Dictionary*, s.v. 'hous-wif', n; Jenni Nuttall, *Mother Tongue: The Surprising History of Women's Words* (London: Virago, 2023), p.181.
5. *The Good Wife's Guide (Le Ménagier de Paris): A Medieval Household Book*, trans. Gina L. Greco and Christine M. Rose (Ithaca: Cornell University Press, 2012), p.303.
6. *Oxford English Dictionary*, s.v. 'Lollard', n.1.
7. *PL* Davis, vol. I, pp.xli–xlii.
8. *PL* Davis, vol. I, p.xl.
9. *PL* Davis 124.
10. J.M. Lambert, J.N. Jennings, C.T. Smith, Charles Green, and J.N. Hutchinson, *The Making of the Broads: A Reconsideration of their Origin in the Light of New Evidence* (London: Royal Geographical Society/John Murray, 1960).
11. 'How the Goode Wife Taught Hyr Doughter' in *The Trials and Joys of Marriage*, ed. Eve Salisbury (Kalamazoo, MI: Medieval Institute Publications, 2002), lines 27–28.
12. 'Troilus and Criseyde', book II, l.651, in *The Riverside Chaucer*, ed. Larry D. Benson (Boston, Mass.: Houghton Mifflin Co, 1987).

Chapter 2

1. 'The General Prologue', l.460, in *The Riverside Chaucer*, ed. Larry D. Benson (Boston, Mass.: Houghton Mifflin Co, 1987).
2. *PL* Davis 124.
3. *PL* Davis 125; *SL* Watt 21.
4. *PL* Davis 230.
5. *Middle English Dictionary*, s.v. 'fetis, -ice', adj.2.
6. 'The Romaunt of the Rose', ll.776, 821 and 1241, in *The Riverside Chaucer*, ed. Benson.

7. The 'Liber de Diversis Medicinis' in the Thornton Manuscript (MS Lincoln Cathedral A.5.2), ed. Margaret Sinclair Ogden, Early English Texts Society, original series 207 (London: Oxford University Press, 1938), p.56. Since the publication of this edition, the Thornton manuscript has been renumbered as MS 91.

8. Monica H. Green, 'Women's Medical Practice and Health Care in Medieval Europe', *Signs* 14.2 (1989): 434–73 (at 450).

9. *The Trotula: An English Translation of the Medieval Compendium of Women's Medicine*, ed. and trans. Monica H. Green (Philadelphia: University of Pennsylvania Press, 2002).

10. *The Lais of Marie de France*, trans. Keith Busby and Glyn S. Burgess, 2nd edition (Harmondsworth: Penguin, 1999), p.62.

11. *The Book of Margery Kempe*, trans. Anthony Bale (Oxford: Oxford University Press, 2015), pp.21–2.

12. *PL* Davis 151.

13. Jacobus de Voragine, *The Golden Legend: Readings on the Saints*, trans. William Granger Ryan, intro. Eamon Duffy (Princeton: Princeton University Press, 1993).

14. De Voragine, *The Golden Legend*, p.369.

15. London, British Library, MS Harley Ch 43 A 14.

16. London, Wellcome Collection, Western MS. 632; see Sarah Fiddyment, Natalie J. Goodison, Elma Brenner, Stefania Signorello, Kierri Price and Matthew J. Collins, 'Girding the Loins? Direct Evidence of the Use of a Medieval English Parchment Birthing Girdle from Biomolecular Analysis', *Royal Society Open Science* 8.3 (2021), http://doi.org/10.1098/rsos.202055.

17. Sue Niebrzydowski, 'Marian Literature' in *The History of British Women's Writing, 700–1500*, eds Liz Herbert McAvoy and Diane Watt (London: Palgrave, 2012), p.117.

Chapter 3

1. *PL* Davis 126; *SL* Watt 22.
2. *PL* Davis 177.
3. Monica H. Green, *Making Women's Medicine Masculine: The Rise of Male Authority in Pre-Modern Gynaecology* (Oxford: Oxford University Press, 2008).
4. Thomas Benedek, 'The Roles and Images of Medieval Women in the Healing Arts' in *The Roles and Images of Women in the Middle Ages and Renaissance*, ed. Douglas Radcliffe-Umstead (Pittsburgh, PA: Center for Medieval and Renaissance Studies, Institute for the Human Sciences 1975), pp.145–59 (p.152).
5. 'A Petition to the Parliament of 1421 for Protective Legislation' *Sources for the History of Medicine in Late Medieval England*, ed. Carole Rawcliffe (Kalamazoo, MI: Medieval Institute Publications, 1995), pp.62–4.
6. The ballad is reproduced in its entirety online on the Walsingham Archives website at https://www.walsinghamanglicanmedieval.org.uk/pynson.htm. The sole surviving copy of the pamphlet is Cambridge, Magdalene College, MS Pepys 1254.
7. *PL* Davis 399.
8. An inventory of the goods in the Priory dating to c.1422, which includes descriptions of the statues and relics, is edited and translated by W.T. Bensly, 'St Leonard's Priory, Norwich', *Norfolk Archaeology* 12 (1895): 189–227.
9. *English Hawking and Hunting in* The Boke of St Albans, ed. Rachel Hands (Oxford: Oxford University Press, 1975).
10. *The Good Wife's Guide: Le Ménagier de Paris, A Medieval Household Book,* eds Gina L. Greco and Christine M. Rose (Ithaca: Cornell University Press, 2009), p.233.

11. Robin S. Oggins, *The Kings and their Hawks: Falconry in Medieval England* (New Haven: Yale University Press, 2004), pp.118–19.
12. *The Good Wife's Guide,* eds Greco and Rose, p.233.

Chapter 4
1. *PL* Davis 130; *SL* Watt 26.
2. *PL* Davis 36.
3. *PL* Davis 131; *SL* Watt 27.
4. *PL* Davis 132; *SL* Watt 28.
5. *PL* Davis 264; London, British Library, MS Add. 43489, f.47r.
6. See the 3D reconstruction at 'This is Paston: Gresham Castle', at https://www.thisispaston.co.uk/gresham01.html.
7. 'This is Paston: Gresham Walk', at https://www.thisispaston.co.uk/ux/file/ref=15&ty=DOCS
8. London, British Library, Royal MS 10 E IV, f.43v. However, the same manuscript also includes humorous and parodic representations of war, such as giant snail attacking a knight on f.107r. The image of the knight fighting a snail is common in thirteenth- and fourteenth-century manuscripts and its meaning or symbolism is widely debated.
9. *PL* Davis 127; *SL* Watt 23.
10. *English Historical Documents I: c.500–1042),* ed. Dorothy Whitelock (2nd ed., London: Eyre Methuen, 1979), p.470.
11. *The Lais of Marie de France*, trans. Glyn S. Burgess and Keith Busby, 2nd edition (Harmondsworth, Penguin, 1999), pp.68–72.

Chapter 5
1. *PL* Davis 141; *SL* Watt 30.
2. *Middle English Dictionary*, s.v. 'pestilence', n.1.a and 1.b.
3. Monica H. Green, 'Putting Africa on the Black Death Map: Narratives from Genetics and History *Afriques* 9 (2018), https://journals.openedition.org/afriques/2125.

4. Giovanni Boccaccio, *The Decameron*, trans. John Payne (New York, Walter J. Black, n.d.), p.2.
5. *The Black Death*, trans. and ed. Rosemary Horrox (Manchester: Manchester University Press, 1994), p.66.
6. 'The Pardoner's Tale', ll.675–6 and 679, in *The Riverside Chaucer*, ed. Larry D. Benson (Boston, Mass.: Houghton Mifflin Co, 1987).
7. *The Black Death*, trans. and ed. Horrox, p.78.
8. *PL* Davis 25; *SL* Watt 10.
9. *PL* Davis 26; *SL* Watt 11.
10. *PL* Davis 147.
11. *PL* Davis 220; *SL* Watt 69.
12. J.P. Griffin, 'Venetian Treacle and the Foundation of Medicines Regulation,' *British Journal of Clinical Pharmacology*, 58.3 (2004): 317–25.
13. *PL* Davis 313.
14. *PL* Davis 381.
15. *PL* Davis 751 and 755. This book has been identified as Boston, Harvard Medical School, Countway Library of Medicine, Ballard MS 19.
16. *PL* Davis 389.
17. *PL* Davis 7.
18. *PL* Davis 220; *SL* Watt 69.
19. *PL* Davis 711.
20. Christine de Pizan, *The Treasure of the City of Ladies or The Book of the Three Virtues*, trans. Sarah Lawson (London: Penguin, 1985), p.50.
21. *PL* Davis 128; *SL* Watt 24.
22. *PL* Davis 135.

Chapter 6
1. *PL* Davis 146; *SL* Watt 32.
2. Colin Richmond, 'Elizabeth Clere: Friend of the Pastons' in *Medieval Women: Texts and Contexts in Late*

Medieval Britain: Essays for Felicity Riddy, eds Jocelyn Wogan-Browne et al. (Turnhout, Belgium: Brepols, 2000), pp.251–72 at p.252.

3. *PL* Davis 145; *SL* Watt 31.

4. *The Paston letters, A.D. 1422–1509*, ed. James Gairdner, 6 vols (London: Chatto and Windus, 1904), no.235.

5. *PL* Davis 496.

6. *PL* Davis 512.

7. William Shakespeare, *Henry VI, Part 3*, ed. Randall Martin (Oxford: OUP, 2001), I.iv.111–15.

8. *PL* Beadle and Richmond 1029.

9. 'Houses of Benedictine Monks: The Cathedral Priory of the Holy Trinity, Norwich', *British History Online* at https://www.british-history.ac.uk/vch/norf/vol2/pp317-328.

10. Nikolaus Pevsner, *The Buildings of England: Northeast Norfolk and Norwich* (Harmondsworth: Penguin, 1962), p.207.

11. Thomas of Monmouth, *The Life and Passion of William of Norwich*, ed. Miri Rubin (Harmondsworth: Penguin, 1994).

12. See the transcription of the will in Jane Clayton, 'A Study of the Letters and Wills of the Lesser-Known Paston Women' (University of Surrey PhD thesis, 2021), pp.262–72.

13. *PL* Davis 230.

14. *PL* Davis 320.

15. *PL* Davis 206; *SL* Watt 63.

16. Jane Clayton, 'Elizabeth Clere and Marriage between the Clere and Paston Families in the Late Fifteenth Century', *Notes and Queries* 66.2 (2019): 214–16.

17. *PL* Davis 500, 600 and 724; *SL* Watt 77, 78, and 79.

18. *PL* Davis 190; *SL* Watt 51.

19. *PL* Davis 209; *SL* Watt 64.

20. Richmond, 'Elizabeth Clere: Friend of the Pastons', pp.270–2.
21. Marian Campbell, *Medieval Jewellery in Europe, 1100–1500* (London: V&A Publishing, 2009), pp.10–11 and plate 4.
22. Campbell, *Medieval Jewellery in Europe*, pp.55–7 and plate 54.

Chapter 7

1. Georgine de Courtais, *Women's Hats, Headdresses and Hairstyles* (Mineola, NY: Dover Publications, 2006), pp.27–37.
2. Nikolaus Pevsner, *The Buildings of England: Northeast Norfolk and Norwich* (Harmondsworth: Penguin, 1962), p.270.
3. *PL* Davis 144.
4. *PL* Davis 147.
5. *PL* Davis 150; *SL* Watt 34.
6. C.M. Woolgar, *The Great Household in Late Medieval England* (New Haven, CT: Yale University Press, 1999), p.65.
7. *PL* Davis 446; *SL* Watt 76.
8. *PL* Beadle and Richmond 1040.
9. *PL* Beadle and Richmond 1012.
10. 'The Tale of Gamelyn' in *Robin Hood and Other Outlaw Tales*, eds. Stephen Knight and Thomas H. Ohlgren (Kalamazoo, MI: Medieval Institute Publications, 1997).
11. *PL* Beadle and Richmond 1039.
12. *PL* Davis 28; *SL* Watt 12.
13. *PL* Davis 121; *SL* Watt 18.
14. *PL* Davis 123; *SL* Watt 20.
15. *PL* Davis 122; *SL* Watt 19.
16. *PL* Davis 266.
17. *PL* Davis 800.
18. *PL* Davis 145; *SL* Watt 31.

Chapter 8

1. *PL* Davis 83.
2. *PL* Davis 509.
3. *PL* Davis 583.
4. *PL* Davis 54.
5. *The Paston letters, A.D. 1422–1509*, ed. James Gairdner, 6 vols (London: Chatto and Windus, 1904), no. 385.
6. *PL* Davis 153; *SL* Watt, 36.
7. William Shakespeare, *Henry IV, part 1*, ed. David M. Bevington (Oxford: OUP, 1987), I.ii.2–3.
8. William Shakespeare, *Henry V*, ed. Gary Taylor (Oxford: OUP, 1982), III.iii.10–11.
9. *PL* Davis 372.
10. *PL* Davis 64.
11. H.S. Bennett, *The Pastons and their England*, 2nd ed. (Cambridge: CUP, 1932), p.111.
12. Colin Richmond, *The Paston Family in the Fifteenth Century: Fastolf's Will*, (Cambridge: Cambridge University Press, 1996), p.70.
13. 'The Wife of Bath's Prologue', l.692, in *The Riverside Chaucer*, ed. Larry D. Benson (Boston, Mass.: Houghton Mifflin Co, 1987).
14. Richmond, *Fastolf's Will*, pp.72–3.
15. Book of Hours, Los Angeles, The J. Paul Getty Museum, MS 5, f.170v.
16. Oxford, Bodleian Library, MS. Laud. misc. 570.
17. John the Blind Audelay, *Poems and Carols (Oxford, Bodleian Library MS Douce 302)*, ed. Susanna Greer Fein (Kalamazoo, MI: Medieval Institute Publications, 2009), XXXIV, carols sequence, carols 6–11.
18. *PL* Davis 275.
19. Cambridge, Trinity College, MS R.2.64 r (fragment); 'Robyn Hod and the Shryff off Notyngham' in *Robin Hood*

and Other Outlaw Tales, eds Stephen Knight and Thomas H. Ohlgren (Kalamazoo MI: Medieval Institute Publications, 1997).

20. *Oxford English Dictionary*, sv 'card', n.2 I.1.a

Chapter 9

1. *PL* Davis 168; *SL* Watt 39.
2. *PL* Davis 158; *SL* Watt 37.
3. Rachel M. Delman, 'Gendered Viewing, Childbirth and Female Authority in the Residence of Alice Chaucer, duchess of Suffolk, at Ewelme, Oxfordshire,' *Journal of Medieval History* 45.2 (2019): 181–203.
4. *PL* Davis 163; *SL* Watt 38.
5. *PL* Davis 191; *SL* Watt 52.
6. Margery Bassett, 'The Fleet Prison in the Middle Ages,' *The University of Toronto Law Journal* 5.2 (1944): 383–402.
7. *PL* Davis 323.
8. *PL* Davis 340.
9. *PL* Davis 323.
10. *PL* Davis 77.
11. *PL* Davis 192; *SL* Watt 53.
12. *PL* Davis 193.

Chapter 10

1. *PL* Davis 148; *SL* Watt 33.
2. *PL* Davis 175; *SL* Watt 41.
3. *PL* Davis 232.
4. *PL* Davis 319.
5. *PL* Davis 234.
6. *PL* Davis 176.
7. *PL* Davis 72.
8. *PL* Davis 178; *SL* Watt 42.

9. *PL* Davis 73.
10. Richmond, *The Paston Family in the Fifteenth Century: Endings* (Manchester: Manchester University Press, 2000), p.56 n.156.
11. *PL* Davis 174; *SL* Watt 40.
12. *PL* Davis 341.
13. Corinne Saunders, *Rape and Ravishment in the Literature of Medieval England* (Cambridge: D.S. Brewer, 2001), pp.1–31; *Middle English Dictionary*, s.v. 'rape', n.2.a.
14. See Jenni Nuttall, *Mother Tongue: The Surprising History of Women's Words* (London: Virago, 2023), pp.227–8.
15. *PL* Davis 45.
16. *PL* Davis 395.
17. *Sir Gawain and the Green Knight*, eds. J.R.R. Tolkien, E.V. Gordon and Norman Davis (Oxford: Clarendon Press, 1967), ll.168–72.
18. 'The Awntyrs off Arthur' in *Sir Gawain: Eleven Romances and Tales*, ed. Thomas Hahn (Kalamazoo, Michigan: Medieval Institute Publications, 1995), l.554.

Chapter 11
1. *PL* Davis 180; *SL* Watt 44.
2. *PL* Davis 179; *SL* Watt 43.
3. *Oxford English Dictionary*, s.v. 'captainesse', n.1; cf. *Middle English Dictionary*, s.v. 'capteness', n.; and Jenni Nuttall, *Mother Tongue: The Surprising History of Women's Words* (London: Virago, 2023), pp.180–2.
4. Christine de Pizan, *Ditié de Jehanne D'Arc*, trans. Angus J. Kennedy, Kenneth Varty (Oxford: Society for the Study of Mediaeval Languages and Literature, 1977), part 2, p.68.
5. William Shakespeare, *Henry VI, Part 1*, ed. Michael Taylor (Oxford: OUP, 2003), V.ii.
6. *PL* Davis 74.

7. *PL* Davis 31; *SL* Watt 15.
8. *PL* Davis 32; *SL* Watt 16.
9. *PL* Davis 33; *SL* Watt 17.
10. *PL* Davis 30; *SL* Watt 14.
11. *PL* Davis 23; *SL* Watt 8.
12. *PL* Davis 222; *SL* Watt 71.

Chapter 12

1. *PL* Davis 690.
2. *PL* Davis 188.
3. Avicenna, 'On the Signs of Melancholy's Appearance' in *The Nature of Melancholy: From Aristotle to Kristeva*, ed. Jennifer Radden (Oxford: Oxford University Press, 2000), p.77.
4. *PL* Davis 688.
5. *PL* Davis 194; *SL* Watt 54.
6. *Oxford English Dictionary*, s.v. 'Dog bolt', n. and adj.
7. *PL* Davis 195.
8. Lovers in a Garden, comb, The Françoise and Georges Selz Gallery, Victoria and Albert Museum, London, accession number A.560–1910: https://collections.vam.ac.uk/item/O72949/lovers-in-a-garden-comb-unknown/.
9. See Hollie L.S. Morgan, *Beds and Chambers and Late Medieval England: Readings, Representations and Realities* (York: York Medieval Press, 2017), pp.24–39.
10. Morgan, *Beds and Chambers*, p.7.
11. *PL* Davis 196; *SL* Watt 55.
12. *PL* Davis 694.
13. *The Paston Letters, A.D. 1422–1509*, ed. James Gairdner, 6 vols (London: Chatto and Windus, 1904), no. 637.
14. *The Paston Letters*, ed. Gairdner, no. 637.
15. Nikolaus Pevsner, *The Buildings of England: Northeast Norfolk and Norwich* (Harmondsworth: Penguin, 1962), p.81.
16. *PL* Davis 198; *SL* Watt 57.

Chapter 13

1. *PL* Davis 200; *SL* Watt 58.
2. *PL* Davis 201; *SL* Watt 59.
3. *PL* Davis 201; *SL* Watt 59.
4. *PL* Davis 332.
5. Alison Weir, *Elizabeth of York: The First Tudor Queen* (London: Vintage, 2014), p.9.
6. *PL* Davis 861.
7. *PL* Davis 203; *SL* Watt 60.
8. *Middle English Dictionary*, s.v. 'brethel', n.
9. *Oxford English Dictionary*, s.v. 'brethel', n.
10. *Oxford English Dictionary*, s.v. 'brethe', v.
11. *Middle English Dictionary*, s.v. 'brothel', n.2.
12. *PL* Davis 208.
13. *PL* Davis 238.
14. *PL* Davis 204; *SL* Watt 61.
15. Jim Bradbury, *The Medieval Siege* (Woodbridge, Suffolk: The Boydell Press, 1992), pp.180–2.
16. *PL* Davis 244.
17. *PL* Davis 334; Bradbury, *Medieval Siege*, p.309.
18. *PL* Davis 316.
19. William Caxton, *The Game and Playe of the Chesse*, ed. Jenny Adams (Kalamazoo, Michigan: Medieval Institute Publications, 2009), Book 4, ll.307–310; see *PL* Davis 316.
20. Holger Afflerbach and Hew Strachan, *How Fighting Ends: A History of Surrender* (Oxford: Oxford University Press, 2012), p.57.
21. *PL* Davis 213; *SL* Watt 66.

Chapter 14

1. *PL* Davis 201; *SL* Watt 59.
2. *PL* Davis 417; *SL* Watt 89.
3. *PL* Davis 206; *SL* Watt 63.

4. *PL* Davis 216; *SL* Watt 67.
5. *PL* Davis 270.
6. *PL* Davis 282.
7. *PL* Davis 352.
8. John Lydgate, *The Siege of Thebes*, ed. Robert R. Edwards, TEAMS Middle English Texts Series (Kalamazoo, MI: Medieval Institute Publications, 2001).
9. *PL* Davis 397.
10. See, for example, Mary Beth Long, '"Woful Womman, Confortlees": Failed Maternity and Maternal Grief as Feminist Issues', *postmedieval*, 10.3 (2019): 326–43.
11. *Oxford English Dictionary*, s.v. 'miscarriage', n; 'abortion', n.
12. *Middle English Dictionary*, s.v. 'abortif, ive', adj. and n. 1(a), (b) and (c).
13. *Medieval English Prose for Women: Selections from the Katherine Group and Ancrene Wisse*, eds. Bella Millett and Jocelyn Wogan-Browne (Oxford: Clarendon Press, 1992), p.31.
14. *The Lais of Marie de France*, trans. Keith Busby and Glyn S. Burgess, 2nd edition (Harmondsworth: Penguin, 1999), pp.61–7.
15. *PL* Davis 151.
16. *Medieval English Prose for Women*, eds Millett and Wogan-Browne, p.31.
17. Mary E. Lewis and Rebecca R. Gowland, 'Brief and Precarious Lives: Infant Mortality in Contrasting Sites from Medieval and Post-Medieval England (AD 850–1859),' *American Journal of Physical Anthropology* 134.1 (2007): 117–29.
18. NHER Number: 61871, Norwich Heritage Explorer, https://www.heritage.norfolk.gov.uk/record-details?MNF69064

19. *Pearl*, ed. Sarah Stanbury (Kalamazoo, Michigan: Medieval Institute Publications, 2001), l.234.
20. '"Tragic Death" of Medieval Paston Family's Daughter Revealed,' BBC News, 9 June 2019, https://www.bbc.co.uk/news/uk-england-norfolk-48530068; M.J. Clayton, 'Looking for Anna: The Search for Anne Paston,' *Norfolk Archaeology* 48.2 (2019): 218–23.

Chapter 15

1. *PL* Davis 220; *SL* Watt 69.
2. Middle English Dictionary, s.v. 'secretari(e)' n. (1) (a).
3. *PL* Davis 129; *SL* Watt 25.
4. British Library MS Add. 39848, f.2r.
5. *PL* Davis 212; *SL* Watt 65.
6. *PL* Davis 353.
7. *PL* Davis 355.
8. *PL* Davis 282.
9. *PL* Davis 402.
10. *The Oxford Book of Oxford*, ed. Jan Morris (Oxford: OUP, 1978), p.33.
11. J.H. Harvey, 'Architecture in Oxford 1350–1500' in *The History of the University of Oxford: Volume II: Late Medieval Oxford*, eds J.I. Catto and T.A.R. Evans (Oxford: Oxford University Press, 1992; online edn, Oxford Academic, 3 Oct 2011), https://doi.org/10.1093/acprof:oso/9780199510122.003.0017.
12. *PL* Davis 263.
13. *PL* Davis 353.
14. *PL* Davis 733.
15. *PL* Davis 734.
16. *PL* Davis 227.
17. *PL* Davis 403.
18. *PL* Davis 404.

19. *PL* Davis 405.
20. *PL* Davis 397.

Chapter 16
1. *PL* Davis 665.
2. *PL* Davis 144.
3. Barbara Cornford, 'The De Mautby Family at Mautby,' *Yarmouth Archaeology* (1991): 23–5.
4. *PL* Davis 230.
5. See the Villa del Principe website, which includes images and descriptions of the tapestries: https://www.doriapam-philj.it/en/genoa/the-art/the-tapestries/.
6. Samuel R. Howard, *Mautby Remembrance: A Personal Observation of the Norfolk Villages* (Hemsby, Norfolk: Desne, 1996), p.116.
7. *PL* Davis 221; *SL* Watt 70.
8. *PL* Davis 216; *SL* Watt 67.
9. *PL* Davis 214.
10. *PL* Davis 274.
11. *PL* Davis 291.
12. *PL* Davis 316.
13. MS Harley 4014, f.153; 'Detailed Record of MS Harley 4014', *Catalogue of Illuminated Manuscripts*, available online at: https://www.bl.uk/catalogues/illuminatedmanu-scripts/record.asp?MSID=4496.
14. London, British Library, MS Lansdowne 285; *PL* Davis 245.
15. *PL* Davis 222; *SL* Watt 71.
16. *PL* Davis 399.
17. R.G.K.A. Mertes, 'The Household as Religious Community' in *People, Politics and Community in the Later Middle Ages*, eds Joel Rosenthal and Colin Richmond (Stroud, Gloucester: Sutton, 1987), pp.123–37.

18. Margaret Wood, *The English Mediaeval House* (London: Bracken Books, 1965), p.242.
19. Washington, DC, Dumbarton Oaks Collection, mus. no. HC.T.X.XXXX.21.(E); *English Medieval Embroidery: Opus Anglicanum*, eds Clare Browne, Glyn Davies, M.A. Michael, with Michaela Zöschg (New Haven: Yale University Press, 2016), plate 37.
20. *PL* Davis 14; *SL* Watt 2.
21. Howard, *Mautby Remembrance*, p.116.

Chapter 17

1. *PL* Davis 226; *SL* Watt 73.
2. *PL* Davis 791; *SL* Watt 82.
3. *PL* Davis 304.
4. *PL* Davis 790; *SL* Watt 81.
5. *PL* Davis 415; *SL* Watt 87.
6. Chaucer, *The Parliament of Fowls* in *The Riverside Chaucer*, ed. Larry D. Benson (Boston, Mass.: Houghton Mifflin Co, 1987), ll.309–310; Henry Ansgar Kelly, *Chaucer and the Cult of St Valentine* (Leiden, the Netherlands: E. J. Brill, 1986), pp.79–84 and 127.
7. *PL* Davis 791, *SL* Watt 82.
8. John Lydgate, 'The Lyfe of Seynt Margarete' in *Middle English Legends of Women Saints*, ed. Sherry L. Reames (Kalamazoo, MI: Medieval Institute Publications, 2003), ll.209–10; Juliana Dresvina, *A Maid with a Dragon: The Cult of St Margaret of Antioch in Medieval England* (London: British Academy/Oxford University Press, 2016), p.113.
9. *PL* Davis 416; *SL* Watt 88.
10. *PL* Davis 791; *SL* Watt 82.
11. *PL* Davis 378.
12. *PL* Davis 773.

13. *PL* Davis 792.
14. *PL* Davis 236.
15. *PL* Davis 213.
16. *PL* Davis 350.
17. *PL* Davis 351.
18. *PL* Davis 362.
19. *PL* Davis 373.
20. *PL* Davis 417; *SL* Watt 89.
21. *PL* Davis 418; *SL* Watt 90.

Chapter 18
1. *PL* Davis 228; *SL* Watt 74.
2. *PL* Davis 295.
3. *PL* Davis 367.
4. *Les heures d'Étienne Chevalier par Jean Fouquet: les quarante enluminures du Musée Condé*, ed. Patricia Stirnemann (Paris: Somogy, 2003), pp.54–5.
5. The Fayrey Pall, V&A, accession number Loan: St.Peter.2, https://collections.vam.ac.uk/item/O122998/the-fayrey-pall-funeral-pall-unknown/.
6. *English Medieval Embroidery: Opus Anglicanum*, eds Clare Browne, Glyn Davies, M.A. Michael, with Michaela Zöschg (New Haven: Yale University Press, 2016), cat. 82.
7. *PL* Davis 311.
8. *PL* Davis 311.
9. *PL* Davis 753; *SL* Watt 85.
10. *PL* Davis 781; *SL* Watt 86.
11. *PL* Davis 381.
12. Jane Clayton, 'Discovering Constance: Reconstructing the Life of the Illegitimate Daughter of John Paston II,' *Medieval Feminist Forum: A Journal of Gender and* Sexuality 56.2 (2021): 93–124.
13. *PL* Davis 383.

14. *PL* Davis 386.
15. *PL* Davis 230.
16. *PL* Davis 353.

Epilogue

1. Peter Bance, *Sovereign, Squire and Rebel: Maharajah Duleep Singh and the Heirs of a Lost Kingdom* (London: Coronet House, 2009), pp.117–31. Nikolaus Pevsner and Bill Wilson, *Norfolk 2: North-West and South* (New Haven, Connecticut: Yale University Press, 2002), pp.209–10.
2. Virginia Woolf, *A Passionate Apprentice: The Early Journals, 1897–1909*, ed. Mitchell Alexander Leaska (London: Hogarth Press, 1990), p.312.
3. Woolf, *A Passionate Apprentice*, p.311.
4. 'Virginia Woolf's "The Journal of Mistress Joan Martyn,"' eds Susan M. Squier and Louise A. DeSalvo, *Twentieth Century Literature* 25.3/4 (1979): 237–69; *The Flight of the Mind: The Letters of Virginia Woolf, 1888–1912*, eds Nigel Nicolson and Joanne Trautmann (London: Hogarth Press, 1975), vol. 1, no.283.
5. Woolf, 'The Journal of Mistress Joan Martyn,' p.242. Woolf takes the name Martyn from Thomas Martin of Palgrave, who was born in Thetford, and an early owner of many of the original the Paston letters: David Stoker, '"Innumerable Letters of Good Consequence in History": The Discovery and First Publication of the Paston Letters,' *The Library*, 17.2 (1995): 107–55.
6. Woolf, 'The Journal of Mistress Joan Martyn,' p.242.
7. Woolf, 'The Journal of Mistress Joan Martyn,' p.257.
8. Woolf, 'The Journal of Mistress Joan Martyn,' p.243.
9. Woolf, *A Passionate Apprentice*, p.311.

INDEX